THE GREAT FULL

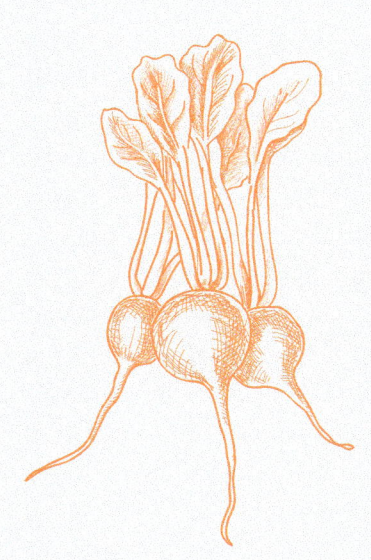

THE GREAT FULL

Sustainable Eating with Purpose and Joy

Michelle Grant

*This book is dedicated to all the people
who make our food.*

Michelle Grant is a food systems and sustainability professional with over 16 years' experience working at the interface of research, education and practice. She was the founding Executive Director of the World Food System Center at the Swiss Federal Institute of Technology (ETH Zurich), where she continues her work as Faculty and Education Director. In parallel, Michelle runs The Great Full, a platform that supports individuals and organizations to contribute to personal, societal and environmental wellbeing through intentional eating, living and leading. Michelle studied environmental engineering at the University of Queensland and management, technology and economics at ETH Zurich. She is also a certified advanced yoga and meditation teacher and leadership coach. In 2016, Michelle was nominated by the Swiss government to serve on the Swiss National Committee of the UN Food and Agricultural Organization, advising on national and international food systems policy issues. In 2017, she was awarded the University of Queensland Distinguished Young Alumni Award, and, in 2019, the Advance Australia Award (Food and Agriculture). Originally from Australia, Michelle now lives in Zurich, Switzerland.

INTRODUCTION
Welcome — 13
My Story — 14
Where Does Your Food Come from? — 14

FOOD AND PEOPLE
Food and Nourishment — 19
   Hunger — 20
   Hidden Hunger — 20
   Obesity — 21
Food and Wellbeing — 27
   The Hands that Feed Us — 27
   Human Rights on Our Fork — 27
   The Faces Behind Your Food — 29

FOOD AND PLANET
What is Natural? — 37
Eating the Planet — 39
   Biodiversity Loss — 39
   Soil Quality — 39
   Nutrient Cycles — 41
   Climate Change — 41
   Water Stress — 42
The Absurdity of Waste — 45
Biodiversity on Our Plates — 49

WHAT CAN I DO?
Now I Feel Thoroughly Miserable. What Can I Do? — 53
You Are More Than Just an Eater — 54
Choose Your Own Adventure with Food System Change — 55

INTENTIONAL EATING
We Are What We Eat — 61
   The Invisible Fork — 61
   Eating Is An Emotional Act — 61
   Not You and Them but Us and Our — 63
Can't You Just Tell Me What I Should Eat to Save the World? — 65
   What Does Science Say? — 67
   Start Where You Are — 69

INTENTIONAL SHOPPING
Buy Labelled Products (but Know Their Limits) — 71
Buy Seasonal (but Know It's Not That Simple) — 72
Buy From Diverse Places (but Don't Dismiss the Big Players) — 72
Buy Much Less Meat (but Buy Better) — 73
Buy the Ugly and the Unusual — 75

COOKING UP CALM

Giving Us Time	81
Making Healthy Choices Easier	81
Rescuing Nutrients	83
The Chance to Learn and Create	83

THE PLANT-BASED KITCHEN

Plant-based Pantry	85
Vegetables, Fruit and Herbs	*85*
Legumes and Pulses	*85*
Whole Grains	*86*
Pasta and Noodles	*86*
Nuts and Seeds	*86*
Sweeteners	*86*
Oils, Fats and Sauces	*87*
Dry Herbs and Spices	*87*
Dairy and Meat Substitutes	*88*
Other Essentials	*88*
Animal Source Foods	*88*
Equipment Basics	89
The Basics of Plant-based Meals	91
How to Use the Recipes	91
Global Instructions and Conversion Tables	93

RECIPES

BREAKFAST

Stracciatella Overnight Oats	97
Chocolate Orange and Maple Overnight Oats	99
Chai Spiced Breakfast Smoothie	101
Mixed Berry Millet and Oat Bake	103
Carrot Cake Oatmeal	105
Blushing Oatmeal	105
Rooibos Apricot and Maple Granola	106
Vegan Pancakes	109
Orange Chia Compote	111
Berry Chia Compote	111
Rhubarb Ginger Compote	113
Apple Cinnamon Compote	113

STARTERS AND SIDES

Tangy Salad Boats	117
Roasted Cauliflower with Mint Mousse and Hazelnut Sumac Dukkah	118
Easy (and Possibly Turkish) Bread	121
Shiitake Truffle and Mustard Crostini	123
Guacamole Potato Bites	125
Mini Millet Burgers	126

SALADS AND SOUPS

Salad Basics	131
Soup Basics	133
Roasted Chickpea Zucchini and Pomegranate Salad	134
Tropical Soba Noodle Salad	137
Mediterranean Rice Salad	139
Strawberry Balsamic Salad with Roasted Puffed Grains	140
Summer Pea Salad	143
Refreshing Coconut Lime and Nut Slaw	145
Warm Winter Salad	147
Watermelon Gazpacho	149
Quick Vegan Ramen	151
Meditative Minestrone	152
Warming Vegetable and Corn Chowder	154
Creamy Roast Potato Lemon and Dill Soup	157
Spiced Harissa Carrot and Lentil Soup	159
Green Magic Soup	161

MAINS

Warm Pumpkin Spinach and Quinoa Salad	164
Aubergine Napoletana Pasta	166
Sweet Potato Burrito Bowls	168
Easy Mac and Sundried Tomato Sauce	170
Sweet Potato Noodle Pad Thai	171
Dominican Black Beans and Rice	172
Lasakopita	175
Creamy Beetroot Sweet Potato and Feta Layered Bake	176
Falafel and Fries	178

Sri Lankan Jackfruit Curry	180
Roasted Tofu and Greens Noodle Bowl	182
Artichoke and Easy Green Pesto Pasta	185
World's Easiest Risotto	187
Sunshine Buddha Bowl	189

SWEET TREATS

Chocolate Cherry and Coconut Truffles	193
Date and Chestnut Banana Bread	194
Pineapple Ginger Carrot Cake	196
Chocolate Nut Rice Crackles	199
Summer Peach Tart	200
Sweet Potato Prune and Hazelnut Muffins	202
Raspberry Cherry Rose Chocolate Kisses	204
Vitamin Bites	207
Beetini Brownies	209
Make Your Own Chocolate – Three Ways	213
Spiced Orange Upside Down Cake	215
Chocolate Indulgence Tart	219
Lemon Tarts	221
Chocolate Stuffed Dates	223
Salted Cacao and Nut Butter Popsicles	225
Aprichoc Hazelnut Blondies	227
Berry Cherry Crumble Cake	229

DRINKS

Syrian Lemon Mint Polo	233
Go to Green Smoothie	235
Turmeric Mango Smoothie or Popsicles	237
Green Elixir	238
Apfelshorle	239
Chia Fresca	241
Blood Orange Raspberry and Buckwheat Smoothie	243

SAUCES, SPICES, TOPPINGS

Creamy Honey Mustard	246
Sesame Vinaigrette	246
Tahini Honey Lemon	247
Peanut Sesame Tamari	247
Garlic Dressing	247
Sundried Tomato Harissa Dip	248
Zaatar Hazelnut Dukkah	249
Turmeric Latte Spice Mix	250
Turmeric Latte	251

WITH GRATITUDE	**252**
ENDNOTES	**254**
Figure Endnotes	257
INDEX	**258**

INTRODUCTION

THE GREAT FULL

INTRODUCTION

WELCOME

Most of us know that food can bring us joy. We spend so much of our busy lives running from one thing to the next. Then, if we are one of the lucky ones, we have the opportunity to sit down and delight in a delicious meal three times a day. For a few moments, our awareness is diverted from incessant thinking and doing, and we dive into a sensory experience that serves us a little slice of joy.

Rarely do we see that each meal is also an opportunity to fulfil a bigger purpose. Food connects us to ourselves but also to the rest of the world – the ones we share a meal with, the ones who have grown, processed and transported our food and the ones from generations past and yet to be born. Our food also entwines us with the natural world – with climates, landscapes and ecosystems we inhabit and those we may never visit. Each time we eat, we get the chance to do so with a purpose. This might be with the intention of nourishing our families or making sure that those involved in providing our food earn enough to look after theirs. Or it might be about minimizing the impact of our diet on the environment so that future generations can also nourish themselves.

Despite these two wonderful motivations – eating for joy and eating with purpose – our relationship with food is often hijacked by an emotive and confusing food culture. We are inundated with propaganda about how the latest diet can help us conform to a particular body image. At the same time, we watch aspirational television shows of people cooking elaborate and luxurious feasts. We take photos of our meals to share with strangers. We line up in droves to try out the latest food hype, such as a donut that thinks it's a croissant. All of this takes our energy and attention away from the things that really matter when it comes to food, namely, nourishing ourselves while also being conscious of our impact.

It is my hope that reading this book helps you to explore some of the meaningful discussions around what is on our plates today. Most importantly, I hope that it supports you to eat with greater intention – being mindful of the impact your food choices have on you, others and the planet. To help you with this, Part 1, Food and Purpose, unpacks how modern food systems are performing against their purpose – that of nourishing us while supporting the wellbeing of those producing our food and respecting the natural environment. We will see that these issues are relevant for every eater and talk about how each of us can participate in creating change, beginning at our kitchen tables. In Part 2, Food and Joy, we will meet in the kitchen to explore how we can cook delicious and healthy meals that support this purposeful eating.

My intention is that this book helps you:

+ Understand how food connects us to some of the major challenges facing humanity.

+ Be motivated to contribute to positive change, in whatever way you can.

+ Be inspired to shop, cook and eat with intention, gratitude and kindness for yourself and others.

From my kitchen to yours,

Michelle

MY STORY

My relationship to food changed dramatically at the age of 20. After reading the jolting book *Fast Food Nation* I decided, overnight, to become a vegetarian. The book sheds light on the difficult conditions for the men and women working in industrial meat processing. Although I was already concerned about some of the environmental impacts of intensive meat production, I was completely unaware of what it meant for the workers. At the time, boycotting meat seemed like one thing that I could do to say I was not ok with this.

Food would eventually become my professional focus. When I became a vegetarian, I was studying chemical and environmental engineering at university. After graduation I went on to work in a variety of roles related to sustainable development. Basically, I was exploring how we can take care of our planet and the people on it, so that we can have a high quality of life for present and future generations.

Researching and teaching on topics such as climate change, energy, water, international development, education and health kept leading me back to a central theme – our food system. It seemed to be at the interface of every major issue facing humanity. As a result, food increasingly became the focus of my work. In 2011, I took up the role of founding Executive Director of the World Food System Centre at ETH Zurich, one of top 10 universities in the world. Here I was responsible for building up a research and education centre of excellence that would engage with some of the biggest food challenges of our times.

After 6 years in this role, I felt called to consolidate the interesting work I was engaged with, but in a way that would connect with anyone who cooks and eats. The result is this book. It combines my love of cooking and eating with my conviction that food can be a tool to tackle some of the biggest challenges we are facing in the world.

WHERE DOES YOUR FOOD COME FROM?

Let's start with a seemingly simple question: where does your food come from? At first thought, this may seem pretty straightforward. Your food probably comes from some sort of market, most likely a supermarket. For many people, this is the extent of their knowledge of their food's origin. But there is an intriguing journey behind every ingredient, and I would love to take you on it.

The next time you sit down to a meal, I invite you to pause for a moment, take a breath and look at what is in front of you. What you see is not just a mix of carbohydrates, proteins, fats and nutrients. Actually, what is on your plate connects you to people you will never meet; links you to natural landscapes you may never see; and involves you in politics, economies and cultures you may never know. What is really behind that forkful of food you are about to put into your mouth?

Regardless of what you are eating, it is likely that it began its journey to your plate on a farm. Maybe one next door or even on the other side of the world. Let's take, for example, a simple loaf of bread that you might buy at the supermarket or bakery. It started its life as a seed of wheat in the soil, using water to germinate and the sun's rays to produce its own food in the form of sugar. To grow properly, it needed nutrients, more water and some help to manage pests and weeds. This had to be done by people, on land, with or without the help of machinery and chemicals.

When the wheat was ready to harvest, it was collected from the field and cleaned, dried and stored, before being sold, transported and traded one or many more times. Next it arrived at the mill, where it was graded, cleaned and milled before being packaged, stored and transported again.

Only now is it finally at the baker, ready to be mixed with water, yeast and a few other ingredients and made into the bread you are enjoying with your meal. All of this work, resources, and effort for us to quickly eat a sandwich between meetings or leave it on the bench to be thrown away. Or alternatively, to be slowly savoured and appreciated with every bite.

How this network functions and who benefits from it reflects many things. The policies of the different countries the wheat moved through, be that agricultural, trade, employment, development or food safety related, play a fundamental role. This includes the type of production system the wheat can be grown in, if there are subsidies or tariffs when it is imported or exported, if there is a minimum wage for workers in the field or serving you at the bakery. Then there are economic factors working on your loaf of bread, shaping how much you pay for it, how much people along the value chain earn and if it will be enough to buy the food they need.

And what type of bread did you decide to buy? Was it sliced white, artisanal sourdough, gluten-free, whole-wheat, multigrain, a baguette or a loaf? Your preferences for the bread, and all the food you eat, are shaped by a complex set of social and cultural factors, like what you grew up eating, what the media is telling you, what your religion is, what your personal taste preferences are, what is available and what you can afford.

Then there are the thousands of different environmental factors that are silently shaping your diet without you knowing it. Perhaps there was a drought in Russia or Ukraine this year that impacted wheat yields, effecting prices and availability. Or a depletion of soil fertility and rising salt levels in Western Australia, contributing to lower harvests.

Now, this was just an example of a "simple" loaf of bread. You can think about any item of food in your kitchen in the same way, and very quickly your head will spin. There is so much time, energy, resources, sweat and even tears behind every piece of food we get to consume. *I believe the privilege of a diverse and healthy diet brings with it a great responsibility: to eat with gratitude and compassion for ourselves, others and the planet.* This means learning whatever we can about what we are eating and the impacts of our choices. Above all, it means appropriately valuing our food – and the people and environment that make it available – so that we can build a healthier and more equitable world.

What Is a Food System?

A food system includes all of the activities, people and organizations involved in producing, storing, transporting, distributing and consuming food. It considers the environmental, political, economic, social and cultural drivers and boundaries that shape how food is produced and consumed. The main outcomes of a well-functioning food system should be food and nutrition security, social wellbeing and environmental sustainability for all. With all of these elements interacting, the food system is inherently complex. Whenever we engage with it or attempt to change something, we face a lot of different perspectives, trade-offs and consequences. Therefore, there is no single solution that works everywhere.

For example, someone living in rural Assam in India may get a lot of their food from local markets and their own kitchen garden, with a limited number of steps or people involved from the soil to the stomach. Contrast that to someone living in Dubai where most food is imported from around the world, connecting the consumer to endless people and resources globally. Each of these contexts is completely different, as are the challenges the people face. It is important for us to remember that each ingredient we purchase is part of a much bigger picture. And while you may be a tiny part of a giant structure, your choices matter. To find out how, read on…

THE GREAT FULL

PART ONE

Food and People	19
Food and Planet	37
What Can I Do?	53
Intentional Eating	59
Intentional Shopping	72

FOOD AND PEOPLE

THE GREAT FULL

PART ONE | *Food and People*

FOOD AND PEOPLE

FOOD AND NOURISHMENT

These days there are countless media articles asking, "How will we feed 10 billion people in 2050?" Rather than jumping into the future, I think we need to talk about how our food system is, or isn't, serving people today. The sad fact is that a huge number of people on the planet today are suffering because they don't get the food they need for a healthy life. The easiest way to grasp the magnitude of what we are facing is to imagine 7 of your friends standing in front of you. If they represent the world population, 2 of them would be overweight or suffering from obesity[1]. One person would be undernourished, not getting the basic food they need on a regular basis[2]. Finally, at least 2 of your friends would be suffering from hidden hunger, meaning they get enough food, but it doesn't have the vitamins and minerals they need to live a healthy life[3].

We are used to thinking about these issues in terms of hunger in "poor countries" and obesity in "wealthy countries". But times have changed. Today, we see these multiple forms of malnourishment within the same country, city, family and even individual. For example, you can be suffering from obesity but also be malnourished – just because you are eating enough, or even too much, in terms of volume or calories doesn't mean you are getting the nutrients your body needs. Also, if you are undernourished as a child, you are at greater risk of being overweight or suffering from obesity later in life[4]. Every country in the world today is grappling with at least one form of malnutrition, and most are dealing with multiple forms of malnutrition at the same time. This is referred to as the double, or triple, burden of malnutrition[5].

Because of the health, social, emotional and economic impacts of hunger, hidden hunger and obesity, we have a lot of diet related suffering on the planet today. Let's look at these different areas in more detail.

The Great Full | 19

Hunger

Each year the UN Food and Agricultural organization releases a report on global hunger. When I opened the report in 2016, I was surprised to see that for the first time in over a decade, the number of hungry people in the world had increased. Conflict and climate variability have turned around the progress we were making and today we are back to having 11% of people on the planet going hungry[6].

Now, statistics can be hard to internalize – they are numerical, impersonal. But what does it mean to go to bed hungry day after day? What is it like to be a parent of a malnourished child, knowing you cannot afford to give them the food they need? Hunger is closely linked to poverty, and both rob children and adults of their basic human rights. If you are hungry, you are not able to grow, learn or develop to your full potential. If a child does not get the nutrition that they need in the first 1000 days of their life (from conception until their second birthday), they are likely to face stunted growth, not only physically and mentally but also socially and emotionally[7]. This period of time sets the foundation for lifelong health and can stop a child from reaching their full potential, often trapping them in a poverty cycle which then carries this burden across generations. It is a tragedy for the individuals and for the whole of society. This is why access to nutritious food needs to be seen as a human right. We need policies that provide a safety net for people who cannot access this, appreciating the first 1000 days as an important window of opportunity to break the intergenerational cycles of hunger and malnutrition.

Actually, we have more than enough food in the world today to feed everyone (on a calorie basis). Why then, do so many still go hungry? Firstly, not all the food we grow is used to feed us humans. In fact, 36% of global crop calories are used to feed animals and 9% are used to feed cars in the form of biofuels[8]. Food waste and loss then takes away another 1/3 of all the food we produce[9]. What is left is food for humans.

Provided, that is, you can afford it. There are many hungry people in the world who are living where there is an abundance of food. However, they cannot access it because they are unable to pay for it, making it impossible to separate hunger from poverty and inequality. This means eradicating hunger is not just about growing more food it is about changing systems.

There are others who live in remote areas where food may be abundant at certain times of the year. However due to poor roads and a lack of proper storage, that food spoils easily. This forces small farmers to sell at harvest time, when prices are lowest, and buy in scarce times, when prices are highest. Add to that the harsh reality of conflict, war, or natural disasters like droughts or floods, and we end up with famines. In 2018, 124 million people in 51 different countries were facing crisis food shortages like this, a 15% increase from the year before[10].

This is where organizations like the UN World Food Program have a critical role to play. As the world's largest provider of emergency food assistance, on any given day they will have 5000 trucks, 20 ships and 70 planes moving food to people in need[11]. Traditionally, the organization received and distributed in-kind donations of food – for example, taking a blend of corn and soy grown in the United States and shipping it to people in crisis situations. In recent years, there has been a push to find other ways to support hungry people in crisis, one that looks at their needs more holistically. For example, offering people vouchers that can be used in local markets to buy healthy food. Such a method is often cheaper, more effective in delivering nutritious food and more supportive to local farmers and economies, helping break the cycle of poverty[12].

Organizations like Meds and Foods for Kids in Haiti take another approach. In a country where 1 in every 5 children is malnourished, they developed a solution to simultaneously nourish children, provide jobs and improve local agricultural production[13]. They source peanuts from local farmers and combine them with other ingredients to make Medika Mamba, which means "peanut butter medicine" in Haitian Creole. This is a ready-to-use therapeutic food, the gold standard for treating acute malnutrition, as it contains all the energy, protein, vitamins and minerals a malnourished child needs in a single meal. Through this approach the organization has saved the lives of nearly 380,000 children, trained 2,403 farmers and created jobs for 65 people, despite a continual onslaught of hurricanes, earthquakes and cholera outbreaks over the last years[14].

Hidden Hunger

We have been trying to tackle hunger for a long time, but our efforts sometimes create other problems. The 1960s saw a huge push to tackle global hunger through a series of technologies and practices that came to be known as the Green Revolution. This poured a lot of funding into a few crops – mostly corn, wheat and rice – as well as technologies like irrigation and mechanization to support increased productivity[15]. This made these basic staple foods more affordable, but it made a diverse diet more expensive[16].

As a result, we pulled many people out of hunger, but shifted a larger number of people into a state of hidden hunger[17]. When someone is suffering from hidden hunger, it means that they are getting enough food in terms of quantity, but not in terms of quality. Their diet lacks vitamins and minerals like vitamin B, vitamin A, zinc, iron and iodine, which are only needed in small quantities but are critical for the healthy functioning of our bodies. This often happens to people who rely on cheap staple grains like rice or maize for their meals and who eat very few vegetables, fruits, nuts, pulses or animal-source foods. There are 2 billion people living in the world today who do not have the micronutrients they need for a healthy life[18]. Often this remains invisible, silently impacting people's immunity, stamina and longevity. But it can also become very severe, as we see when people develop night blindness from vitamin A deficiency, goitre from iodine deficiency or anaemia from iron deficiency. Hidden hunger is also the reason that 1.1 million children die each year[19]. The largest burden of hidden hunger is in developing countries, yet deficiencies to micronutrients such as iron, vitamin D and vitamin B_{12} also exist in the west[20].

To tackle this in the long term, we need everyone on the planet to be able to access a diverse and balanced diet. The provision of supplements, such as a multivitamins, and fortified foods, such as iodized salt, can help us on the way to this goal. Ultimately, we need solutions that make diverse and healthy food available and affordable, while simultaneously educating people on the importance of a diverse diet and how to integrate these foods into their everyday meals.

On a work trip to Sri Lanka a few years ago, I had the chance to visit an inspiring project looking to tackle hidden hunger and its underlying causes. The Sustainable Agricultural Development Program has worked with over 17,000 families living on or below the poverty line to improve food and nutrition security, resilience and income[21]. Rather than offering direct financial assistance, the program offers resources and training to families to set up organic kitchen gardens around their home, with a focus on empowering women. Over a 2.5 year period, each family works with field officers to prepare their land for cultivation, set up compost pits for organic fertilizer, plant seeds for vegetable production, cultivate mushrooms and beehives and create local networks to exchange and learn from one another. I remember visiting one family and the smallest son guided us proudly around his garden, showing the innovations families in the area had created and shared. I saw clever ideas like planting vegetables in old rice bags with a pipe in the middle with holes in it so that only a little water was needed during the dry season, but during the wet season the plants would not get water logged. The goal of the project is to first increase the food and nutrition security of the family, improving their level of self-sufficiency in food production and diversifying their diet. Eventually, families may be able to sell excess production on the local market and increase their household incomes.

A recent study on kitchen gardens in Sri Lanka found that families with organized kitchen gardens, such as those supported through this program, have a more diverse diet and a higher uptake of micronutrients compared to families in the same region with non-organized kitchen gardens[22]. Projects like this are so important, helping families directly meet their nutritional needs while creating new livelihood opportunities, tackling hidden hunger at its roots.

Obesity

I was in high school around the time obesity started making headlines in Australia. I remember watching news pieces that talked about a "crisis of personal responsibility", broadly stating that people were eating too much and not exercising enough and we were all paying the price. This made it sound like a case of the overweight individuals failing society, something that always felt deeply wrong to me.

Many years later, when I started to view this topic through a professional lens, I was not surprised to find a large amount of evidence showing just how complex the obesity puzzle really is. One report that widened my view was a 2007 foresight study in the UK that set out to identify the main drivers of obesity[23]. It narrowed them down to 109 drivers, linking food consumption and energy expenditure to a broader range of things such as how food is produced, how it is consumed, our individual physiology and activity, the activity environment we live in as well as individual and social psychological factors. The more we learn about obesity, the longer this list grows.

If we get too much energy from our food and do not use it, it is likely that we will put on weight. But so many things outside our direct control impact this energy loop. For example, when we are surrounded by cheap, convenient and highly palatable food designed and marketed to be addictive, we lose our ability to stop eating when we are full. This type of food becomes especially hard to resist when we are feeling stressed or depressed. In fact, obesity is often accompanied by depression, with one influencing the other in a negative cycle that is hard to escape[24]. To add fuel to this fire, a number of medications prescribed for depression have also been associated with weight gain[25].

According to Gallup's annual Emotions Report, in 2018 our world was more stressed, worried, sad and in pain than it has ever been[26]. This is pretty sobering information on its own, but it also has a link to obesity. As we all know, anxiety

and stress, be that from work, financial pressure, lack of sleep or physical or emotional pain, can significantly impact our eating patterns. When we experience chronic stress, it leads to elevated levels of cortisol in our body. This can increase our appetite and has been linked to weight gain and metabolic syndrome[27].

Moreover, an environment where sugary drinks and highly processed food are cheap and abundant makes avoiding them more challenging. Sugary drinks have been in the spotlight over the last years, as evidence linking the consumption of these drinks to obesity is very strong. In fact, children who consume sweetened drinks daily have a 55% higher risk of being overweight[28]. This prompted a number of governments to trial a "soda tax" – raising the prices of sugary drinks to disincentivize people to buy them. From Mexico to South Africa, this approach has gained momentum with policy makers around the world. The city of Berkeley in California implemented the tax in 2014 and saw a 21% drop in consumption of sugary drinks in low-income neighbourhoods in the first year[29]. In Mexico City, consumption dropped nearly 8%[30]. Revenues from these taxes can be used by governments to support those vulnerable to obesity and to subsidize access to nutritious food for those who need it[31].

When it comes to the movement part of the equation, many of us know first-hand how hard it is to fit an adequate amount of exercise into our day when we sit at a desk for hours on end. But what about living somewhere where it is too dangerous to exercise or walk around outside before or after work? Or when high housing prices force you to live far away from where you work, leading to extremely long commuting times that leave little room for healthy eating or exercising. Or when you have to work multiple jobs to make ends meet, on top of caring for your family, erasing the privilege of time needed for cooking and exercising[32].

As time goes on, we continue to learn new things about obesity and what drives it. For example, we now know that some ethnic groups are genetically more susceptible to becoming overweight[33]. That exposure to toxins and endocrine disruptors in our environment, or in the environment of our parents and grandparents, can impact how we gain weight across generations[34]. Or how altering the gut microbiota, for example through eating more prebiotic foods, may help treat obesity[35]. The more we learn, the more complex it gets.

Understanding how to navigate all this complexity is more important than ever. Obesity is no longer just a challenge in wealthy countries; these drivers play out all over the world and the figures are startling. You may not know, for instance, that the tiny Pacific island nations, which are barely visible on the world map, have the highest rates of adult overweight and obesity in the world. In Nauru, for example, 88.5% of the adult population is overweight or suffers from obesity. The Middle East also has a very high burden, with Kuwait at 73.4% and Qatar at 71.7%. The more widely known situations, like the United States or Australia, have rates of 67.9% and 64.5% respectively[36].

Thankfully we are slowly starting to see some initiatives that appreciate the multiple challenges that individuals and societies face when trying to tackle obesity. In the United States, a 2012 study showed that most doctors have a prejudice against patients with obesity, impacting the type of care they provide and reducing the trust of the patient. Centres like the IDEAL Clinic in Washington DC are trying to change that, spending adequate time with patients to understand the many different factors that impact their weight and health. In bi-weekly meetings, the patients and their families are met with respect, using communication that helps them feel listened to and understood. Patients have access to a range of professionals, including doctors, psychologists, nutritionists, health coaches and educators who provide holistic support for changes that are very difficult to manage alone[37].

The reality is, almost anywhere you live in the world today, you or someone near you is struggling with their weight and associated health issues. Yes "food in" and "exercise out" matters, but it is much more complex than that.

We have to be very careful about where we draw lines of personal and societal responsibility and engage with the struggle we collectively face. This connects us all, regardless of what we weigh.

I recently read a deeply moving article in The Atlantic by Tommy Tomlinson, the exceptionally talented author of the book *The Elephant in the Room: One Fat Man's Quest to Get Smaller in a Growing America*. Tommy graciously allowed me to share an excerpt from his book here. I hope it inspires you to read the whole thing and hear his profoundly touching personal account of navigating the many drivers of obesity.

Eat less and exercise.

That's what some of you are saying right now. That's what some of you have said the whole time you've been reading. That's what some of you say—maybe not out loud, but you say it—every time you see a fat person downing fried eggs in a diner, or overstuffing a bathing suit on the beach, or staring out from one of those good-lord-what-happened-to-her? stories in the gossip magazines.

"Eat less and exercise."

What I want you to understand, more than anything else, is that telling a fat person, "Eat less and exercise" is like telling a boxer, "Don't get hit."

You act as if there's not an opponent.
Losing weight is a fucking rock fight. The enemies come from all sides: The deluge of marketing telling us to eat worse and eat more. The culture that has turned food into one of the last acceptable vices. Our families and friends, who want us to share in their pleasure. Our own body chemistry, dragging us back to the table out of fear that we'll starve.

On top of all that, some of us fight holes in our souls that a boxcar of donuts couldn't fill. My compulsion to eat comes from all those places. I'm almost never hungry in the physical sense. But I'm always craving an emotional high, the kind that comes from making love, or being in the crowd for great live music, or watching the sun come up over the ocean. And I'm always wanting something to counter the low, when I'm anxious about work or arguing with family or depressed for reasons I can't understand.

There are radical options for people like me. There are boot camps where I could spend thousands of dollars to have trainers whip me into shape. There are crash diets and medications with dangerous side effects. And, of course, there is weight-loss surgery. Several people I know have done it. Some say it saved them. Others had life-threatening complications. A few are just as miserable as they were before. I don't judge any people who try to find their own way. I speak only for myself here: For me, surgery feels like giving up. I know that the first step of 12-step programs is admitting that you're powerless over your addiction. But I don't feel powerless yet.

- Tommy Tomlinson[38]

Now we have explored some of the bigger issues around nutrition and who our food system is not serving as it should. To summarize this in one sentence that may surprise you – unhealthy diets are responsible for more disease and death in the world than unsafe sex, alcohol, drug and tobacco use combined[39]. Worldwide, 1 in every 5 deaths is due to a poor diet (one low in wholegrains, fruit, nuts and seeds and high in fat, sugar, red and processed meats)[40]. It seems we are not really doing a great job of nourishing ourselves on a global scale.

Next, we will look at who is suffering the most. Let me give you a hint – in one of the world's greatest paradoxes, it is often the people involved in producing our food.

PART ONE | *Food and People*

FOOD AND WELLBEING

The Hands that Feed Us

When we buy food at the store, our final act is to place money in the hands of the person at the cash register. This is the last in a long line of hands, hearts and minds that feed us. When I began working with food systems, my thoughts usually jumped from the hands at the register to the hands of the farmer, completely bypassing of all the other people involved in making my food.

Then I started working with someone who opened my eyes to the bigger picture of social wellbeing in our food system. Aimee, a colleague and friend, had done a lot of research around fair trade and social conditions for agricultural workers and she motivated me to explore what I think is the biggest, and least spoken about, paradox of our food system: the fact that the people who produce, process, distribute, retail and serve our food cannot always access a nutritious diet themselves. Globally, the food and agricultural sectors have some of the most challenging and poorly paid working conditions in the world. The people who do this work are the ones who pay the ultimate price for our cheap food. It is a painful irony that is now permanently in my awareness.

This is a very difficult topic to talk about. It is also a massively under-researched area, because it is complex and sometimes dangerous to understand what is going on, and each context and individual has its own nuance and story. This is also the topic I find the most challenging to engage with personally, where the dance between joy and purpose is a difficult one.

Human Rights on Our Fork

Last summer my husband and I joined the throngs of people journeying south to the beaches and olive groves of Puglia. During the drive along the length of Italy, my thoughts constantly wandered to the workers I was seeing in the fields, toiling under the blazing sun to harvest crate after crate of tomatoes and other crops. This produce was sold for less than 2 euros a kilo at the supermarkets nearby.

The agricultural workers on the field in Italy are some of the 1.1 billion people in the world who try to earn a living in this way[41]. People working in agriculture make up nearly 1/3 of the world's total workforce[42]. Around half are farmers, the majority of whom are smallholders or subsistence farmers, and the other half are people employed as waged and temporary workers on farms and plantations[43].

The agricultural workers most vulnerable to dangerous working conditions are those who work on their own small plots of land as subsistence farmers; the individuals toiling in plantations as day labourers; seasonal and migrant workers (who are often undocumented); and child labourers[44].

Here is where we start to see the paradox playing out, because these are also the people who make up the majority of the world's poor and hungry[45]. And so it is, that the people who go to bed hungry at night are more likely to be involved with producing food. It is nourishment at the price of undernourishment, and I find it both perplexing and deeply troubling.

But the human price of cheap food doesn't end there. Aside from low wages agricultural workers often face informal work arrangements, dangerous working conditions and a lack of social protection such as health insurance. And this is important, because the health risks of agricultural work are high. This work is, by nature, very physically demanding. The risk of injury or illness is compounded by exposure to extreme temperatures, operation of dangerous equipment, and exposure to chemicals, such as pesticides, especially when protective equipment is not available or not used. In fact, *workers in agriculture run twice the risk of dying on the job than workers in any other sector*[46]. In many parts of the world, these workers do not have any type of social protection from the government and are not covered by national legislation. If regulations do exist, they are often not enforced[47].

A pretty sobering example of how serious this can be has been playing out quietly over the last 2 decades, somehow under society's radar. Chronic kidney disease has now reached epidemic proportions in agricultural communities in Central America[48].

The Great Full | 27

Imagine for a moment you are out harvesting sugar cane in a field in Central America. It is hot. Really hot. And with climate change, it is just getting hotter. You are doing strenuous, unrelenting manual work, without easy access to clean drinking water. You get paid based on the amount you deliver, and to make ends meet you push yourself to the limit and avoid breaks because pausing work means lost wages. Finding a bathroom is not necessarily easy. In the course of your day, you may also be exposed to toxic substances such as pesticides. So, what happens? You get severely dehydrated and your kidneys get stressed, which can eventually lead to chronic damage and even death. In fact, you may even end up as one of the 20,000 people in Central America who have died from this in the last 10 years[49]. This phenomenon is playing out all around the developing world, in India, Sri Lanka and more recently in the southern parts of the US, in Florida and California, as well[50].

There is another dirty little secret that is hiding in our food system: the high rates of sexual assault that female agricultural workers face. This happens all around the world, but the #metoo movement recently gave a platform to the voices of female farm workers in the USA. Let me share their words with you, from an open letter from 700,000 female farmworkers published in Time magazine in November 2017[51]:

Dear Sisters,

We write on behalf of the approximately 700,000 women who work in the agricultural fields and packing sheds across the United States. For the past several weeks we have watched and listened with sadness as we have learned of the actors, models and other individuals who have come forward to speak out about the gender based violence they've experienced at the hands of bosses, coworkers and other powerful people in the entertainment industry. We wish that we could say we're shocked to learn that this is such a pervasive problem in your industry. Sadly, we're not surprised because it's a reality we know far too well. Countless farmworker women across our country suffer in silence because of the widespread sexual harassment and assault that they face at work.

We do not work under bright stage lights or on the big screen. We work in the shadows of society in isolated fields and packinghouses that are out of sight and out of mind for most people in this country. Your job feeds souls, fills hearts and spreads joy. Our job nourishes the nation with the fruits, vegetables and other crops that we plant, pick and pack.

Even though we work in very different environments, we share a common experience of being preyed upon by individuals who have the power to hire, fire, blacklist and otherwise threaten our economic, physical and emotional security. Like you, there are few positions available to us and reporting any kind of harm or injustice committed against us doesn't seem like a viable option. Complaining about anything — even sexual harassment — seems unthinkable because too much is at risk, including the ability to feed our families and preserve our reputations.

We understand the hurt, confusion, isolation and betrayal that you might feel. We also carry shame and fear resulting from this violence. It sits on our backs like oppressive weights. But, deep in our hearts we know that it is not our fault. The only people at fault are the individuals who choose to abuse their power to harass, threaten and harm us, like they have harmed you.

In these moments of despair, and as you cope with scrutiny and criticism because you have bravely chosen to speak out against the harrowing acts that were committed against you, please know that you're not alone. We believe and stand with you.

In solidarity,

Alianza Nacional de Campesinas

Alianza Nacional de Campesinas is an organization comprised of current and former farmworker women, along with women who hail from farmworker families.

Slowly but surely these stories are starting to be heard. And as we start to lift the netting, we find that the rotten roots run deep. Take a recent example from Sicily, the southern Italian island normally associated with fresh, locally grown culinary delights. In 2018 a police investigation in the Ragusa province of Sicily led to the arrest of 15 men involved in trafficking Romanian women into the area as exploited agricultural workers. It is estimated at least 5,000 Romanian women working on farms in the area face conditions of forced work, sexual assault and unsanitary and isolated living conditions[52].

When it comes to the country as a whole, the 2018 Global Slavery Index estimated there are 50,000 enslaved agricultural workers in Italy and 400,000 agricultural workers who are vulnerable to exploitation and labour abuse[53]. The government has recently passed new laws and guidelines to try and tackle some of these issues, however the implementation on the ground remains very light. New social certification schemes and private sector initiatives, are also trying to improve conditions for workers in agriculture fields. All of this is an important start, but we have a long way to go. It seems that a healthy Mediterranean diet is not healthy for everyone.

When we hear about the conditions that some farm workers face, it is probably not surprising to learn that there is a labour shortage in agriculture in many parts of the world.

Because these are not the most attractive jobs, if people have another option, they tend to take it. This leaves a gap that is filled in the same way, all around the world. People from poorer countries or contexts move to richer ones, fleeing poverty to seek out a better life elsewhere. That may mean a journey from Romania to the UK to pick strawberries or from Burkina Faso to Ivory Coast to harvest cocoa. These are the only hands desperate enough to harvest our food in such conditions. At what point do we start to notice the taste of exploitation?

The circumstances are particularly grim for agricultural workers, but we should not forget about the many other people who get food onto our plates – those driving trucks, working in slaughterhouses and packing houses, stacking shelves and serving food.

It is really hard to find figures on this globally. The most comprehensive research into conditions for workers across the food system was a 2016 study by the Food Chain Workers Alliance (FCWA) and the Solidarity Research Cooperative in the United States. Their findings are extremely sobering and make me want to see a study like this for every country in the world. The FCWA found that in the US, 1 in every 7 workers is employed in the food system, making it the largest sector of employment[54]. Yet this group has an annual median wage below all other industries. Rates of injury and illness have been increasing since 2010. And the most distressing finding: food systems workers are more food insecure than workers in other industries. The very people responsible for bringing food to tables in the US are 2.2 times more likely than workers from other industries to rely on government food assistance.

That is the situation in the United States. It is of course different in every country in the world. And in every field, truck, warehouse, store and restaurant. It is always difficult to globalize and generalize. I don't want you to finish reading this section thinking that every person working in the food system is a victim. There are of course jobs in the food system that pay a living wage and offer social protection and all the other things we deserve from work. There are stories where food has provided livelihood, opportunity, a fulfilment of dreams or the creation of an enterprise that supports and nourishes others. Like a café in Australia that serves up delicious food while training at-risk youth in hospitality. Or a social enterprise in Kenya that collects rejected produce from farms and cooks it into nutritious school meals. An online platform in Switzerland that connects local farmers with urban consumers, helping them to directly access new markets and better margins.

A large international ice-cream company that uses fair trade ingredients and also pays their own workers a living wage, recalculating this each year based on the actual price of living. Or a winery in South Africa that puts the health of the soil and its employees at the forefront of how it produces wine.

But food is a difficult business. Unfortunately, the margins are extremely low and the risks very high, particularly for those at the beginning of the value chain. Farmers often receive very little for their products while also dealing with a whole range of shocks, like bad weather or drought. Even in cases where they would like to pay their workers more, it is really challenging because of the low and often fluctuating prices the market offers for their products. This makes poor working conditions and pay a harsh reality for too many in this system.

The Faces Behind Your Food

I was recently eating at one of my favourite plant-based restaurants, a place where I feel bursts of delight when I read the mouth-watering menu. But this time, my feelings of joy got a little clouded by my feelings of purpose. I kept thinking about how annoyingly trendy and virtuous everyone around me seemed as they Instagrammed their vegan smoothies and avocado toast. Sure, eating this way was doing good for the health of the wealthy consumer, but was it doing much for the people who grew, distributed and prepared this food? The hours of research I had been doing about labour conditions for agricultural workers was swooshing around in my head. All of a sudden, I felt like the main character of Aimee Bender's The Particular Sadness of Lemon Cake, a book about a girl who can taste the emotions of the people who prepared her food. My delicious smoothie took on a sour taste and I was overwhelmed with sadness about this system, nearly to the point of tears.

My husband, always a little perplexed by how heavily I feel things that seem far away, brought me back to the moment with a piece of simple wisdom. He reminded me that eating with sadness was not helping anyone. In fact, it devalued all of the people who had worked hard to make this meal possible. I pulled myself together and shifted the paralyzing guilt of privilege to a perspective of gratitude and possibility. I then did what I now do whenever big, distant and complex challenges feel overwhelming and make me shut down. I asked myself: what tiny contribution can I make right here, right now? This. Felt. Possible.

PART ONE | *Food and People*

And it was here I reconnected with the joy again. Firstly, I could go and speak with the kitchen staff and tell them what a wonderful job they did and how much I appreciated it. I could tip the staff generously while verbally sharing my heartfelt thanks. I could write to the restaurant, telling them how much I loved their food, and asking if I could learn more about their social and ethical practices – how were they sourcing their food and taking care of their staff?

No, this was not going to radically change the system, but it would contribute in a tiny way. And that is what I believe we all need to get more comfortable with. Taking the small steps right where we are. Through that, we can start to collectively engage with the bigger issues in a practical way.

Which brings me to what else we can do. The first is to acknowledge that the people impacted by this are motivated to improve their situation but are often powerless to do so. They are actors, not victims, and need to be seen and heard. They need support to be able to organize and to collectively speak up and change the situation. Those who can need to be willing to pay more to factor in the true cost of our food. We also need to campaign for new regulations, a better sharing of value across shorter supply chains, greater visibility for the voices and needs of workers, support for ethical standards, improved transparency and greater connection between the people on the field and the final consumer. You can do this through how you vote, which organizations you lend support to, by raising awareness in your networks and through how you shop and where you eat.

Fair Food Program — Consumer Powered, Worker Certified

It's the 1990s in Florida and farmworkers picking tomatoes are fed up. They face wage theft, discrimination, harassment and abuse while they work more than 70 hours a week, all to earn less than $US 10,000 a year. A group of them form the grassroots organizing group that is now known as the Coalition of Immokalee Workers (CIW) to raise awareness on what is happening in the fields[55]. In 2000, their movement gains momentum and they decide to focus their attention on large, consumer-facing companies that use the tomatoes they are picking in their products. Working with student and religious groups, they organize a boycott of Taco Bell on university and school campuses. The aim is to put pressure on the company to pay an extra penny per pound of tomatoes to improve workers' wages and to make growers comply with a worker-designed code of conduct. The boycott and media coverage works, and Taco Bell is followed by McDonalds in signing on to their requirements[56]. Eventually, one of Florida's largest tomato growers signs on, opening the door for others. In fact, the clever structure of the program makes it harder for non-compliant growers to sell their product. Through all this, the CIW work to get the financial support from philanthropists, politicians, consumers and public interest groups while continuing to put pressure on big tomato buyers such as fast food companies and supermarkets.

It has taken over 20 years of hard collective work, but today CIW's Fair Food Program agreements cover 90% of Florida's tomato production, with 14 of the biggest food buyers on board, including the likes of Burger King, McDonalds, Walmart and Subway. The Fair Food Program has improved wages and working conditions for 30,000 workers and now has its sights set on expanding across the country and to other agricultural sectors. More recently, there has been talk of expanding the program to Spain, Italy and other Mediterranean countries where many migrant labourers face difficult work conditions as they feed Europe's demand for fresh fruit and vegetables.

What is unique about this approach, compared to many other labels or initiatives, is that it is completely worker driven. It is a human rights program designed, monitored, and enforced by workers themselves. The Washington Post referred to the Fair Food Program as "one of the great human rights success stories of our day". It is a wonderful example of all actors demanding a voice and seat at the table to collaborate and design a solution that works for all.

The Great Full | 33

When Clean Eating Gets Dirty

We need to talk about cashew nuts. Maybe you have noticed the cashew cheese, cashew butter, cashew cheesecake and cashew milk popping up everywhere you look lately? You name it, we will milk a cashew to make it. Which means there has been a dramatic rise in demand for these nuts, as more and more people use them as dairy substitutes in a vegan diet or as healthy snacks.

First of all, it is important to know how cashew nuts grow. This is often mind boggling to people, because it is not actually a nut at all. In fact, it's a fruit (the cashew apple), which looks like a cross between a bell pepper and a pear. At the bottom of each fruit is ONE seed and inside its hard protective layer is the kernel, which is what we usually call the cashew nut. To get the "nut", you have to pick the fruit, remove the seed and then extract the crescent-shaped kernel from its shell. This isn't so straightforward; it involves sun drying, roasting, cutting off the hard shell, heating and peeling.

The processing of cashews mostly happens in India and Vietnam. In India, the job is usually done by hand, and mainly by women's hands. Although their work is skilled it is often poorly paid and performed under difficult conditions. On top of that, shelling cashews is a dirty business. There is an acid that lies between the shell and the kernel, and it can, and does, seriously burn the skin. These burns have become a fact of life for people trying to make a living from shelling our cashews. Even when gloves are available, they are not always worn because it slows down the work, which is an issue when you are paid by volume. Gloves can also lead to other injuries or make the burns even worse.

In Vietnam mechanized processing is more common, which allows the producers to meet (at least in part) the price pressure exerted by western supermarkets on global cashew markets. Yet not all of Vietnam's processing of cashews is done by machines. Several years ago a Human Rights Watch report exposed "blood cashews" – nuts that were being hand-processed in Vietnam by drug addicts imprisoned in forced labour camps [57].

But here is the other odd thing about cashews: a lot of them are not actually processed where they are grown. India and Vietnam import around 60% of the cashews they process, mostly from West Africa, the region growing the largest number of cashews in the world[58]. With 90% of all cashews grown in West Africa exported raw, only a minor amount of processing actually happens there[59]. When you buy cashews at the shop, it is not usually declared where they were grown or where or how they were processed. It is a value chain that is not very transparent.

So, what can you do as a consumer? Probably, this means paying more and consuming less, eating cashews more like a delicacy than a substitute for everything. If we buy them, then we should at least buy fair trade, which generally speaking improves the conditions for workers. The best thing to do is to find organizations that care about their sourcing practices, the conditions for workers and upholding transparency in their operations. In Switzerland, there are a few organizations, like Gebana, Crowd Container or Pakka, who take a "more than fair trade" approach to create ethical value chains. This means building long-term relationships directly with farmers, offering stable prices and pre-financing and guaranteeing decent working conditions[60]. You quickly notice the difference in price and quality.

FOOD AND PLANET

THE GREAT FULL

FOOD AND PLANET

We have explored how food systems are serving people, but what about the planet? Of all human activities, food production has the greatest impact on our natural world and is the largest driver of environmental change[61]. Let's find out how what is on our plates links us to the soil, land and ecosystems that may be far away from our kitchen table.

WHAT IS NATURAL?

Even though we don't really know what is behind it, many of us will seek out and pay more for food labelled "natural"[62]. Yet, there is very little food in the world today that is truly natural. Take the humble and ubiquitous banana. A beloved food you can find in most parts of the world, providing a naturally packaged snack for little and big kids alike.
It grows on a tree and isn't processed, so it is natural, right? Well, in some ways. But if you trace it back thousands and thousands of years to its distant cousin, the original banana, you would barely recognize it. Small, fat, pod-like, full of seeds and more like okra than the sunshine yellow fruit we know and love. What we know as a banana today only exists because of centuries of human interference. The same is true for almost every plant, and animal, that exists on our farms and shelves today.

We tend to look back on history in terms of battles of power and technological development. Strangely, food doesn't often feature in our retelling of the past, yet it has shaped the entire history of humanity[63]. About 10,000 years ago, humans started planting crops and domesticating animals. This made it possible for us to settle in one place, rather than roaming around to hunt and gather, creating villages, towns and cities that have changed not only our social structures but also the natural world.

Today, of all human activities, food production is the largest driver of environmental change[64]. A lot of this comes from modern agriculture. Through the creation of modern plant breeding, the use of machinery, irrigation, fertilizers and crop protection, we were quickly able to feed more people with less land and less labour. All of this helped us to achieve the objective we had at the time – saving more people from starvation. It seems in this regard we were partially successful – this aforementioned suite of practices, often called the Green Revolution, has been credited with saving millions of people from hunger[65]. It also created the foundation for the modern food system, which feeds those who are able to pay very well. The problem is, whenever we impose a uniform solution on a complex system, we end up with some unintended consequences. In this case, we are now coming to understand the other impacts of the Green Revolution. Namely, we have reduced hunger, but have created the persisting challenge of hidden hunger or micronutrient deficiency that continues to affect 2 billion people in the world[66]. Beyond that, it is a system that contributes to a degradation of the environmental basis that is essential to our ongoing food production. This increase in food production per unit of land area is due to the intensive planting of a few plant species together with the use of external inputs and irrigation water. As a result, feeding the world takes a major toll on our planet, especially when you consider the conversion of natural ecosystems to agricultural land, one of the major drivers of the rapid extinction of species we are witnessing today.

Figure 1

The Sea of Plastic in Almeria, Spain – The region of Almeria in Spain has the largest concentration of greenhouses in the world, where nearly half of the fresh produce consumed in Europe is produced. Water use in the area is around 5 times higher than the rainfall, with the additional water being drawn from underground aquifers at a faster rate than they are replenished, leading to salination. Farmers struggle to survive economically and there are routine reports of exploitation from migrant farm workers. Retailers and governments are under increasing pressure to deal with the wide-ranging issues in the area.

EATING THE PLANET

Producing food has a big impact on the environment, yet without a healthy environment we will not be able to produce food in the future. Let's have a closer look at this relationship.

Biodiversity Loss

Biodiversity is the variety of animals, plants and micro-organisms that are needed to keep our ecosystems healthy. Biodiversity provides us with services such as healthy soil, fresh water, pollination of plants, pest control and flood protection. But unfortunately, our current mode of food production threatens the very biodiversity it relies on. A recent global assessment report highlighted that 1 million plants and animals are currently facing extinction – more than at any other time in human history[67]. The greatest drivers of biodiversity loss are clearing land to use it for agriculture and using land more intensively.

To give you a concrete example of biodiversity loss, let's talk about insects. Researchers expect that 40% of the world's insects will soon be extinct[68]. Great, you may think, less bugs on the windscreen and nasty insect bites. But these creatures are actually responsible for pollinating 2/3 of all food crops in the world[69]. Plus, they provide food for birds, replenish soil and keep pests under control. This rapid decline of insects is mostly due to agriculture: the loss of habitat as a result of clearing land to grow or graze food and the excessive use of fertilizers and pesticides[70]. Without our little flying friends, we are going to have trouble feeding ourselves, yet in our efforts to feed ourselves we are killing them.

Biodiversity literally keeps us alive – a pretty good reason to do whatever we can to protect it. This can start with small steps, like cooking with heirloom or forgotten varieties of vegetables, buying from farmers who prioritize building diversity on their farms or setting up a wild bee home in your back garden.

Soil Quality

Healthy soil is the foundation of healthy food. Yet today we face extensive soil degradation – over the last 40 years, we have lost 1/3 of the world's arable land[73]. The main drivers of soil degradation are overgrazing, deforestation, pollution, the mining of nutrients (by harvesting crops without replenishing the nutrients they take with them) and inappropriate water and soil management that leads to erosion[74]. A lot of these practices are driven by land shortages, poverty, migration and economic pressures on farmers[75]. Some soil degradation is irreversible and leads to desertification; this is currently happening at a rate of 12 million hectares per year[76]. To put that in perspective, that is an area of land 3 times the size of Switzerland.

"We speak a lot of the importance of sustainable food systems for healthy lives. Well, it starts with soils. Soils also host at least one quarter of the world's biodiversity. They help us to mitigate and adapt to climate change. They play a role in water management and in improving resilience to floods and droughts. The multiple roles of soils often go unnoticed. Soils don't have a voice, and few people speak out for them. They are our silent ally in food production."

– *José Graziano da Silva, Director General, United Nations Food and Agriculture Organization* [77]

There are around 300,000 edible plant species in the world, but less than 200 are used by humans[71]. Over the past hundred years, 3/4 of diversity once found in agricultural crops has been lost. Today, just 3 crops (rice, maize and wheat) provide nearly 60% of the calories consumed by humans[72].

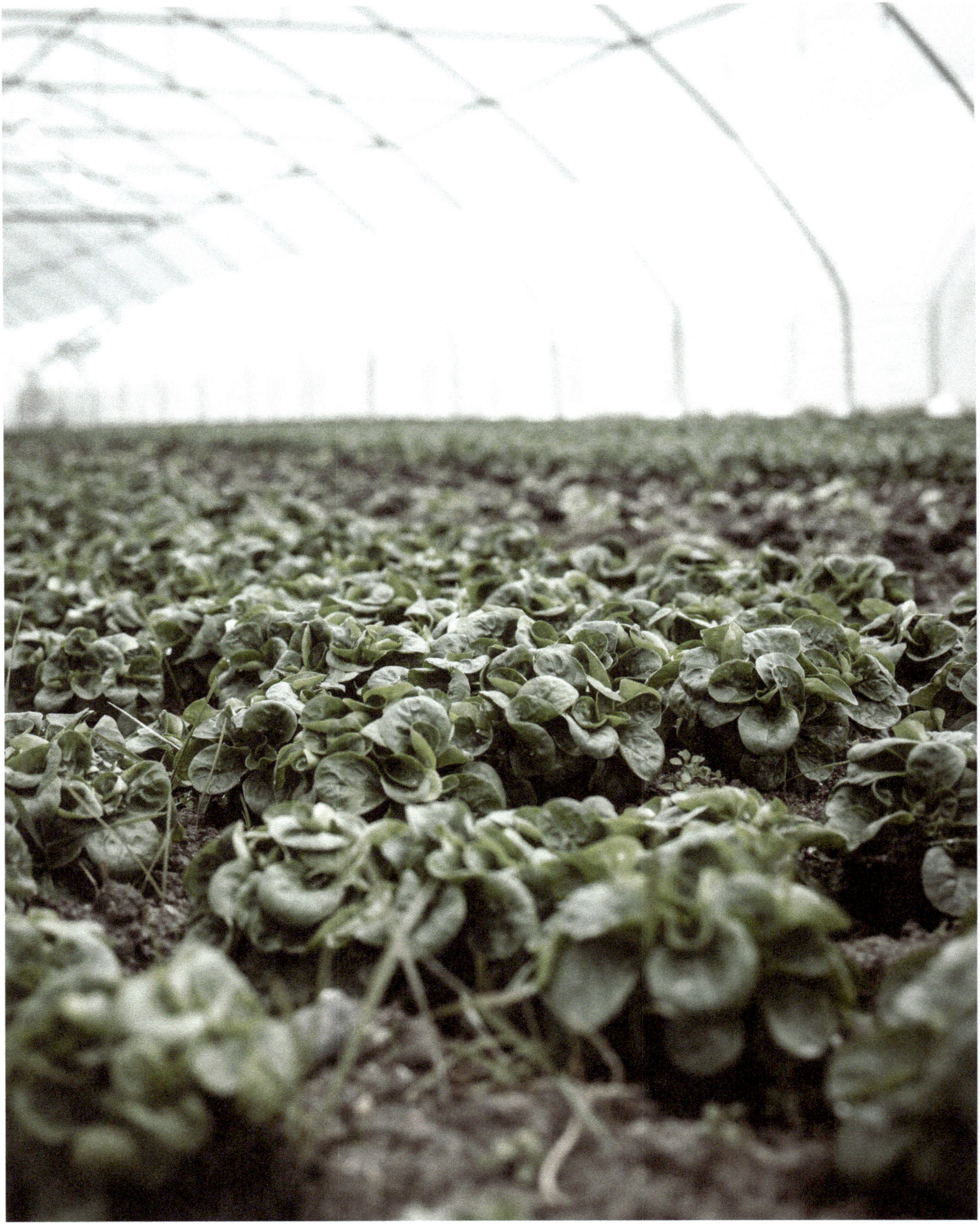

Nutrient Cycles

Although we spend time thinking about which foods are more nutritious for us, we often don't think about where those nutrients are coming from or where they go. For as long as we have existed, human beings have been connected to the earth's nutrient cycles. Nutrients in the soil are taken up by plants, we then eat these plants and whichever nutrients are not used up by our bodies are excreted and released back to nature. The only problem is that we now mostly live in urban areas, and these nutrients end up far away from where they began. When we harvest plants, we take nutrients away from the soil. This means we need to replace those nutrients, with either synthetic fertilizers or natural ones, such as manure or compost. When we apply more than the plant needs, which is often the case in western agriculture, the excess can run off into groundwater, rivers and lakes and this contamination can lead to eutrophication, the death of fish and acidification of water and soil. To deal with this, we need to reduce nutrient applications to the optimum required amount, precisely dosing the right quantity at the right place and time. In addition, we need to find ways to recycle nutrients on a large scale, including what we lose in urban areas through food waste but also human waste.

Tackling this is a part of building a circular economy, where we start to close the loops by making the waste of one the food of another, using what we usually throw away to build capital instead. Examples of this include using treated sewage sludge in agricultural fields, using or recovering phosphorus from sewage ash or utilizing urine as fertilizer. The Swiss Federal Institute of Aquatic Science, for example, has developed a technology to separate human urine and process it into a nutrient rich fertilizer, recovering valuable nutrients, conserving natural resources and reducing water pollution along the way. They have successfully trialled this approach in pilot plants in Switzerland and South Africa, and it offers a promising solution to closing nutrient cycles.[78]

Climate Change

When it comes to our changing climate, there is a lot of focus on reducing fossil fuels for energy use. But strangely we rarely talk about food. Scientists estimate that the activities that make up our food system contribute around 30% of all human related greenhouse gas emissions[79]. Most of this happens in agriculture, which alone is responsible for around 80% of these food system related GHG emissions[80]. Agricultural emissions primarily come from methane generated by ruminant livestock (like cows and sheep) and flooded rice fields, nitrous oxide created by fertilized soils and carbon dioxide produced when we clear land to grow food. Off the field, the food system generates greenhouse gas emissions through the manufacturing, transportation, packaging, storage and cooking of food.

Generally speaking, foods with the highest overall climate impacts are ruminant meat (beef, lamb), followed by other meat (chicken, pork, seafood) and then products from animals (eggs, milk and cheese). Plant-based foods tend to have the lowest impact, though this can still be high if the plants are grown in heated and lit greenhouses or transported by air[81].

The recent EAT-Lancet Commission paper estimated that changes in food production practices could reduce agricultural greenhouse gas emissions by 10%, increased consumption of plant-based diets could reduce emissions by up to 80% and halving the amount of food lost or wasted could contribute to a further 5% reduction.

Water Stress

Of all the fresh water extracted by humans on the planet, 70–80% is used for food production[82]. Although we do not see it in the end product, each piece of food we eat has a hidden backpack of "virtual water" – water that was used to grow it, process it and package it but that is not in the final product. Certain foods are particularly water intense; nearly 30% of the total water footprint of humanity is due to animal products, with beef and dairy cattle being the highest. This is mostly due to the water used to grow animal feed. However, the amount of water used depends on the production system – industrial cattle production typically uses more water and creates more water pollution than pasture raised cattle[83].

Virtual Water[84]

Apple	125 L per apple
Apple Juice	230 L per glass
Coffee	130 L per cup
Tea	27 L per cup
Wine	109 L per glass
Chocolate	1,700 L per 100g
Beef	1,540 L per 100g
Chicken	432 L per 100g
Almonds	1,600 L per 100g
Avocados	320 L per avocado
Lentils	600 L per 100g
Dates	227 L per 100g

When we are enjoying food from other parts of the world, we are also indirectly using that region's water supply. In some places this can be sustained, but in many water-scarce areas it is not. Over one quarter of the world's food is currently grown in water scarce areas and a lot of popular crops, like wheat, nuts and avocados are grown in areas with high water stress[85]. This makes water-smart agriculture not only a buzzword but an absolute necessity if we want to produce food on a hotter, drier planet.

Agroecology

Agroecology considers social and ecological concerns in the design and management of agriculture. It is a scientific discipline, a set of farming management practices and also a social movement. It aims to work with the natural environment based on the local context to build sustainable and resilient systems that support human, animal and environmental health and wellbeing. The most well-known agroecological approach is organic farming; others include biodynamic farming, regenerative agriculture or agroforestry, and management practices such as integrated pest management, crop rotations or intercropping. Agroecology is not a certification system, but it is an umbrella term for approaches to agriculture that are adapted to the local context, use natural processes and integrate knowledge from a range of different perspectives. As agroecology has received less investment in research and development, is often knowledge and labour intensive and may have lower yields in the short term, products from agroecological systems can be more expensive. But this is where you have to think of the true cost of food, not just the price on the tag.

There are countless examples of the principles of agroecology being applied all around the world. Like in Santa Cruz, California, where researchers and farmers worked together over a period of 3 years to redesign strawberry production systems on Swanton Berry Farm. Strawberries are traditionally grown in monocultures that rely on a large number of chemical inputs – especially chemical fumigants. Through integrating scientific and practical knowledge the collaborators implemented more sustainable agroecosystems, using a range of approaches like crop rotation, intercropping and "push-pull" natural pest management techniques[86].

10 Elements of Agroecology

Diversity	Co-creation & sharing of knowledge	Synergies	Efficiency	Recycling
Resilience	Human & social values	Culture & food traditions	Responsible governance	Circular & solidarity economy

Figure 2

The FAO identified 10 elements of agroecology - underlying principles that can be used to design and evaluate agroecological systems.[i]

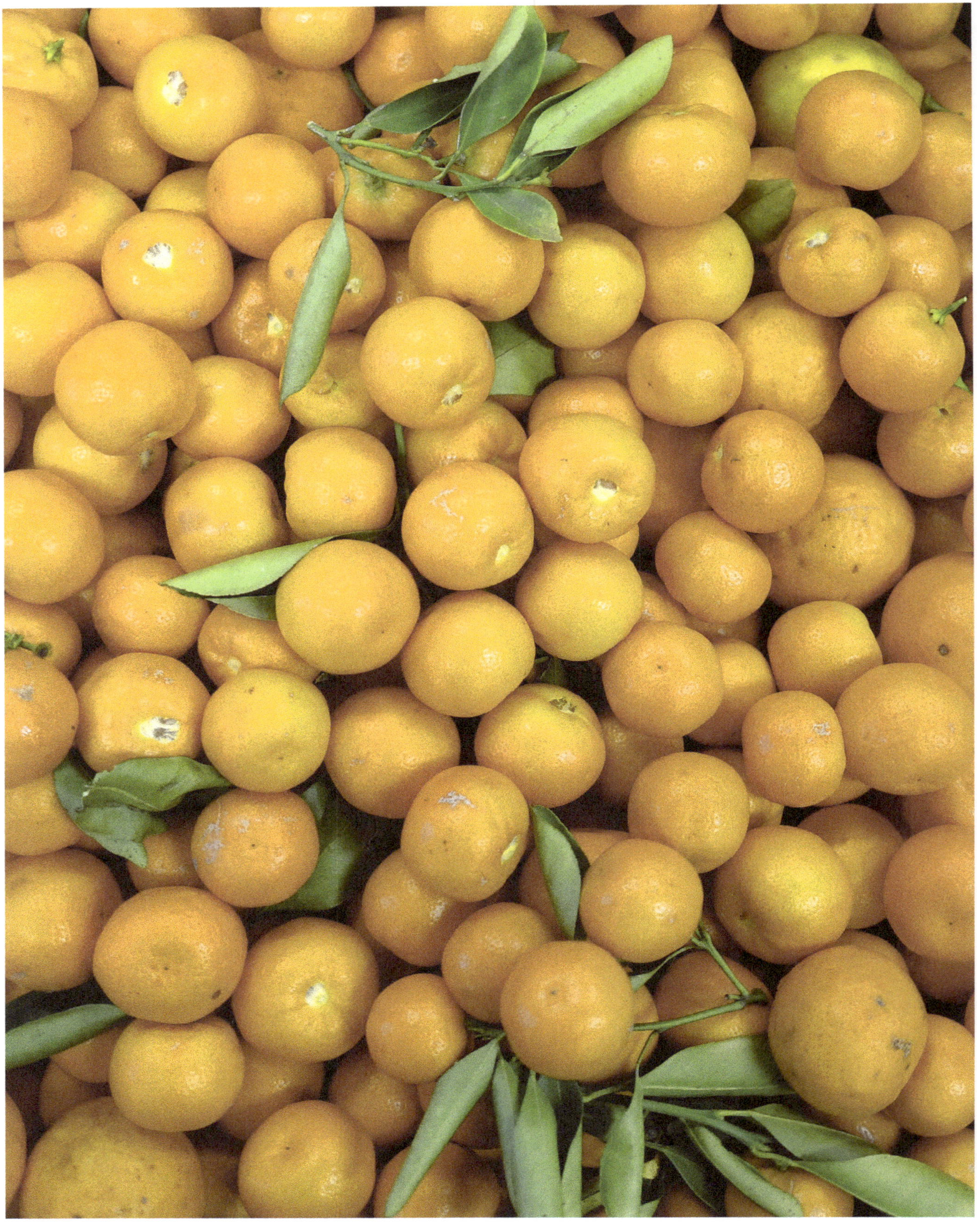

THE ABSURDITY OF WASTE

I'll let you stop for a moment to digest just how many environmental impacts our food actually has. It is a little crazy, right? Even more crazy is the fact that after we have used all those resources, as well as people's time, energy and wellbeing to produce our food, we let at least 1/3 of it go to waste[87]. This happens at the same time as millions of people on the planet suffer from hunger or hidden hunger because they can't access enough nutritious food. Our world has a massive food waste problem and we need to talk about it.

To help give a perspective to the scale of food loss and waste here is an example: if food waste was a country it would be the nation with the third largest emissions of greenhouse gasses globally[88]. Food waste uses 28% of the worlds agricultural area and costs food producers $US 750 billion annually[89].

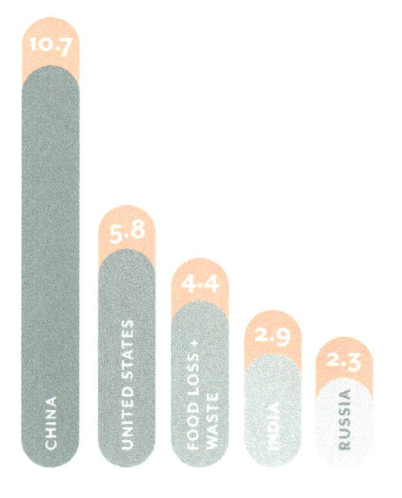

CHINA 10.7
UNITED STATES 5.8
FOOD LOSS + WASTE 4.4
INDIA 2.9
RUSSIA 2.3

GT CO_2 Equivalent (2011/12)

Figure 3

If food loss and waste were its own country, it would be the third largest emitter of greenhouse gases.[ii]

How this waste happens depends on which part of the world you inhabit. In low-income countries, a lot is actually food loss, as it happens closer to the farm and involves food that was meant to be for human consumption. This is when insects or mould destroy food after it is harvested, or when you don't have good roads or decent storage, which means produce spoils on the way to the market. Here relatively simple technologies can really help. For example, hermetic storage bags that keep grains dry and insects and mould out. This allows small farmers to store their crops for their own consumption or to sell at a time when the market rate is better. The World Food Program is currently working with industry partners in Sudan to provide these bags to farmers at a low cost. A similar research initiative in Tanzania found that improving storage options on the farm, by using items such as these bags, could reduce the number of people suffering from hunger in the area by 1/3[90].

Other incidents of food loss happen because of decisions on the other side of the world, such as the standards of retailers who may reject a harvest at the farm gate because of a minor quality or aesthetic issue. Often this is not related to the important features of the product such as its taste, safety or nutritional value.

If you think our society has ridiculous ideals around human beauty, consider the ones we have for our fresh produce.

To be accepted by many large buyers a tomato can't be too big, too small, out of shape or discoloured. Supermarkets say this is all consumers will buy, though it is a bit of a chicken-or-egg question. Have these standards changed what consumers think is normal for how food should look? Either way, the end result is a lot of food that goes to waste somewhere along the value chain.

Love Food, Hate Waste

Did you know a family of 4 in the US could save around $US 1,500 a year by cutting down on food waste? Here are some tips to help you get started:

- Plan your meals for the week, shop for what you need and batch cook a few meals at once. There are lots of meal planning guides with recipes available to download for free.

- Use the freezer as a pause button, creating more time to enjoy your food before it goes bad.

- Learn the best way to store produce to extend its shelf life. Did you know tomatoes should be stored at room temperature? Or that you should only wash produce right before you use it?

- Experiment with cooking. Use food scraps, left overs and ugly produce as a part of your next meal. Have a once a week "fridge clean out" meal where you challenge yourself to create something from whatever you have left over.

- Keep track of what is in your fridge. Check it out each morning to avoid buying what you already have.

- Avoid clutter in the fridge and stock it using the "first in, first out" principle.

- Take best before dates as an indicator only. Use your senses to see if really needs to be thrown away.

- Serve smaller portions and let people get more if they want it.

- Especially avoid wasting any meat or animal products, they are the most resource intensive to produce.

- There are endless apps out there to help you manage your own food waste or pick up food that is going to be thrown out. Download and use them.

- Outside of your own kitchen, you could volunteer or support a food redistribution organization that rescues food that would be otherwise be wasted and donates it to people in need.

But those of you reading this are probably more likely to be connected to food waste – when we throw away perfectly good, edible food. In middle- and high-income countries this is mostly done by retailers or by us consumers, in our own homes. If you take a moment to think about your own food waste story, you will see you are also playing a role here, and probably a bigger one than you realize. From leaving vegetables at the back of the fridge, to serving too much, to letting meat pass its expiry date, most of us contribute to this every day. The underlying drivers of it are clear – we are increasingly urban, busy and overwhelmed. This means we are disconnected from how our food is produced, eat less often at home, rely on convenience and pre-prepared food (which spoils faster and creates more waste). Many of us reading this do not actually pay a lot for our food relative to our income – in the US, UK, Switzerland and Australia people spend less than 10% of their income on food[91]. All this leads us to undervalue our food and feel we can afford to waste it.

Food waste in the household is actually a pretty simple issue to overcome, but it really requires us to change how we value and prioritize food. It can help to think about the real cost of food waste – in the form of nutrients, water, land, soil, chemicals, biodiversity loss and emissions that we are throwing in the bin. But we are also wasting people's time, energy and wellbeing. These are all costs that are usually not included in the actual price of our food.

There is a final element to food waste, and that is what happens to it after we throw it away. In most countries, our food waste ends up in landfill, where it decomposes and releases methane and carbon dioxide into the air. Methane from food rotting in landfill is the largest source of greenhouse gas emissions from the entire waste sector globally[92].

This alone is a problem. But so is the fact that food waste actually contains nutrients that we need to produce more food and meet our nutrition needs. So, if we are going to throw away food, we can at least make sure we are composting it. This may not seem easy if you live in an urban area, but you would be surprised. When you start looking into it, you will find a bunch of options, from starting your own compost, getting a worm composter, taking your waste to a community urban farm or connecting with the municipal composting system. Then all you need to do is start separating the waste, which is also a great way to start monitoring just how much food is getting thrown away in your house.

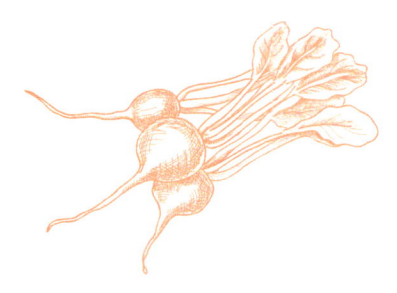

OzHarvest – Fighting Food Waste in Australia

Australians like to call their land the lucky country. In many ways it is. Yet nearly 1 in every 5 people living in Australia is food insecure[93]. At the same time, 1 in every 5 bags of groceries bought is wasted[94]. OzHarvest tackles this paradox head on – with a fleet of yellow vans and a swarm of yellow-shirted volunteers. Now Australia's leading food rescue organization, OzHarvest began with just one van and a simple concept to rescue good food that would otherwise go to waste and deliver it to people in need. It now operates across the country and has delivered 120 million meals and saved more than 37,000 tonnes of food from ending up in landfill. OzHarvest collects food from more than 3,500 businesses including supermarkets, hotels and airports and delivers it to 1,300 charities that support people in need. Beyond food distribution, OzHarvest also works on education and skill building. This includes teaching children about food waste and sustainability, educating at-risk adults on cooking healthy and affordable meals and providing vocational training in hospitality to at-risk youth. OzHarvest's charismatic founder, Ronni Kahn, is also recognized for creating legislative change to make food redistribution possible and for holding the Australian Government to account to halve food waste by 2030. Want to know more? Check out the new film about Ronni and Oz Harvest called "Food Fighter – One Woman's Crusade Against Waste". Maybe you could organize a food waste dinner and a film screening with friends?

BIODIVERSITY ON OUR PLATES

One of the reasons I love to travel is to experience the amazing diversity of food on offer around the world. From pad thai on the street in Bangkok to vegetable tagine in the Medina in Marrakech, it's the new aromas, flavours and ingredients that are highlights of my trips. When we think about how people eat all around the world, we are certainly left with an impression of variety and contrast. This makes it easy to overlook what is happening in reality – that diets around the world are becoming increasingly similar.

To try and understand what the world is eating, and how it is changing, a group of researchers compared diets by country and tracked the changes over 5 decades[95]. The results tend to shock people a little bit. They found that globally we are increasingly eating the same types of food; getting more and more of our calories from wheat, rice, corn, sugar, oil crops and animal products like meat, milk and cheese. At the same time, the global consumption of traditional crops such as buckwheat, amaranth, millet, rye, sorghum, cassava and yams is falling. The regions that have experienced the most dramatic changes in diet are Africa and Asia. In the Democratic Republic of Congo, for example, sugar consumption has increased a mind-boggling 858% since 1961[96].

This is linked to the fact that around the world, more and more of us are eating a western diet – one that is high in animal products, sugar, fat and processed food and rather low on fruit, vegetables, whole grains and pulses. The decreasing availability of diverse local foods and the increase in processed and convenience foods has been associated with multiple health issues such as obesity, Type 2 diabetes, hypertension and cardiovascular disease [97].

The trend towards a more uniform diet is having a profound impact not only on our health, but also on the health of the planet. Today, an estimated 12 crop species and 5 animal species provide 75% of all our food[98]. Now we find ourselves in a very vulnerable situation. Cultivating large areas with just a few crops makes them incredibly susceptible to pests and diseases. These threats are even more likely in the face of climate change. A recent study showed that in extreme weather events, like drought, farmers with greater biodiversity were less likely to suffer a loss of income than those in areas with low biodiversity[99].

The good news is you can play a role in bringing diversity back into the landscape. Eating a healthy and diverse diet is not only good for you, it also helps create a demand for different crops that can increase diversity in our agricultural systems. An important part of this is reconnecting with the traditional crops that used to be grown in your local area but have been neglected in the last decades. This means foods like kakadu plum and bush tomato in Australia, buckwheat in Europe, the 2,800 traditional varieties of potato in Peru, pearl millet in India or baobab leaves in eastern or southern Africa[100].

This is also an opportunity to add greater diversity to the voices at the table shaping the future of food systems. In many countries, traditional crops are intricately linked with indigenous knowledge and cultures. Australia, for example, is currently experiencing a boom in traditional bush foods, yet indigenous people participate in only 1% of the industry production and value[101]. We must recognize traditional knowledge and ownership in the commercialization of traditional foods. Several organizations are striving to do this, from IndigiGrow to Orana Foundation, supporting the creation of indigenous owned businesses where value is shared fairly, and crops are cultivated sustainability with a respect for the land.

If we change nothing, the UN predicts that by 2050:

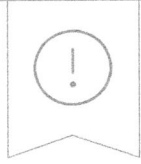

The global population will reach

10 billion people

68% of people on the planet will live in cities

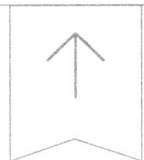

Demand for food will increase by

50%

Meat consumption will increase by

73%

Most of this demand increase will come from changing consumption patterns — as people earn more money, they buy more resource intensive, animal source foods.

When we reflect on all these challenges we have just explored – nourishing ourselves, ensuring the wellbeing of people producing our food and protecting the natural environment – we see that it is food that connects us to some of the biggest issues of our times. Food really matters. In the face of climate change, population growth, a massive increase in demand for animal sourced foods and rapid rural to urban migration, the future does not look bright unless we all participate in creating change. **Let's talk about how each of us can get started.**

WHAT CAN I DO?

THE GREAT FULL

WHAT CAN I DO?

NOW I FEEL THOROUGHLY MISERABLE. WHAT CAN I DO?

After reading the last sections, I can imagine you feel a little overwhelmed. You probably want to know how we can use food as a tool to create positive change for people and the planet. The good news is you can. The bad news is that it isn't always easy.

When we start to learn about challenges with food, we all find ourselves with a similar dilemma: knowing what we now know, do we a) bury our heads in the sand and continue as we have; b) change our own behaviour; or c) change the system? Each of these choices comes with its own nice little set of trade-offs.

Let me tell you about my own experience managing this dilemma. Like most people, when I started learning about food I buried my head in the sand for some time. I then launched quite dramatically into changing my own eating, and with it my shopping and cooking behaviour. I then decided I wanted to dedicate my professional life to this topic, with the aim of contributing at a larger, systemic level. Through this I came to learn what changing the system actually means.

Actually, it took me years of working in food systems to realize what now seems obvious. That underlying all of the big sticky issues is the fact that cheap food is the basis of our current political economic system.

This means we undervalue people and the environment to make food cheap for consumers, using price as a proxy to ensure widespread access. But this doesn't serve everyone, and it means we cannot tackle food system issues without taking on poverty, inequality and exploitation. It also means we need to put a value on the social and environmental costs and benefits of food so we can understand what it actually costs us, beyond just the monetary price. At the moment, more sustainable and ethical choices tend to cost consumers more, even though these choices have a greater net benefit for society.

Many people have started to engage with change by voting with their forks. In other words, they are using the extra money they have as wealthy consumers to align their purchasing with their values[102]. While it is important to start somewhere, every choice you make about what to eat is loaded with trade-offs. Imagine you decide you want a green smoothie – the bastion of healthy choices. Now you start wondering … it looks healthy, but is it loaded with so much fruit that it's going to send my blood sugar through the roof? What were the conditions for the farmworkers growing the bananas? What were the impacts on the environment from growing, processing, storing and transporting all the different ingredients? Augh. You quickly feel paralyzed because with one small purchase you are trying to change a big system. Possibly all in the 5 minutes you have before running to your next commitment. It feels overwhelming so we push the thinking aside, make a quick decision that meets our need for convenience and taste and move on. If we only engage with change at the time of purchase, it is easy for our ideals to be run over by time pressure and meeting our immediate needs.

The other issue with the "voting with your fork" approach is that it is only the people who are benefiting from the current system who are able to "vote" this way, because it depends on having disposable income. This leaves the ones who are suffering the most with little say in creating change.

When we focus only on what we should do as consumers, it can also put a greater burden of change on those who are traditionally the food providers in households, namely women. Across a range of countries, on average 85–90% of household food preparation is done by women[103].
I have spoken to so many mothers who start to engage with these issues when they have kids, mostly out of concern for their children's health and for the world their children will inherit. What I see is a huge burden in providing food for their families overlaid with an almost paralyzing responsibility of having to ethically screen every food purchase. This creates its own form of suffering and puts a burden on the part of the population that has experienced systematic disadvantage. (Of course, there are many fathers in the same boat, but when we consider where the burden of household management lies for the majority of families around the world, it is still with women.)

When we only focus our energy on alternative ways of buying, eating or preparing food, we don't always put as much effort into nudging, or pushing, the bigger actors like government and industry to create new policies and approaches that drive a more sustainable system. We might be enjoying our organic local produce, or our plant-based diet, but in parallel the large number of people who cannot or do not vote with their forks continue to participate in the existing system. These are topics that critical food scholars have been writing about for many years and that popular food journalists are now starting to explore as well.

YOU ARE MORE THAN JUST AN EATER

The point in all of this is that the burden is not all ours. True, when we have a choice we have responsibility. However, government and industry need to prioritize producing food in a way that is socially ethical and environmentally sustainable. To support this, we need to look at ourselves as more than just eaters in the food system. We are also citizens, voters, professionals and members of different communities. It is up to each of us to write our own narrative for how we want to participate in creating change in a way that links to our own values, skills and what brings us joy in this life.

PART ONE | *What Can I Do?*

CHOOSE YOUR OWN ADVENTURE WITH FOOD SYSTEM CHANGE

Indeed, we have to begin with ourselves before we want to shape others. – Max Frisch

A big part of working out how you want to contribute to change is getting clear on your own values, the things you stand for. This can help you to make decisions about how to contribute and to weigh up the inevitable trade-offs. Being clearer on our own values makes it easier to become more intentional about your food related choices and to avoid making decisions on autopilot.

So, what are your values when it comes to food? In other words, what key things do you believe are important for how we produce and consume food? Here is an exercise to help you understand your own food values. You will need a pen and paper and a bit of time to sit and reflect.

1. Think of some inspiring people, stories or initiatives you have come across in the food system. This might be a huge project of an international organization, a national policy, a start up in the food space, or your neighbour starting to grow their own vegetables. What are the key principles and goals behind these initiatives that really speak to you or inspire you? Jot down your answers.

2. Take a deep breath and let yourself settle for a moment. Brainstorm a list of words that are important to you when it comes to food, in terms of yourself, others and the planet. These might include equity, sustainability, inclusivity, community, health, joy, taste, cost, safety and quality or wellbeing, to give just a few examples.

3. From 1 and 2 look at which words came up most frequently. Consider which of these feel most important to you when you think about the type of food system you want. Condense your list to the 3–5 words that you feel are most important to you.

4. You can consider these your core food system values. Write them down on a clean sheet of paper. Next to each one, place a score from 1–5 (1 = not aligned, 5 = very well aligned) reflecting how aligned your actions are today. How does this leave you feeling?

Here are some of my core values when making decisions in the food system:

Wellbeing – to support the wellbeing of myself, others and the planet.

Diversity – to support diversity in diets, in production systems, and in who participates in framing problems and designing solutions.

Equity – to support equity for all actors in the food system to access what they need to live healthy lives, requiring that people's work is valued appropriately, and surplus in the system is distributed fairly.

Gratitude – to engage with food with joy and gratitude.

With your values in mind, have a think about how you want to contribute to change. Firstly, consider how you eat, shop and cook. What are some things you could do to encourage alignment with your values? You will find many examples to help you in the next section. But to get started, have a think about what immediately comes to your mind. Is it eating more fruits and vegetables and less meat, cooking more and getting takeaway less or buying from organizations that support sustainable and ethical production?

Secondly, have a think about ways you could contribute to changing the bigger system. Could you engage with government or policy makers, businesses, not-for-profit organizations, entrepreneurs, unions and worker movements, the education or research sector, to transform the system? This can feel overwhelming, so it helps to think about skills and talents that might equip you to contribute. For example, you might be an artist or designer, which initially feels far away from political action on food, but isn't – you could lend your creative skills to support organizations or movements championing values you care about.

If you are someone who likes to do such exercises in a structured way, *turn the page over for a table you can fill out.*

The Great Full | 55

My Values	Score – Current Alignment (1 not aligned – 5 fully aligned)	Individual actions to change how you shop, cook and eat.	Collective actions you could engage with to change the system.

This might leave you with a large list of ideas. To help you pick out which ones you want to act on, why not take the advice of Mikki Halpin in her piece titled *"Practical Activism: If You Want to do Something, Don't Try to Do Everything"*.
She recommends identifying 3 things to take action on:

1. Choose one you will be a leader on – here you set goals and inspire others, maybe starting a project, group or initiative or leading change within your circle of influence.

2. Choose one you will be a follower on – here you can be an active participant in something someone else is driving but take on less of the responsibility. Sometimes this might not be glamorous but it's the work that needs to be done.

3. Choose one you will make a habit of – this is something small you can commit to building into your daily or weekly routine. It might be changing habits around how you or your family eats or hosting a film night twice a year or volunteering at an organization doing something you care about.

I would add to this – choose to engage with things that you can find joy in doing. I really believe that this is a big part of making what you do sustainable. In the end, it may not matter so much what we do, but how we do it.

I hope that reflecting in this way helps you find areas where you want to make a contribution. It is simply not possible for a single individual to tackle everything, and if you try you may burn yourself out in the process. We each need to find the things we can engage with in a way that is aligned with our values, uses our skills and brings us joy. This helps keep us motivated and energized to engage over a sustained period of time. Because real change takes time.

INTENTIONAL EATING

THE GREAT FULL

PART ONE | *Intentional Eating*

INTENTIONAL EATING

Understanding the bigger purpose behind our food is an invitation to become more intentional with our eating. The purpose is the WHY; our intention is HOW we want to live that out. Intentional eating can help us move away from the autopilot that mindlessly drives much of our lives.
I like to think of it as follows:

Intentional eating is a commitment to act with awareness, align our choices with our values and focus on what matters. It invites us to slow down, find the joy in simplicity and resolve to start wherever we are and to begin again each time we forget. Eating with intention asks us to reflect on when, how and what we eat and consider: is this nourishing me? Others? The planet? Intentional eating helps us direct how we eat towards a bigger purpose and to consider how we can make each meal a contribution.

In the next sections, we will explore why we eat like we do and how we can change it to become more intentional eaters.

Why do we eat what we eat?

WHY DO WE EAT WHAT WE EAT?

Inner ring (blue): COMFORT, VALUES, HABIT, NEED, ENTERTAINMENT, NURTURE, SOCIABILITY, PLEASURE, GUILT, RITUAL, SATISFACTION, STATUS, BRIBERY, POWER, LOVE

Outer ring (orange): TECHNOLOGY, WHAT'S AFFORDABLE, ECONOMY, TRADE, WHAT WE KNOW, BIOLOGY, EDUCATION, RELIGION, CLASS, WHAT'S "NORMAL", MEDIA, WHAT'S MARKETED, GOVERNMENT, WHAT'S LEGAL, INDUSTRY, INSTITUTIONS, WHAT'S AVAILABLE, GEOGRAPHY

Figure 4

Why do we eat what we eat? Each decision we make is driven by many internal and external factors that you may not be aware of. iii

WE ARE WHAT WE EAT

As we have discussed, change can happen on a lot of levels. But when it comes to food, it makes sense to start with ourselves and what is on our plate. Here we have an opportunity at least 3 times a day to shape our choices and actions, and to let this be a bridge to other action to change the system. This all sounds wonderful. But in reality, this whole eating thing is a very tricky topic. Food is incredibly emotional, because, as Geneen Roth says, *our relationship to food is a microcosm of our relationship to the whole of life*[104]. Exploring how we eat means looking at our most deeply held personal, emotional and even spiritual beliefs.

The Invisible Fork

For all our obsessing about food, I find it strange that we very rarely actually stop and ask ourselves a pretty fundamental question: why do I eat what I do? Think back to your last bite of food. What actually made you eat it?

You may think everything you eat is your own choice, but often it is not a conscious one. This individual choice is actually shaped by history, evolution, culture, politics and marketing and a whole range of other things that are going on subconsciously every time you take a bite. Figure 4 gives an overview of some of the internal and external factors that may actually shape what you eat.

Regardless of all these factors, studies show us that it is actually taste, price and convenience that are the major drivers of what we decide to eat[105]. Health or sustainability concerns usually come much lower down the list. Regardless of what positive values we might espouse, when it comes to actually paying more for ethical or sustainable food, we don't always put our money where our mouth is.

So the next time you sit down to eat, I invite you to pause for a moment and ask yourself "What actually led me to choose this food?"

Eating Is An Emotional Act

When we are privileged enough to buy whatever food we want, and are surrounded by an abundance of both healthy and unhealthy options, we can start to look to food to deliver us more than physical nourishment. It can become our primary source of pleasure, fulfilment, entertainment and even love. Those little opioid hits are what we turn to in dealing with the chronic dissatisfaction that is often part of the human experience.

So, it is easy to say that we all need to change how we eat. But I think we have to be careful not to underestimate just how hard it is for an individual to change their eating habits. There are many drivers behind our behaviour, but it is the workings of our mind and emotions that are the most challenging to crack.

I know this personally. When I am stressed, dissatisfied, unfulfilled or sad I reach for food to provide me with temporary relief. When I am more connected to myself and living in a way that is fulfilling, I am more compassionate to myself and others and I naturally gravitate to healthier and more sustainable ways of eating.

Becoming aware of this and turning towards my relationship with food has actually been very transformative, even if at times uncomfortable. Watching how I eat has uncovered some key unconscious habits. For example, I noticed that I was spending a lot of time thinking about my next meal with great anticipation for the joy it would bring me. When the meal came along, I would then eat it so quickly, distracted by thoughts of the next things that were coming up, that I would not really extract the joy from it that I anticipated. I was eating like I was living – fast and focused on what was next, never present and never sure it was enough. *I realized I wasn't just missing out on enjoying meals, I was missing out on enjoying my life.*

The first step to changing anything is to become aware of it. So, I highly recommend exploring your own relationship to food with a gentle curiosity. Through this, you can see the ways that this relationship is bringing you joy or suffering, or both. When you have done this, you are better able to tackle the root causes that come between you and eating in a

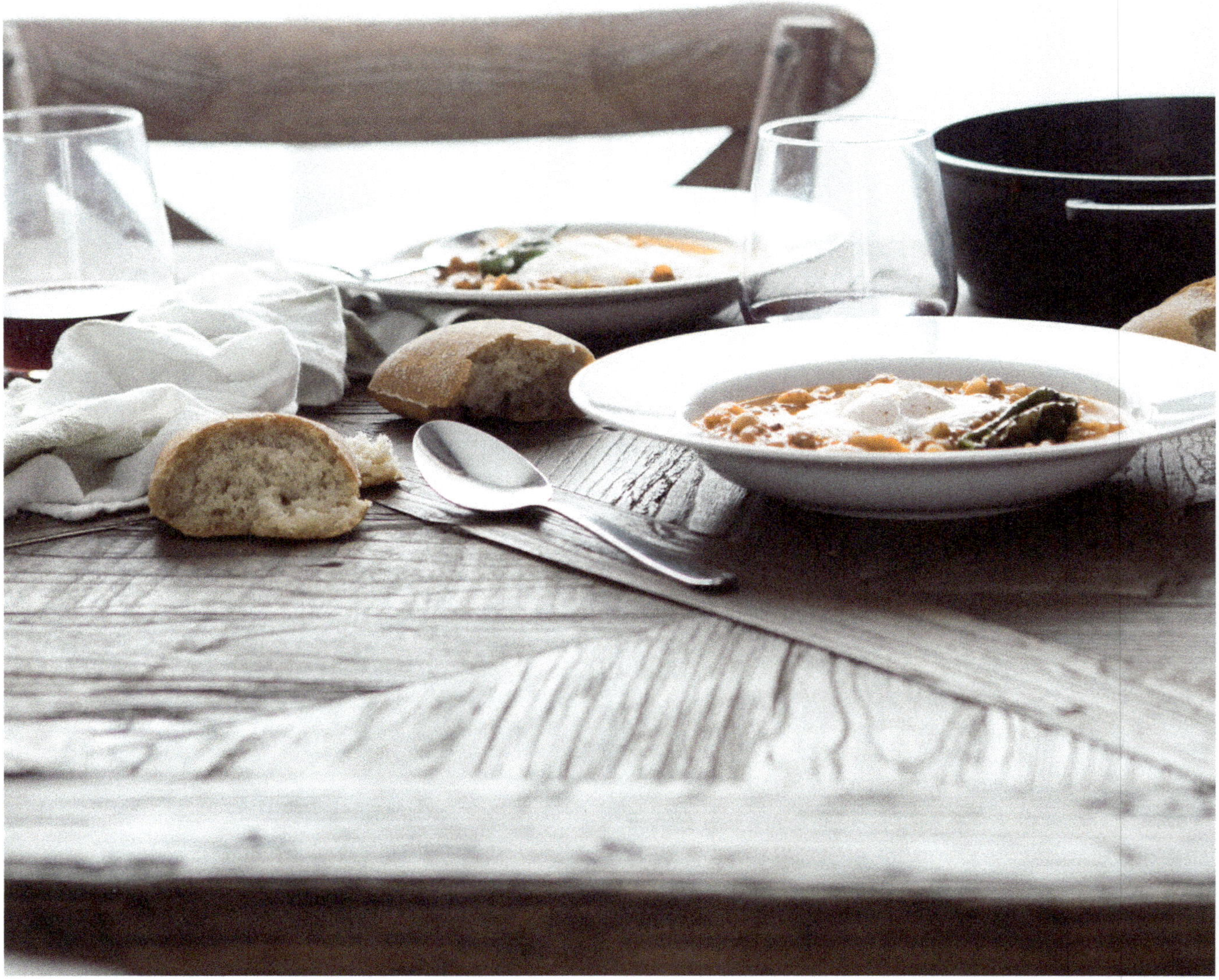

way that is aligned with your values. One of the true powers of food is its ability to open a doorway into how you work with your mind and emotions to live a great and full life. Whatever that may mean for you.

Not You and Them but Us and Our

You are not alone in this food jungle. We all face similar challenges, even though they are unique to context, conditioning and mindset. I believe that if we can collectively work through what we have internalized around food there is great potential to create a healthier basis for our food system. This deeply personal side of eating is not really talked about in the food systems change landscape. I have seen so many global reports and discussions on this topic that point to how we need to eat differently to have a more sustainable food system, with a cursory nod to how difficult it is to change behaviour around food. What is really behind this struggle doesn't get the attention and support it needs in our society and people can feel very alone as they work through it.

But it doesn't have to be this way. We can realize we are not actually alone and start to be more honest with ourselves and others about the challenges we face. We can start to explore how our eating is linked to our living, especially in our modern world. A world where the feeling of never having enough, doing enough or being enough is all pervasive and unconsciously drives so many of our actions. If we start to look at these deeper questions together, we can support one another on our individual and collective journey to more intentional eating and living.

Mindful Eating

One of the best ways to become more intentional with your food is to practice mindful eating. Mindful eating is simply moment-to-moment, non-judgmental awareness of what is happening when you eat. And it is so much harder than it sounds.

It doesn't have to be at every meal to be effective, but perhaps once a day, on the weekend or whenever you remember. The concept is simple (so simple your mind may dismiss it as irrelevant – try it anyway!) and you can do it alone or together with whoever you share a meal with.

Remove distractions – make mealtimes only about eating by removing all distractions: phones, newspapers, televisions, books, games etc. It is just us and our food.

Take a deep breath – before starting to eat, take a long, deep breath and let yourself physically settle and relax.

Take one bite at a time – put the fork down, chew slowly and savour it, taking time to really notice the different flavours and textures. Chew the food thoroughly, waiting until you finish one mouthful completely before you take the next.

Reflect on your choices – what led you to eat what is on your plate or in your hand? Are you eating in response to emotional or physical hunger? Is this supporting your long-term needs?

Reflect on your food – take a moment to think about what is on your plate. Where did it come from? Who produced it? (There's a good chance you won't know the answers to these questions, and this in itself is something to ponder.)

After doing this a few times, you can start to ask yourself some questions about the patterns you are seeing. What insights did you get into how you normally eat, and live? What are the deeper needs behind what and how you eat?

It is important to say that none of the above reflections are about judging what you are doing as good or bad. The key is slowing down and being curious about what is actually happening right now and what is really behind it.

Hijacking Our Control

Do you have a certain food that is your kryptonite? That item that when it is in front of you, you lose all willpower to resist eating more of it? Mine is potato chips. Well, honestly it is just potatoes in any fried and salted form, I am not picky.

Whenever I have asked anyone this, the answer is never a crispy apple or mouthwatering kale salad. It is usually some type of processed food like a chocolate bar, a hamburger with fries or a soft drink – foods and drinks that you can find almost anywhere in the world these days. When I discuss this with my students, who typically come from all around the world, I hold up examples like chocolate bars, chips and cookies. All of them can easily find the equivalent items where they come from, even if it is a rural village in the middle of nowhere. These foods are everywhere.

And they all have some things in common – they are considered hyper-palatable. This means they are designed with the perfect mix of fat, salt and sugar to make them irresistible. Combine these things with flavours, texture and "mouthfeel" (a legitimate industry term!) and you have our kryptonite foods. These foods leave us powerless to resist them, even if we are not hungry.

The theory around why we are so compelled by (and often addicted to) such foods posits that fat, salt and sugar were all rare elements in early human diets. If they did exist, they were in much smaller quantities and seldom packed the flavour punch we see today. However, they were beneficial to our survival as they were energy dense. So, we developed a reward mechanism in the brain to incentivize us to seek them out[106].

When we eat these foods, the opioid circuit in our brain is activated and endorphins – the happy hormones – are released. In the short term, this gives us pleasure, can make us feel calmer and even reduce pain or stress. But this is only temporary.

Indeed, this was all fine back in the day when there was a lot of hunting and gathering to be done to find our food. Today, we are surrounded by these foods and they are cheap. There are constant cues and reminders to eat them, through billboards, product placement in TV series, social media influencers or the clever positioning of such items at every supermarket checkout. These cues, and our own emotional state, can trigger an urge to seek out the reward we have come to associate with them.

Suddenly, we have developed a habit that is hard to break. This completely disrupts and overrides the normal mechanisms we have in our body to regulate our appetite in a healthy way. It can lead to addiction and behaviour that is not all that dissimilar to drug abuse[107]. In fact, lab rats will work harder to get sugar than they will to get cocaine[108].

I am sure you have experienced this yourself at some point. A battle between control and desire rages inside you and the easiest way through is to give in to the desire. But the relief is only temporary, as is the pleasure the food brings.

Realizing why these foods have power over us is the first step to disarming them. The thing that has helped me the most is reading the ingredient list on highly processed foods. I find this quickly diminishes the product's magical power. It also helps slow down the decision, which helps me reflect on the intention behind my purchase. The second step is to avoid buying the item and bringing it home in the first place. Lastly, I substitute the most enticing of these foods with healthier homemade versions. Even with all of this in hand, hyper-palatable temptations will still get me sometimes, but rarely and only when I know I am being complicit in their little game.

Moreover, our individual work needs to be combined with reforms to industry strategy and government regulation, particularly with regard to the marketing of food to children. The brains of children and adolescents are still developing, making them more vulnerable to marketing messages and less able to resist what is being promoted to them, particularly when it comes to hyper-palatable food. In most parts of the world, children and adolescents are exposed to substantially more advertisements for junk food than they are to education around healthy foods. All around the world, as social media personalities and targeted digital advertising become more and more influential in children's lives, regulation is lagging far behind where it should be[109].

"What did we expect to happen when this industry embarked on a highly profitable business model that made foods high in sugar, fat and salt widely available, conditioned us to associate their products with positive emotions and created environments that foster these positive emotions?"

– David Kessler, the End of Overeating

CAN'T YOU JUST TELL ME WHAT I SHOULD EAT TO SAVE THE WORLD?

The basic elements of eating better – for ourselves and for the planet – are not all that complex. Yet I am going to disappoint you because I am not going to give you a list of things you should or shouldn't eat. Health and sustainability mean something different to every person. We are all unique in terms of our nutritional needs, our health issues, what is available to us, our socio-economic circumstances and our values. Everyone on the planet has a different set of challenges and constraints to factor in when choosing what to eat.

What I would like to share with you are the guidelines I use to help me eat in a way that supports my health and the health of the planet, in a way that I find to be delicious and joyful. I have eaten like this for over a decade and find that it works well for me – it is flexible, and I can continually adapt it whenever I get new information or insights from research or my own life experience. This way of eating is not revolutionary and does not lend itself to a fancy name with trendy branding around it. I think this is good, because I don't like attaching too many labels to how I eat. Humans are a pretty amazing species, and we are constantly learning and discovering new things. If we are too righteous or dogmatic about what we eat, we may not be open enough to learn and adapt when new insights emerge.

Here are the foundational guidelines I have crafted for myself around eating:

+ I do what I can to source ingredients that are ethically and sustainably produced, accepting that this is not always possible without also changing the system.

+ I mostly eat a plant-based diet, putting vegetables, whole grains, nuts, seeds, legumes and fruit in focus and minimizing animal source foods (like meat, poultry, eggs and dairy).

+ I eat fresh, seasonal, whole foods whenever possible.

+ I include a diverse range of foods in my diet, especially getting as many different vegetables, greens, grains and legumes into my day as I can and seeking out rare varieties.

+ I keep my consumption of sugar and highly processed foods as low as possible, enjoying treats in moderation, and making them at home as often as I can. (Reducing my consumption of dark chocolate is something I have accepted as a lifelong challenge!)

+ I prioritize drinking water over other drinks and avoid artificially sweetened beverages, coffee and alcohol.

Interestingly, I find it is the last point that sparks the liveliest discussions. Saying no to coffee and alcohol in our busy world of overwhelm seems even more emotionally loaded than saying no to meat!

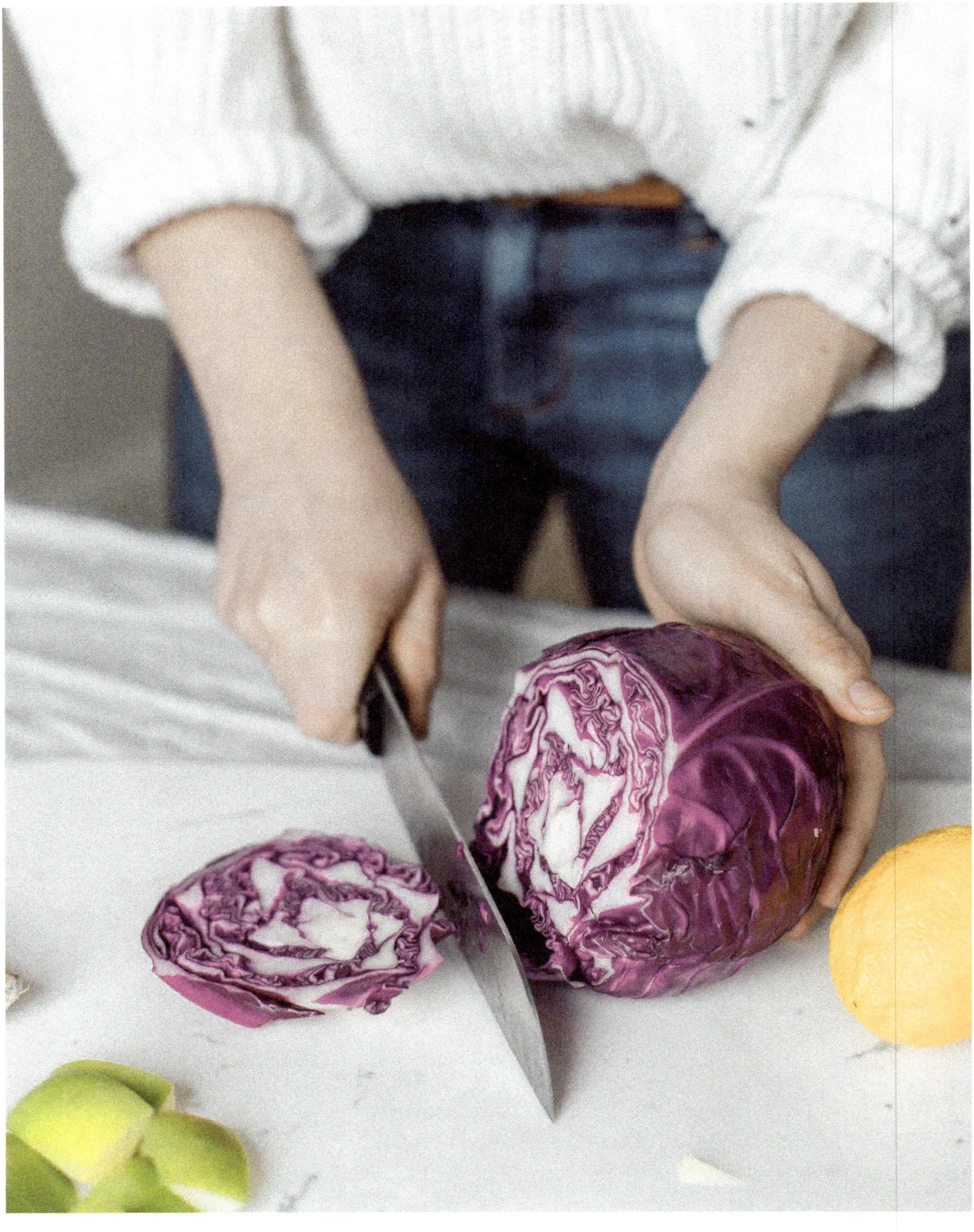

PART ONE | *Intentional Eating*

What Does Science Say?

A lot of research points to this style of eating as a way to support your own health and the health of the planet. The most recent large-scale study to explore the topic was published in early 2019 in the medical journal Lancet[110]. Thirty-seven scientists spent three years reviewing the scientific evidence on diets that could support human health AND reduce our environmental footprint. The final recommendation is a guideline for a Planetary Health Reference Diet. The main recommendations come in the form of a plate, indicating how an average meal should be composed to support our health while also minimizing our environmental impact. Here is what it looks like:

WHOLE GRAINS

VEGETABLES

STARCHY VEGETABLES

DAIRY FOODS

ANIMAL SOURCED PROTEIN

PLANT SOURCED PROTEIN

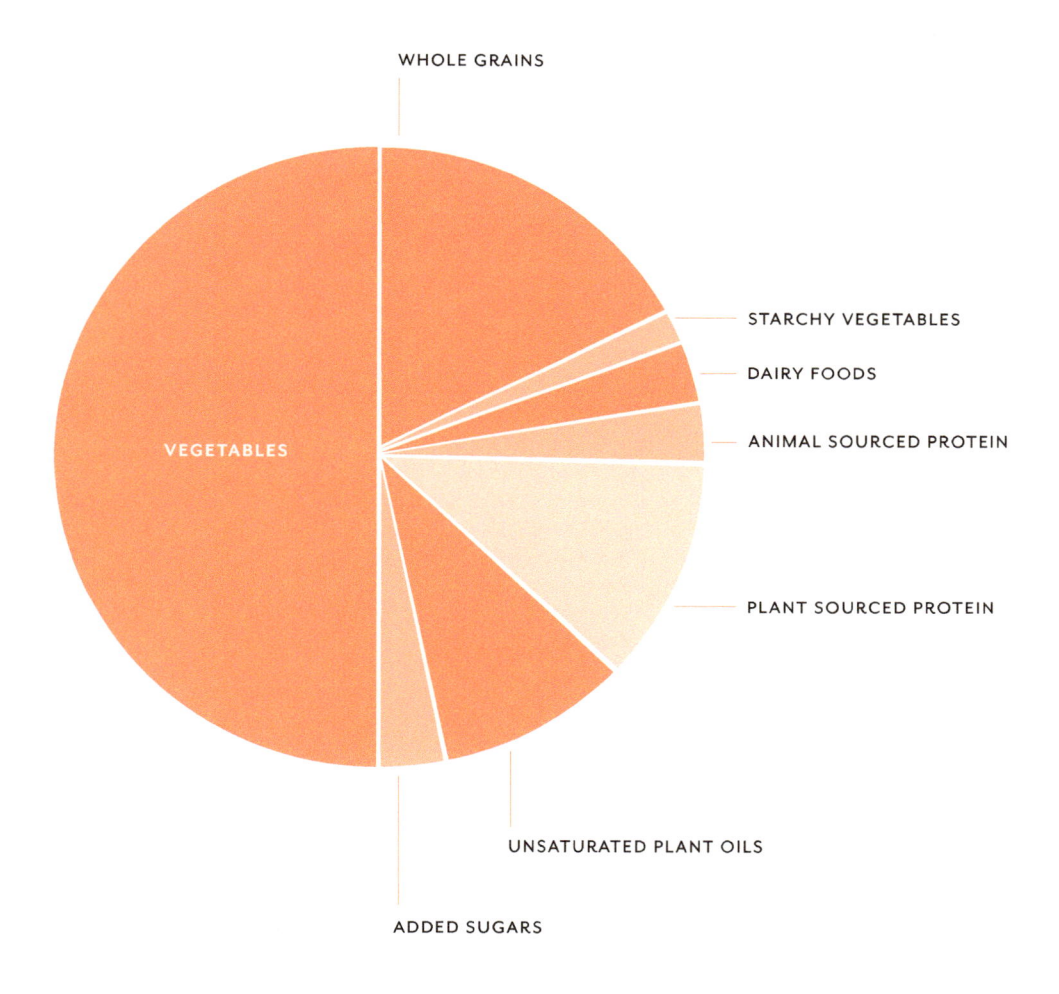

UNSATURATED PLANT OILS

ADDED SUGARS

Figure 5

The Planetary Health Diet on a Plate

The Great Full | 67

As you can see, it puts vegetables and fruit front and centre, followed by whole grains and plant-based proteins (such as beans, legumes and nuts) and fats. Animal sourced foods (such as beef, lamb, poultry, fish, pork, eggs and dairy) are present in very small quantities.

Although this resembles the Mediterranean diet, long considered a healthy way for us to eat, it is intended to be tailored to any cultural context and way of eating. It serves as a useful guideline to see where our eating is now and in which direction we could move it. For most people in the wealthy world, that is a drastic reduction in animal source foods and a large increase in plant sourced foods. Globally, it means a 50% reduction in unhealthy foods (like processed meat and sugar) and a 100% increase in healthy foods (such as nuts, fruits, vegetables and legumes)[111].

Yet for the nearly 1 billion people in the world who are severely undernourished, and the 2 billion who suffer from micronutrient deficiencies, eating some animal source foods could provide important macro and micronutrients that would support their health. In this case, to move towards the reference diet there is a need to improve access to healthy and diverse foods, which could include both plant-based and animal-based foods.

The Planetary Health Diet is aligned with a Whole Foods Plant-based Diet. Studies have shown that eating this way can help treat obesity, diabetes, hypertension and heart disease[112]. The emerging field of nutritional psychiatry is now starting to show that this way of eating can also support our mental health by reducing the incidences and risk of depression. Meanwhile, diets high in saturated fats and refined carbohydrates – common in a western-style diet – are associated with increased incidences of depression[113].

When moving towards a plant-focused way of eating, the main decision is if or how much animal source foods to eat. Most health organizations recommend eliminating processed meat entirely (due to its classification as a carcinogen), reducing red meat consumption to as low as possible and consuming other types of meat in moderation.

If you decide to completely cut animal products, it means learning how to eat a diverse range of plant-based foods so that you get the complete proteins you need, as well as key micronutrients like B12, iron, vitamin D, n-3 fatty acids, calcium and zinc. These nutrients are the ones that may fall short in a poorly planned vegetarian or vegan diet, especially as more unhealthy vegan products come onto the market [114]. It is also a good idea to speak with your healthcare provider to understand your particular health situation. This is especially the case for Vitamin B12, which is mostly available in foods derived from animals. If they are not being eaten, then it is necessary to eat enough foods fortified with B12, take a supplement and eat nori and tempeh, two of the only plant derived foods with notable levels of B12 [115].

Start Where You Are

Getting started or shifting towards this way of eating needn't be an overnight change. It can begin with making meals more vegetable-centric, reducing animal products in your diet by moving them from the centre to the side of your meal, only eating meat on special occasions, letting each meal have diverse ingredients, and finding healthier substitutes for junk foods you crave. You could start with Meat-free Monday then extend that, or make sure you eat one fully plant based meal each day. It also helps to think about what you are adding rather than what you are missing out on. Focus on how you can get the vegetables, fruits, nuts and seeds, legumes and whole grains you need first, and add anything else afterwards.

There are a lot of different words to describe eating in a way that maximizes your own health while minimizing the impact on the planet, with some being more restrictive than others. Here is an overview of the most common terms:

Vegan: A person who seeks to avoid all forms of exploitation and cruelty to animals through eating an entirely plant-based diet, excluding all animal foods such as meat, dairy, honey and eggs, and avoiding any animal derived materials, products tested on animals and places that use animals for entertainment.

Vegetarian: A person who does not eat any meat or fish, but may eat eggs and dairy products.

Flexitarian: A person who mainly follows a vegetarian diet, but eats meat and fish occasionally (also jokingly called "vegetarians with benefits").

Pescatarian: A person who follows a vegetarian diet, but eats fish.

Plant-based Diet: A diet that maximizes the consumption of nutrient-dense plant foods, while minimizing animal-based foods, processed foods and added sugars and fats[116].

Sustainable Diet: A diet with low environmental impact, which contributes to food and nutrition security and to a healthy life for present and future generations. Sustainable diets are protective and respectful of biodiversity and ecosystems, culturally acceptable, accessible, economically fair and affordable; nutritionally adequate, safe and healthy; while optimizing natural and human resources[117].

People typically follow the diets above from a concern for their own health, environmental sustainability and animal welfare. Unfortunately, none of these ways of eating explicitly takes into account the wellbeing and working conditions of people producing our food. That is why we need to look beyond what we eat to how it is produced, reflecting on how we shop, and how we act beyond voting with our forks.

A Contemplation for Grateful Eating

Many cultural, spiritual and religious traditions offer thanks before sitting down to eat. I think it is a beautiful practice to pause before a meal and return to a mindset of gratitude, as a preface to mindful eating. Here is a short contemplation you can use before a meal to help you reconnect to the importance of food in your life.

The food on this plate in front of me is a gift and I am grateful for the people and resources that made it possible. I will eat with joy, awareness, and kindness for myself, others and our planet. May this food nourish me and fuel my contribution to the world.

INTENTIONAL SHOPPING

THE GREAT FULL

PART ONE | *Intentional Shopping*

INTENTIONAL SHOPPING

Remember those food values you defined earlier? Well you might want to have them handy, because it's time to go shopping. The simple eating advice summarized so nicely by Michael Pollan – *"Eat food. Not too much. Mostly plants."* – can go a long way to improving our own health and the health of the planet. But it is not just about what we eat; it is also where it comes from. The minute we start to look at this, we face an overwhelming number of trade-offs. Should I buy the fair trade rice from India or the organic rice from Italy? The local cow's milk or the cashew milk? In these situations, your food values will help you to prioritize. More generally, here are some tips to help your shopping have a positive impact on people and the planet.

BUY LABELLED PRODUCTS (BUT KNOW THEIR LIMITS)

Labels offer a chance for people to pay for products which embody their values. Fair trade, union made, or other labels with explicit and high labour standards can help support ethical working conditions. Those such as organic, biodynamic or soil association can help build more environmentally sustainable production practices. When I can, I buy products with labels that are aligned with my values. I pay special attention to such labels when buying products from countries that do not have strict social or environmental standards enforced by the government.

Labels can get very confusing. There are around 130 different sustainability labels in the European market alone[118]. This means that not all labels are equal, and it is worth researching what is behind each one. For example, the criteria for organic certification are different in every country in the world. There are a few organizations that help out with this, reviewing the hundreds of different labels on the market and highlighting the strengths and weaknesses. These include Ethical Consumer and Good Shopping Guide in the UK; the How Good App, DFTA Label Comparison and Fair World Project in the US; or Label Info or Plush in Switzerland. Generally, it is best to look for labels that are transparent about what they cover and that involve third party certification or are part of a Participatory Guarantee System.

Labels however, have limits. It is difficult to really know which ones are the best, as we can only compare labels based on the written list of criteria they use rather than how they are actually being implemented by producers on the ground. Due to the cost and paperwork involved in the certification process, it is not always easy for small producers to participate. Labels also reduce citizens to consumers, potentially directing us away from political action and towards consumption based action. They make fair working conditions or environmental sustainability the responsibility of consumers who can and will pay more. We will probably never solve labour exploitation through voluntary consumer choice alone. We need stronger governance of these issues by state and industry players.

That said, the good labels can have a positive impact and they provide a foundation and network of people to innovate and improve the existing system. Importantly, they help us signal that as consumers, we care about these things.

The Great Full | 71

BUY SEASONAL
(BUT KNOW IT'S NOT THAT SIMPLE)

It makes sense that we focus on eating food that is grown during its natural growing season. This way we avoid the use of artificial heating or lighting during production, which greatly increases energy use and GHG emissions. But seasonal can mean two things: grown and eaten in the local season or grown in season in one part of the world and transported to be eaten in another. The latter often gets a bad rap, with discussions about food miles becoming an overly simplified way of talking about environmental impact. But this is not so straightforward.

Food miles are only one metric in a complicated landscape. All they indicate is how far the food has travelled; they don't tell us anything about the food's overall impact in terms of greenhouse gas emissions, biodiversity, land use, water use, intensity of inputs like fertilizers or pesticides or how the food was processed. All these things often have a greater impact than the distance the food travels.

Local and seasonal eating can reduce negative impacts in other countries, impacts such as water stress, converting pristine land to farmland, biodiversity loss or labour exploitation. But this really depends on the comparison to how things are being produced where you live. Eating locally also allows us to directly support the food producers in our region and keep us better connected to what is being grown when.

However, if you live in a location with long, cold winters, a strictly local seasonal diet can lead to reduced fruit and vegetable consumption, which may already be too low from a health perspective[119]. International trade and eating food produced abroad can offer greater dietary diversity during these times. It can also help when one growing region experiences some sort of weather or climate shock and is no longer able to feed the local population. In terms of the environmental impact of imported foods, products that are transported by land or sea have a lower environmental footprint. Produce that is transported by air tends to have a higher footprint. This is also the case for food grown in a heated greenhouse.

In fact, environmental impact depends much more on what type of food you choose to eat, namely if it comes from plants or animals, rather than whether it is seasonal. Research has shown that reducing meat consumption has a much greater impact on the environment than eating a seasonal diet[120]. When it comes to eating more plants, some have greater environmental impacts than others because of what it takes to produce them. For example, hardy crops like root vegetables, onions and leeks tend to have a much lower environmental impact that more delicate crops like tomatoes[121].

BUY FROM DIVERSE PLACES
(BUT DON'T DISMISS THE BIG PLAYERS)

Over the last 70 years, supermarkets have quickly changed the way we buy food. Offering a wide range of products at a relatively low price, they are now the most common way for people to source food. Like every other food business, the margins are tight and the risks high, which means there is a lot of consolidation in the food retail space. In most countries, there are only a couple of major supermarkets that serve the majority of consumers. This concentrates negotiating power into a smaller number of hands, allowing supermarkets to buy bigger volumes at lower prices. With this greater influence, supermarkets have a greater opportunity to change the system for the better, which can happen if there is pressure, or incentives, by consumers or policy makers. When there isn't, it can mean the power to maintain the status quo of pushing down margins to the bottom of the supply chain.

Whenever I talk to people working in sustainability for supermarkets, they all say the same things. Supermarkets will change if consumers, and governments, keep pressuring them to do so. Writing letters, creating petitions, spamming the information lines with more complex sustainability related questions, social media campaigns and public discussions on these topics all help push change within these organizations, who are particularly vulnerable to reputational damage.

That said, it doesn't make for a very resilient system when we get all our food from a couple of sources. Although supermarkets are often the most efficient supply chains, efficiency isn't the only thing we might care about. It makes sense to buy at least some of our food from organizations that are trying to build different types of value chains, where there is a more equitable distribution of profit through the supply chain. This could mean shopping at farmers markets, seeking out stands that sell their own produce directly. Or connecting with local food saver organizations where you can rescue some ugly or "imperfect" produce that would otherwise go to waste. Another option is to get a fresh produce box each week through a community supported agriculture scheme. You could use a platform, like farmy.ch in Switzerland, which acts like an online farmers market to help connect producers and consumers without too many intermediaries taking a cut in between. I also like to visit values driven shops, like Bachsermärt in Switzerland. This is a small food retailer that is a part of a broader sustainable regional food network - a connection of organizations that share the same values and use these as a basis for how they do business together. The stores in the wealthier urban centres help cross subsidize those in the rural areas and the product range is adapted to each local market. The products sourced internationally are only from producers that have an alignment of values with the organization and each product is assessed against a range of sustainability criteria before being taken into their range. Their model is now being adapted in different locations, including Nepal and Portugal.

Yes, these options are more expensive and not available to everyone. However, starting with reducing the consumption of meat and animal sourced foods to a minimum can help free up some funds to align with your values. We also have to remember that cheap food just means hidden costs that are carried elsewhere.

BUY MUCH LESS MEAT (BUT BUY BETTER)

It seems the general conclusion regarding eating meat is simple: eat much less but buy better (though you probably want to reduce processed meats like hot dogs and bacon to a minimum – they are classified as class 1 carcinogens by the World Health Organization[122]). In terms of making an impact, the LESS part is the most important. When it comes to defining BETTER, meat that is produced on well managed grasslands or pastures using as little external feed as possible is generally better for biodiversity, animal and human welfare, quality and taste than intensive livestock production systems. Globally, nearly 70% of agricultural land is permanent meadow or pasture land, which is typically not suited for other types of food production[123].

Thus, raising animals in such systems can offer a way to utilize the land to produce food. Ideally, this grazing would only be supplemented by small amounts of external feed or agricultural by-products. For pigs and chickens, it would mean basing their feed on by-products and residues from food production, rather than crops like wheat, corn or soy which are grown on prime agricultural land. If we would aim to produce meat and poultry in this way, modelling shows us that we would have to reduce our consumption of beef and dairy products by at least 50% and our consumption of pork, poultry and eggs by 90%[124]. These are rough numbers that only take into account environmental and agricultural considerations and don't factor in health questions, which is why they are different to the recommendations of the Planetary Health Diet we saw earlier.

Mixed crop-livestock systems, where livestock manure provides nutrients for crop production, can also be a way to sustainably source the animal products you eat. In agroecological approaches to farming, such as organic and biodynamic farming, animal manure is needed as it provides nutrients and organic matter critical for building healthy soils and growing plants without synthetic fertilizers. There is currently a surge of interest in regenerative agriculture, an approach that seeks to produce nutritious food while improving the natural ecosystem. One of the principles of this approach is to integrate crop and livestock production in a sustainable way.

These types of systems may be more sustainable, but they produce a much lower volume of animal source foods than we demand today. If we want systems that are better for human and planetary health, we have to drastically decrease our consumption and curb the ever-growing global demand. That can start at your next meal, and it is urgent that it does. The UN FAO predicts that meat consumption will grow by 73% by 2050, and that much of this new demand will be met by intensive production systems[125].

Sourcing animal products that are produced more sustainably can be done by looking for labels that support this type of production, for example organic or biodynamic where animals are grazed on pastures and treated ethically. Even better, do some research to seek out producers in your area who are pioneering new ways of producing meat more sustainability and ethically. They may not sell through supermarkets, but directly to the consumer, online or through other types of markets.

Buying less but better also means it doesn't have to cost you more money overall – reduce as much as you can and use

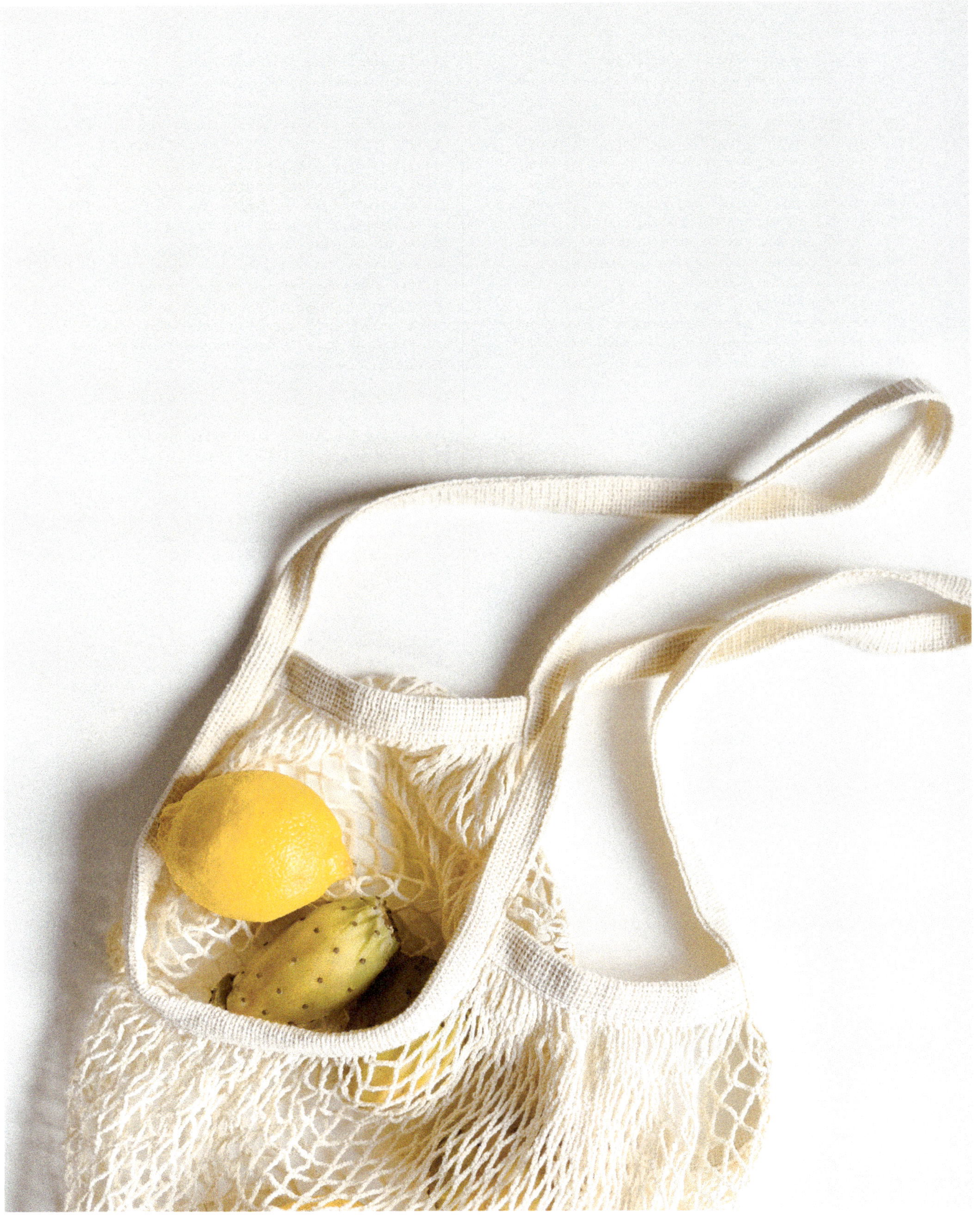

the savings to buy the best quality you can find. You can also save money by participating in nose-to-tail eating, which means eating the less popular parts of the animal that may otherwise go to waste, instead of always taking the prime cuts. In this process we need to recognize meat for the valuable and high-quality resource that it is: what is on your plate took the life of an animal, a lot of resources and human effort to produce. We need to fully appreciate this to avoid over-consuming it, wasting it or taking it for granted.

When it comes to replacing meat, milk or eggs with plant-based alternatives, we also need to be mindful. For example, almond milk has had a massive increase in consumption recently but is linked to very high water and pesticide use. Around 80% of the world's almonds come from California, where water scarcity is a real concern. A recent comparison of plant-based milk alternatives showed that in terms of CO_2 emissions and water use, oat or soy milk are better choices than rice or almond milk[126]. However, all of these options still have a much lower impact than dairy milk.

If you find yourself consuming from the booming "faux meat" or "alternative protein" market, it is a good idea to become conscious of what you are actually eating. These products use plant-based ingredients to create something that resembles meat, hoping to make it easier for people to give up eating something they love. The most famous examples are the Impossible Burger and the Beyond Meat Burger, which have already found their way into a range of fast food restaurant chains[127]. Both have the same key ingredients: water, pea or soy protein isolate and coconut, canola or sunflower oil. Most nutritionists agree that while these products are safe and no worse for you than a normal burger, they are based on highly processed ingredients that should be eaten in moderation. From a nutritional and environmental perspective, you would be better off eating the soybeans or peas in their whole food form.

I think it is important to see the alternative proteins as a part of a bigger picture. Are you buying these products instead of meat, thus actually reducing your meat consumption? Are the products you are choosing using ingredients that support more diverse production systems? What sort of value chains are they a part of? Are they supporting you to eat a healthy diet or simply giving you fast or snack food options? Are you actually already eating enough protein?

There are already a lot of great vegetarian protein sources available that are cheap and simple, like a diverse range of beans, chickpeas, lentils and tofu. It may sound a little 1980s whole foods, but these can be the basis of delicious meals. You can now also buy convenient products like pasta that is made from legumes or contains algae for another easy option to add plant-based proteins into your diet.

These options also tend to be higher in fibre. This is important because most people in the world do not eat anywhere near enough fibre. Yet we rarely hear about this. Instead, clever marketing has made us very focused on protein, despite the fact that most people in the world currently eat more protein than they actually need each day. This means the majority of us can easily cut down on our meat consumption without having to worry if we will still get enough protein.

BUY THE UGLY AND THE UNUSUAL

Why not relax our ridiculous beauty standards for fruit and vegetables and buy the imperfect produce? How fruit and vegetables look actually tells us very little about the flavour, yet it is a major driver of supermarket buying standards and food waste and loss. Ugly produce often doesn't even make it into stores these days, as it is rejected earlier on in the value chain. You may have to seek it out at the farmers market, by ordering an imperfect produce box or find a caterer that cooks from ugly produce (like Zum Guten Heinrich in Zurich). You could even join a local gleaning group and go rescue it from rotting in nearby fields!

We also tend to habitually reach for the ingredients we know and love from the small number of varieties that supermarkets deliver to us year round. Why not seek out the unusual products, like heirloom varieties of grains, fruits, vegetables and livestock that were traditionally grown in your area? You may not find these in a standard supermarket, but you will at farmers markets or when you buy direct from farms that aim to support more diversity in production systems. Although it may take some initial effort to track down these ingredients, it is a great way to bring more diversity into your own diet and into our production systems.

THE GREAT FULL

PART TWO

FOOD AND JOY

Cooking Up Calm	79
The Plant Based Kitchen	85
Breakfast	94
Starters	114
Salads and Soups	128
Mains	162
Sweet Treats	190
Drinks	230
Sauces, Spices, Toppings	244

○ COOKING UP CALM ○

THE GREAT

COOKING UP CALM

If you have made it this far, I am guessing you are intrigued about how you can reduce your consumption of animal foods and integrate more plant-based meals into your diet. Which leads us into the kitchen, where we can cook as an act of service to ourselves and to others. To some, this feels old fashioned or regressive, but actually I consider it a very modern act. It is a chance to take a step away from autopilot and reconnect to our most essential need. It helps us to leave behind unhealthy overly processed foods and get back to simple concepts of nourishment. To get closer to the raw ingredients and to the stories behind how they were grown. To take control over what we are eating, how it is prepared and what value it creates, despite all the other subconscious drivers that pull us away from this. This is an opportunity to take our wellbeing into our own hands, which is the basis of any other contribution we might make in the world.

There is a lot to be said for taking the time to cook at home, going against the pull of our busy lives that begs us to take more convenient options. Firstly, when we eat out, we usually eat less healthily than when we cook for ourselves, as the meals tend to have more energy, fat and salt[123]. Secondly, convenience food and pre-prepared ingredients spoil faster, contributing to food waste. Lastly, the more we eat pre-made food, the less we are building our own cooking skills. This is particularly important for our children – when they are able to develop cooking skills at an early age there are long-term benefits for their health and nutrition[129]. The good news is the joy of cooking can be learned at any age.

Here are some ways I think cooking can help us engage with food systems differently and find joy in the process.

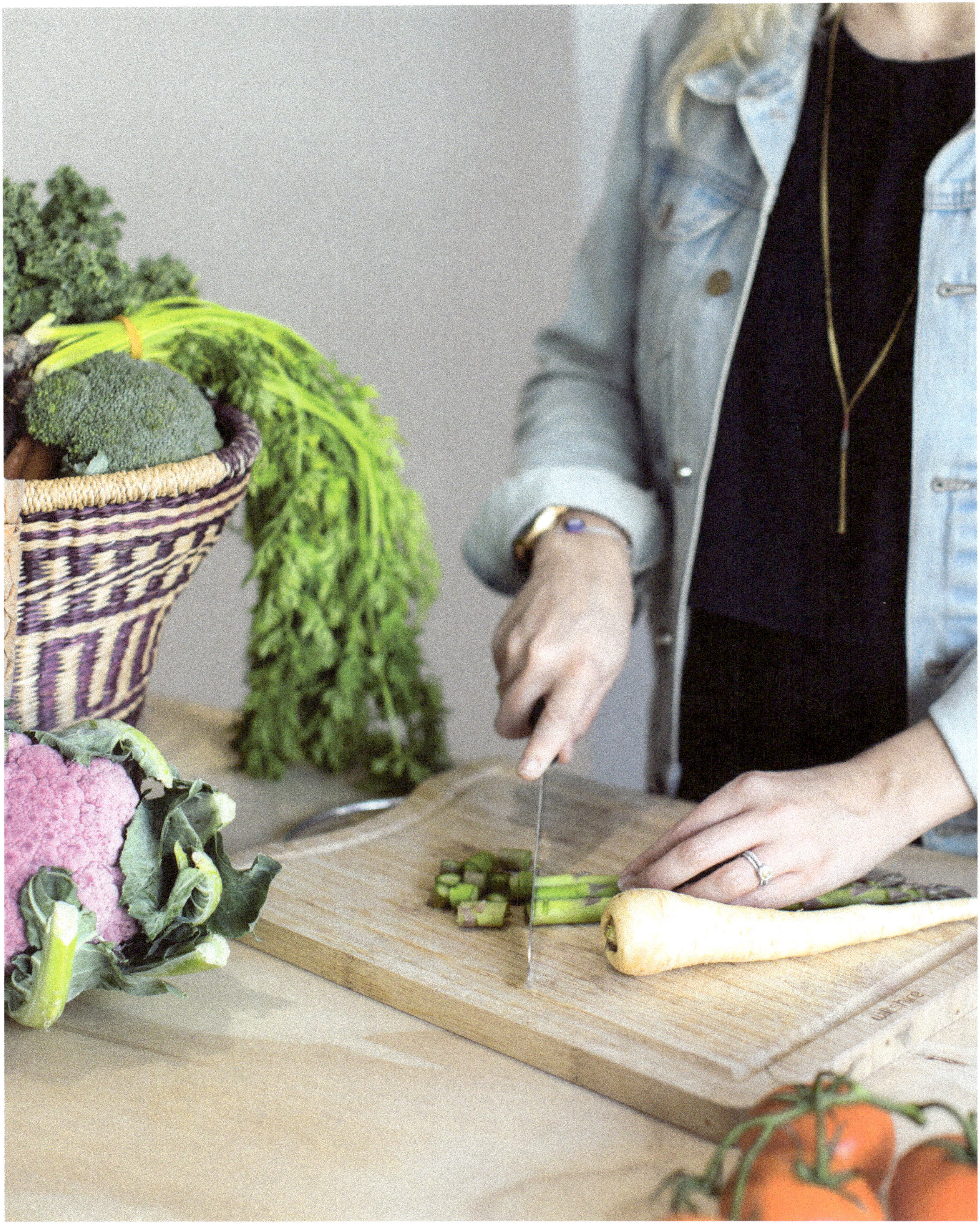

PART TWO | *Cooking Up Calm*

MAKING HEALTHY CHOICES EASIER

When I am busy and running around, it is much harder to eat in line with my values as I have to grab whatever is most convenient. However, if I take a bit of time on the weekend to plan for the week ahead, I am a more empowered eater. I eat and feel better the whole week, save money, reduce waste and know that I am in control of my nutrition. I like to follow these 4 simple steps:

1. On the weekend, I sit down and roughly plan my meals for the week. This usually includes a couple of different breakfasts and four main meals that can double as lunch the next day. I usually plan for 3–4 weekdays and leave a couple of days open so I can shift things around if there is a change in plans.

2. I shop for the ingredients.

3. I spend an hour or two on the weekend to cook up some of the recipes. I do all the breakfasts in advance, and then a couple of the main meals. I leave a couple of meals to cook up mid-week, so they are fresh. Another alternative is to cook up a bunch of ingredients that you can mix and match with dressings for different meals throughout the week.

4. I put a little note on the door to remind me to pick up my lunch from the fridge on the way out! Nothing worse than a left at home lunch.

Some people are calling this The Lunchbox Renaissance. The Wall Street journal wrote about it, saying how it has unexpectedly become chic to bring your own lunch to work. I think they hit on the essence of it: "In order to be in possession of these lovely leftovers, you need to find time for cooking the night before. My hunch is that this is the real source of our packed lunch envy. It isn't the food itself so much as the leisure time it represents"[130]. Which brings me to my next point...

GIVING US TIME

One of the most common complaints I hear from people wanting to cook more is, "I just don't have time." I don't doubt that this is true, especially for people working multiple jobs to make ends meet. But when it comes to cooking, there is an opportunity to reframe by considering how it can give, rather than take, time. Food can be an amazing tool for slowing down and reconnecting with ourselves and others. It requires us to work with our hands and our senses, to step away from our screens and devices and actually create something tangible. At the end of the day, spending time in the kitchen and sitting down to eat with friends or family is a wonderful way to a stretch time, to slow it down and see it as a sequence of precious moments rather than a chaotic blur. To create space to appreciate the joy of food.

You can build on this by letting cooking be a space for mindfulness. This means taking some deep breaths, relaxing your body and then just focusing on what you are doing. When you are chopping the vegetables, just chop the vegetables. Your mind will constantly wander, which is completely normal. When you notice that, smile because it is you becoming aware of yourself being lost in thoughts, then gently bring it back to focus on the task at hand, relaxing yourself in the process and letting go of any frustration that your mind has wandered. This process helps you practice the three skills of mindfulness – ability to focus, ability to sense and ability to find equanimity. These are all skills that can help us find patience, calm and focus throughout our day, not only in the kitchen.

If this sounds like a far cry from your kitchen reality, then cooking can also be a great time to listen to music you love and dance around the kitchen, letting go of anything that happened during the day. It can be a time to learn something new from a podcast, or an opportunity to challenge your brain and your senses by cooking something new or exotic. All of these are things you can invite your kids, partners or housemates to be a part of, making cooking time a chance to connect with each other.

The Great Full

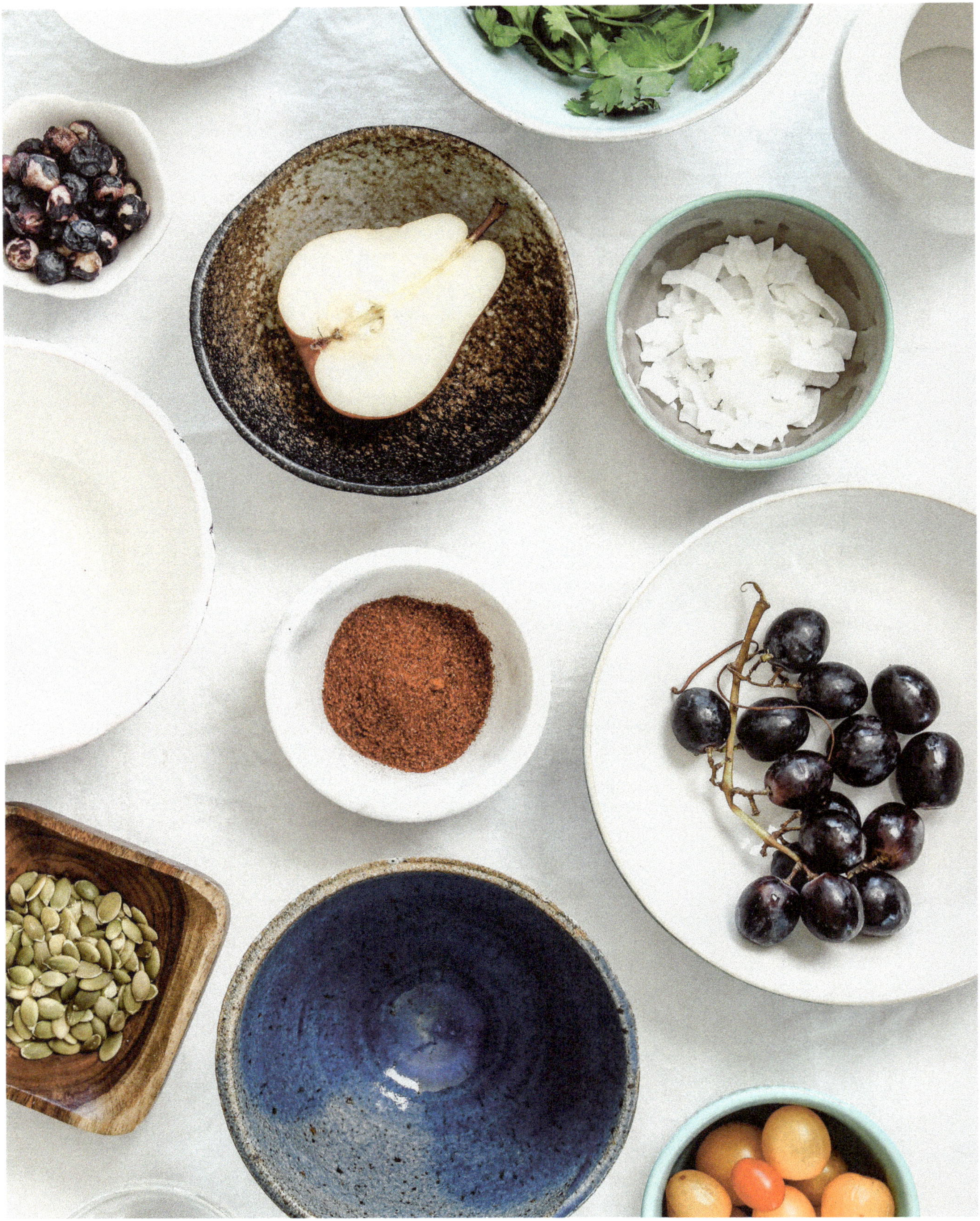

RESCUING NUTRIENTS

By cooking imaginatively and resourcefully, you can tackle the global issue of waste from your very own bench-top. Some of my best recipe ideas have come out of the necessity of combining the random ingredients left in my fridge at the end of the week. You can also get creative with recipes by swapping out what is listed with whatever you have in the pantry or the fridge.

If you do need to throw away food scraps or inedible leftovers, it is really important that they don't just go in the bin. Simply dumping food waste is a fast track to making methane gas in landfill. Plus, it is a massive waste of all the nutrients in the food, which were taken from the soil in which your food was grown. That is why composting food scraps is a really cool thing to do. I live in an apartment, so I totally get that it is not always easy to compost. But there are many solutions now, like mini indoor worm farms or bokashi bins. What works best for me is making use of the green bins available through our local municipality (where I live you have to ask for these) or finding local composters in my area. Community gardens, houses with gardens (including you own!) or small urban farms will welcome your compost, and the nutrients in it, with open arms. It's also an unexpected way to make connections to the community around you.

THE CHANCE TO LEARN AND CREATE

I find it strange that building good cooking skills is not always a part of our formal education systems. This often means we need to take it into our own hands as adults. Rather than see this as a burden, I think it is wonderful to approach it like a new hobby or interest. If you learn the basics of cooking, you can very quickly start to find the joy in getting creative in the kitchen. Often the reason why people feel stuck or stressed is that they haven't had a chance to learn these basic skills, and that leaves them worried about the costs of making a mistake. These days, between blogs, apps, YouTube videos, online courses, TV series and workshops, there is more information than ever that can help us learn how to cook. But I still like to work with old-fashioned cookbooks, reading the first chapters then trying out a few different recipes, learning something new each time. There are three in particular that I have learned a lot from. Samin Nosrat's *Salt, Fat, Acid, Heat* offers a beautiful foundation for good cooking. She helps you understand how the right mix of these elements form the basis of a good dish. From that foundation, you can let yourself get creative. Amy Chaplin's *At Home in the Wholefoods Kitchen* is another great resource to learn more about cooking from scratch with whole foods. Finally, *Naturally Nourished* by Sarah Britton is a wonderful book to find inspiration for everyday meals and tips for how to cook delicious dishes from simple plant-based ingredients.

THE PLANT-BASED KITCHEN

THE GREAT FULL

THE PLANT-BASED KITCHEN

As we explored in earlier chapters, reducing the amount of meat and animal products you eat can make an important contribution to your health and the health of the planet. To make this process easy and enjoyable, it helps to get your kitchen set up for success. This section will help you stock up on key staple ingredients and work out the basic equipment that will help make your life easier.

PLANT-BASED PANTRY

The pantry list below should prepare you to cook up a delicious plant-based storm! Don't feel you need to stock up on everything at once, you can also just buy what you need for each recipe and before you know it you will have all the basics.

Vegetables, Fruit and Herbs

This category of food items is the "bread and butter" of a plant-based kitchen, as fresh fruit and vegetables are the central inspiration for and feature of most dishes. These items you can buy fresh or frozen, depending on the season and what is available.

+ Seasonal fresh fruit and vegetables
+ Leafy greens – kale, spinach, chard
+ Lemons and limes
+ Garlic and onions
+ Frozen fruit – berries, cherries, apricots, bananas
+ Fresh herbs – basil, mint, dill, thyme, rosemary, chives, coriander

Legumes and Pulses

Beans have a bit of a bad reputation as a boring and bland hippy food, but that is starting to change. I guess we can thank hummus and black bean brownies for that rebranding. Legumes and pulses are a source of protein, fibre, calcium, iron, zinc and selenium. They are also an important part of sustainable production systems – as they grow they are able to fix nitrogen from the air and improve the soil quality.

Range of pulses, dry, or canned for example:

+ Chickpeas
+ Lentils
+ Mungbeans
+ Kidney beans
+ Black beans
+ Cannellini beans
+ Butter beans
+ Borlotti beans

Whole Grains

Whole grains are affordable, nutritious and tasty when prepared correctly. Generally speaking, I try to avoid refined grains like white rice or white flour, which have had many of their nutrients stripped.

- Brown rice, wild rice
- Oats
- Quinoa
- Millet
- Buckwheat
- Spelt
- Ancient grains such as freekah, barley, rye, kamut
- Puffed brown rice/quinoa/millet
- Polenta
- A range of flours, for example spelt, brown rice, buckwheat, chickpea

Nuts and Seeds

Nuts and seeds are a great source of healthy fats, protein and minerals. They can be tossed into a salad, thrown on top of oatmeal, made into granola, crackers or nut butter or enjoyed alone as a snack.

- Whole nuts, such as almonds, hazelnuts, walnuts, pecans and, in moderation, cashew nuts
- Seeds such as flaxseed, sunflower seeds, pumpkin seeds, chia seeds, sesame seeds, hemp seeds (keep hemp seeds refrigerated to preserve for longer)
- Nut butters such as peanut butter, almond butter, hazelnut butter
- Seed butters, such as tahini or sunflower seed paste
- Ground almonds or hazelnuts

Pasta and Noodles

Having a range of pasta and noodles on hand makes it easy to whip up a simple meal when you have few ingredients or little time. Just sauté some vegetables with some sort of sauce and fresh herbs and you have a tasty dinner.

- Gluten free, whole wheat, spelt, quinoa or kamut pasta in different forms (spaghetti, penne, macaroni, lasagna sheets)
- Legume pasta (made from chickpeas, lentils or beans)
- Brown rice noodles
- Buckwheat soba noodles

Sweeteners

I like to use a range of different sweeteners in moderation to make homemade treats. These are my go-to sources:

- Maple syrup
- Honey
- Date syrup
- Coconut blossom sugar
- Stevia
- Dried fruit, such as dates, sultanas, prunes, apricots

PART ONE | *The Plant-based Kitchen*

Oils, Fats and Sauces

Oils and fats add texture to dishes, help carry the flavour and act as a cooking medium. Sauces help develop sweet, sour, salty, bitter and umami tastes in your food. Needless to say, both are indispensable in the plant-based kitchen. Here are my go to sources:

+ A range of oils and fats, such as olive oil, sunflower oil, sesame oil, coconut oil, flaxseed oil, ghee and cacao butter
+ Vinegars, such as apple cider, brown rice and balsamic
+ Tamari (the Japanese style of soy sauce that contains little to no wheat)
+ Miso paste
+ Lemon juice – I normally have a bottle of this on hand in case I run out of fresh lemons
+ Seeded and non-seeded mustard
+ Tamarind paste

Dry Herbs and Spices

The use of herbs and spices is really important in plant-based cooking, giving your meals body, flavour and warmth and allowing you to cook with creativity.

+ Herb salt, Maldon salt (plain and smoked), sea salt plus any other salts you like (pink, celtic, kosher)
+ Black pepper
+ Cinnamon
+ Turmeric
+ Cardamom
+ Chilli (powder and flakes)
+ Cayenne pepper
+ Coriander
+ Harissa
+ Paprika
+ Nutmeg
+ Sumac
+ Coriander
+ Cumin
+ Dried garlic
+ Curry powder
+ Ginger
+ Basil
+ Oregano
+ Thyme

The Great Full

Dairy and Meat Substitutes

If you use normal dairy products or alternatives, it makes sense to consume them in moderation and I feel the same about their substitutes.

- Milk substitutes – I tend to use oat or soy milk as a more sustainable choice than almond or cashew
- Yoghurt substitutes (soy or coconut yoghurt)
- Cream substitutes (soy cream, oat cream, coconut cream)
- Tofu (silken and firm)

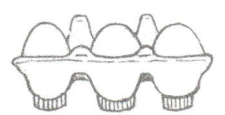

Animal Source Foods

This is the category in the plant-based pantry that varies the most depending on where you land (fully vegan to flexitarian) in trying to reduce your intake of animal source foods. If you decide to eat some animal source foods, it is worth making sure they are produced in a system that is aligned with your values. Here are some of the products you will find used in moderation in this book. (Note – I am lactose intolerant so that guides my choice of cheeses.)

- Eggs
- Ghee
- Goat's or sheep's cheeses (soft, feta)
- Hard cheeses (parmesan, pecorino)

Other Essentials

Some other items can be useful to have on hand:

- Seaweed and algae such as nori sheets or kelp flakes
- Dried mushrooms
- Capers, olives, sauerkraut and other pickled or fermented vegetables
- Baking items like baking soda, baking powder, yeast, agar agar

PART ONE | *The Plant-based Kitchen*

EQUIPMENT BASICS

Aside from the usual kitchen tools there are a few things that are very handy to have in a plant-based kitchen.

An Immersion Blender

This is an appliance that can be used to blend ingredients or puree food in the container they are being prepared in. They often come with attachments such as a mini-food processor, which make them a small and affordable multi-purpose appliance. I use this to puree soups, blend smoothies and make dips.

Food Processor

Food processors are mainly used to chop and combine ingredients, letting you make energy balls and other healthy snacks in no time. They usually come with different attachments that can chop, slice, grate large quantities of vegetables really quickly.

High Speed Blender

It is worth investing in a high-speed blender so that you can make smoothies, nut butters, sauces and soups. No need to buy the most expensive version on the market, just do some research to find the best option in your budget.

Vegetable Spiralizer

This is a simple countertop tool that lets you turn vegetables and fruit into noodles and spiral shapes. It is the best way to make vegetables more fun for adults and kids alike! You can also find smaller, handheld versions or use a julienne peeler for a similar effect. But I have to admit my small investment in a spiralizer was money very well spent.

Mortar and Pestle

I have had to gift many a mortar and pestle to friends over the years, as they do not lend themselves well to moving and travelling. Each time I set up a kitchen I put off buying a new one as they are by no means essential and take up bench space. Then I finally invest in one and wonder why I waited. On a practical level, a mortar and pestle helps you grind spices or crush things into pastes, sauces or dressings. More importantly, there is something therapeutic about slowing down to use this ancient tool that I can't really put into words. I guess it adds a mindful quality to the process, which I think you can almost taste.

Cast Iron Cocotte

This was a relatively recent addition to my kitchen, which is to say it is no means essential. A cocotte is basically a cast-iron pot with a lid (usually round or oval) that stores and slowly releases heat into the food, evenly cooking it and retaining moisture and flavour. You can use it on the stovetop (to make soups and risottos even more delicious) or in the oven (to bake bread). They are certainly an investment piece, but we were able to pick one up at an outlet store for a huge discount as the pot had some tiny discolorations on the outside. You can also find them in second hand stores or online if the budget is tight.

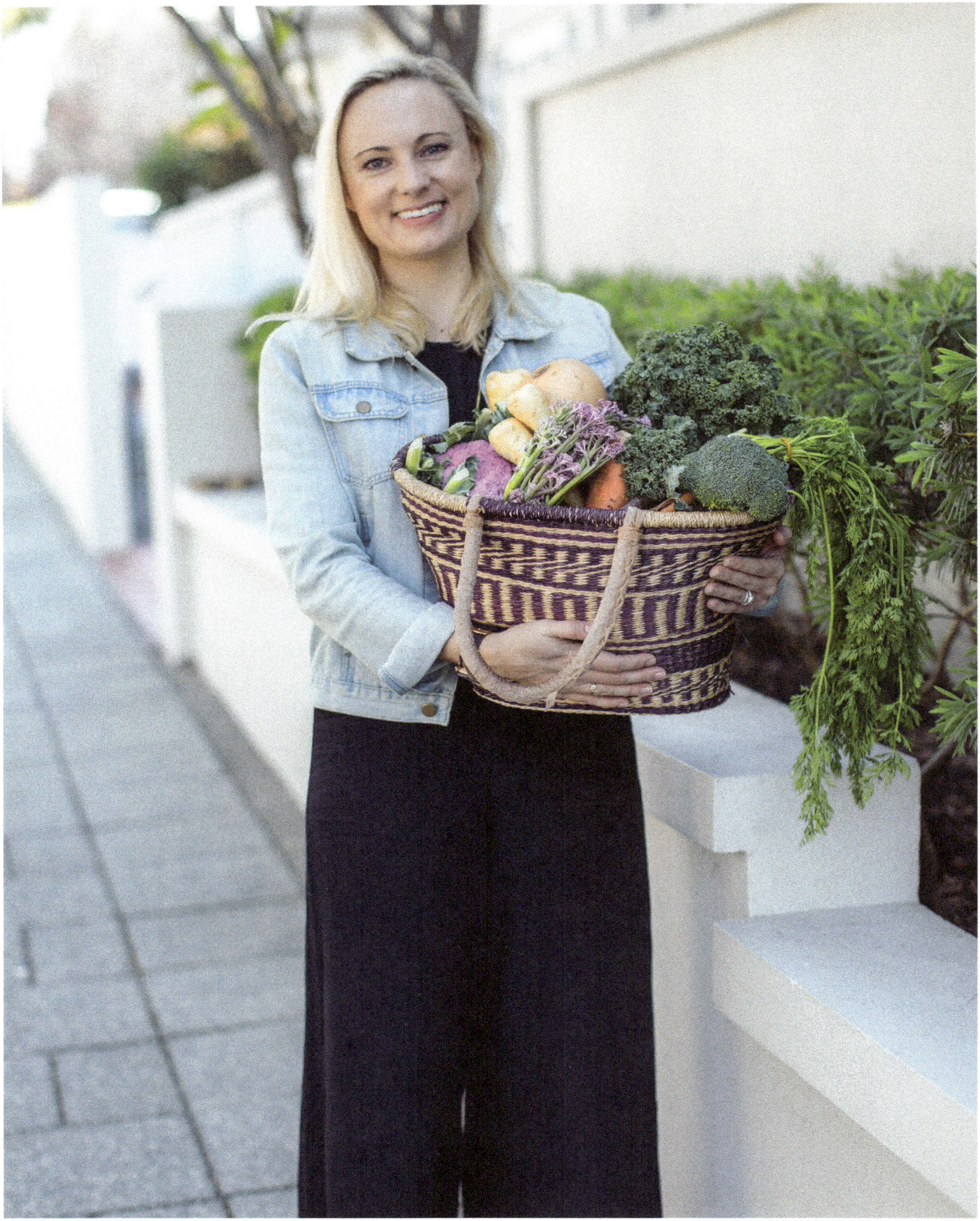

THE BASICS OF PLANT-BASED MEALS

When you get started with plant-based eating it can be helpful to understand some of the basic nutrition principles. Basically, you need to get a mix of the macronutrients (proteins, fats, carbohydrates) and micronutrients (vitamins and minerals) that you need for a healthy life.

This doesn't need to become overwhelming. The most important thing is to eat a diverse and colourful range of healthy foods. When it comes to proteins, there are plenty of plant-based options that will meet your needs, and it is a good idea to try and integrate one into every meal. There are many sources out there that can help you navigate this space so I will not go into great detail here. The blog Nutrition Stripped has a good overview, or for a more scientific summary you can check out "Plant-Based Diets: A Physician's Guide"[131] or the book *How Not to Die* by Michael Greger MD. I found that his concept of a daily dozen was an interesting way to reflect on the diversity I was, or wasn't, getting each day. The daily dozen is a simple checklist of the things you should eat daily for a balanced and healthy plant-based diet. Using this to guide the bulk of your diet, you can then add small amounts of animal source foods if you choose to. You can download it at nutritionfacts.org.

HOW TO USE THE RECIPES

Studies have shown that two of the main barriers for people who want to eat less meat and more plants is that they have a lack of knowledge about preparing vegetarian foods and a strong appreciation for the taste of meat[132]. I hope that these recipes help you to overcome these things and find ease and deliciousness in cooking this way.

The recipes themselves are all straightforward and designed for everyone, regardless of your level of experience in the kitchen. My suggestion is that you read through the recipe thoroughly before starting to cook, so that you have an overview of everything to come. It also helps to prepare all the ingredients first – chop, measure and arrange everything you need before you get started with cooking.

I would love to encourage everyone to integrate diverse and forgotten local ingredients into their dishes. Yet I also want to provide recipes that are helpful to people living all around the world. So, my invitation is always to take the recipes as a suggestion and substitute wherever you can with local ingredients. Try swapping out for diverse local produce, experimenting with flavour and getting creative with seasonal fruit and veggies.

RECIPES

Breakfast	94
Starters	114
Salads and Soups	128
Mains	162
Sweet Treats	190
Drinks	230
Sauces, Spices, Toppings	244

GLOBAL INSTRUCTIONS AND CONVERSION TABLES

*Oven Temperatures**

	Electricity °C	Electricity (fan) °C	Electricity °F	Gas Mark
Very cool	110	90	225	¼
	120	100	248	½
Cool	140	120	280	1
	150	130	300	2
Moderate	160	140	320	3
	180	160	360	4
Moderately hot	190	170	375	5
	200	180	400	6
Hot	220	200	425	7
	230	210	446	8

* Cooking times vary greatly from oven to oven. What I indicate is what works with my oven, but you will need to have a feeling for yours and adjust the timing accordingly.

Volume Measures

I frequently use tablespoons and cups measurements in my recipes. It is important to note that these are actually precise measures of volume, not just any large spoon or cup you might have lying around! A set of measuring cups and measuring spoons are indispensable in my kitchen, they allow me to quickly measure and pour volumes without getting out a kitchen scale. I have outlined to the right the volumes I am referring to when I use this type of measurement in my recipes. I like to have two sets of spoon measurements and two sets of cup measurements on hand. When I am making a recipe, I use one set for wet ingredients and one set for dry, which saves me having to wash them repeatedly.

1 teaspoon (1 tsp)	=	5 mL
½ teaspoon (½ tsp)	=	2.5 mL
¼ teaspoon (¼ tsp)	=	1.2 mL
1 tablespoon (1 tbsp)	=	15 mL
1 cup	=	240 mL
½ cup	=	120 mL
⅓ cup	=	80 mL
¼ cup	=	60 mL

(V) Vegan   (GF) Gluten Free   (DF) Dairy Free

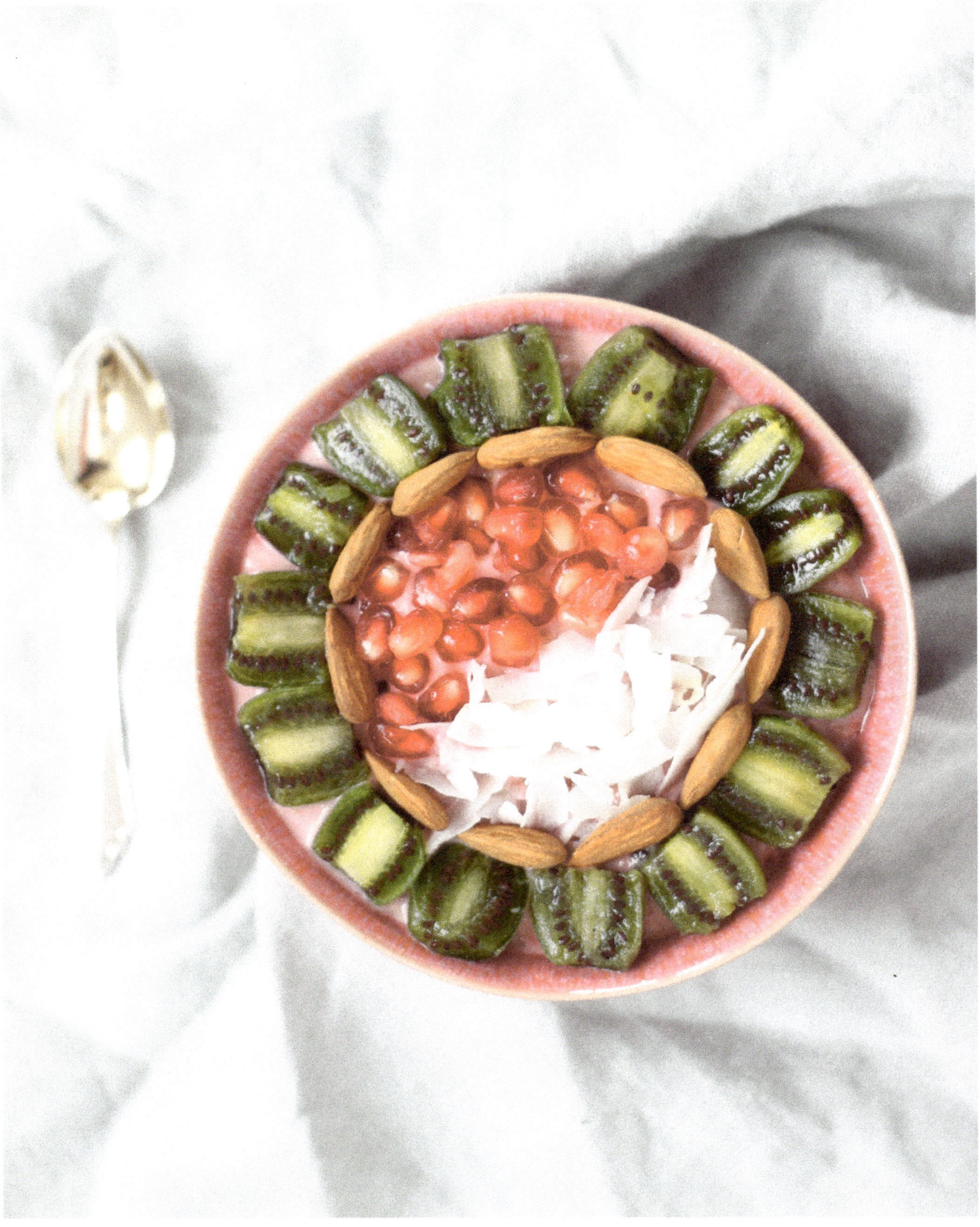

BREAKFAST

Stracciatella Overnight Oats	97
Chocolate Orange and Maple Overnight Oats	99
Chai Spiced Breakfast Smoothie	101
Mixed Berry Millet and Oat Bake	103
Carrot Cake Oatmeal	105
Blushing Oatmeal	105
Rooibos Apricot and Maple Granola	106
Vegan Pancakes	109
Orange Chia Compote	111
Berry Chia Compote	111
Rhubarb Ginger Compote	113
Apple Cinnamon Compote	113

BREAKFAST

STRACCIATELLA OVERNIGHT OATS

5 mins plus overnight soaking | serves 2

These overnight oats are the perfect breakfast for a busy person. You can make them in advance and have them ready to greet you in the fridge every morning. Like many healthy breakfast options these days, this recipe is pretty banana-centric. While bananas are healthy in terms of nutrition, they are also the poster-child of a crazy food system. Poor conditions are often reported by the people who work long hours growing, picking and packing bananas. One of the solutions to this is fair trade, a certification system that takes a premium from consumers and uses that to ensure fair working conditions. This is a good start, but we need to do more. Organizations like Banana Link help with this. They document what is happening in the banana industry and share ways you can get involved with making it more ethical.

Ingredients

Large bananas *(very ripe)*	2
Quick oats	½ cup
Ground hazelnuts or almonds	⅓ cup
Chia seeds	3 tbsp
Cacao nibs *(or sugar free dark chocolate chips)*	1–2 tbsp
Milk *(I use oat or soy)*	¾ cup
Vanilla extract or seeds *(optional)*	½ teaspoon

Method

1. Peel the bananas and place them in a medium sized bowl. Mash them with a fork.

2. Add all other ingredients. Mix well.

3. Cover bowl and leave in the fridge to soak overnight or for a couple of hours. (Alternatively divide the oat mixture into individual jars to make portions you can take with you.)

4. Mix well to recombine before serving, as the banana will brown slightly. Keep in refrigerator for up to 4 days.

V | DF

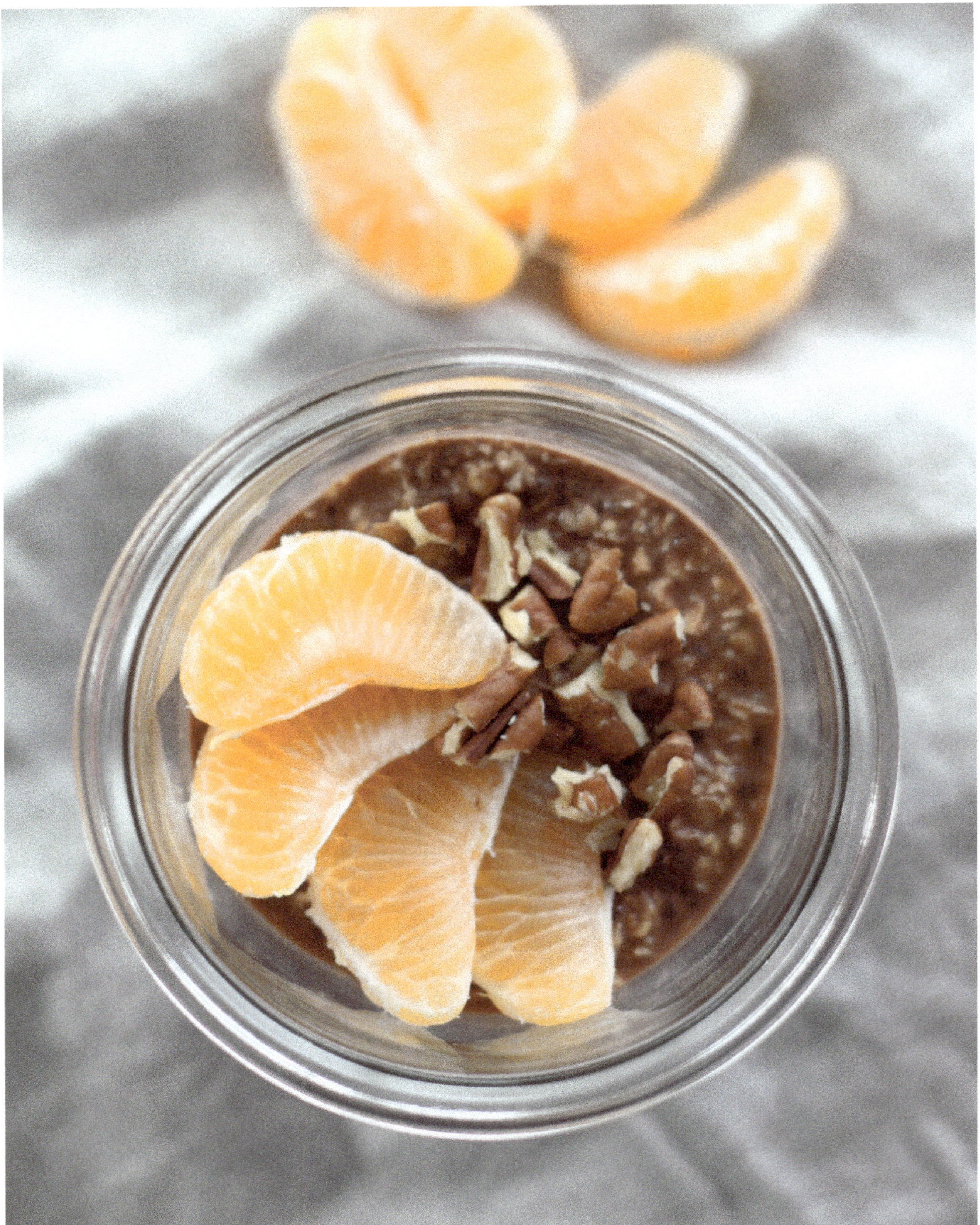

CHOCOLATE ORANGE AND MAPLE OVERNIGHT OATS

5 mins plus overnight soaking | serves 2

Centuries of history, of social, environmental and economic forces shape what food is available to us right now. It actually took a lot to make the cacao powder in this recipe available to you, wherever you are in the world. First, the indigenous people of Mesoamerica had to discover that the cacao plant could be made into a delicious drink. Through colonisation, the Spanish discovered a taste for cacao too. They created plantations to intensify production, relying on the work of slaves or poorly paid workers to produce the volume they needed to feed wealthy Old World appetites. This eventually transformed into the plantations we have today, feeding into value chains that take the cacao beans from the pods, often in West Africa, all the way across the world, eventually processing and packaging it into the cacao powder in your cupboard. I think it's worth reflecting on this history to help us have a deeper appreciation for what is on our plates and fuelling our lives.

Ingredients

Quick oats	⅔ cup
Chia seeds or flaxseeds	¼ cup
Nuts or seeds of your choice	¼ cup
(Ground or roughly chopped)	
Cacao powder	1 tbsp
Milk of your choice *(or orange juice)*	300 ml

To top:
Orange or mandarin slices, pecans, maple syrup (optional)

Method

1. Put all dry ingredients (oats, chia or flax seeds, nuts and cacao powder) into a glass jar that you can keep in the fridge. Pour over milk. Mix all ingredients until combined.

2. Refrigerate overnight. To serve, spoon into bowls, top with additional milk or orange juice, orange or mandarin slices, pecans and a dash of maple syrup.

BREAKFAST

CHAI SPICED BREAKFAST SMOOTHIE

5 mins / serves 2

Life in our busy modern world puts a lot of emphasis on convenience. As we dash from one To Do list item to another, we want food that is easy to grab on the move. Rather than relying on takeaway or delivery food, which often involves a lot of plastic, it helps to find some simple, healthy meals to prepare in advance and take along with you. Or some delicious options that you can whip up in a few minutes, like this breakfast smoothie.

Ingredients

Frozen pear	1
(Core and quarter the pear before freezing)	
Frozen banana	1
(You can replace this with a handful of ice for a less sweet version)	
Quick oats	½ cup
Oat milk	¾ cup
Pecans	¼ cup
Cinnamon	½ tsp
Cardamom	⅓ tsp
Nutmeg	⅓ tsp
Ground ginger	⅓ tsp

Method

1. Combine all the ingredients in a blender.
2. Blend until smooth.
3. Top with additional chopped pecans and nutmeg before serving.

V | DF

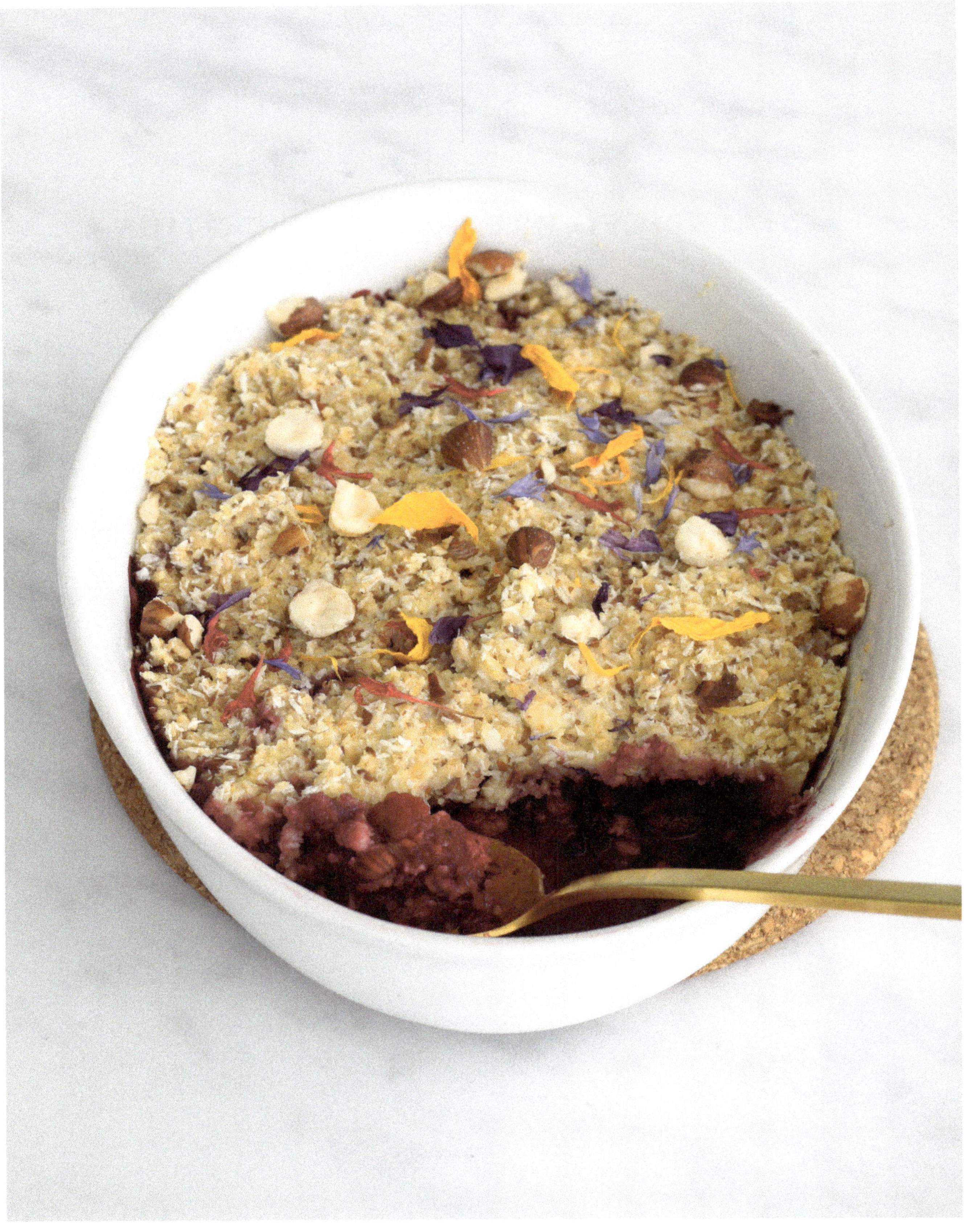

MIXED BERRY MILLET AND OAT BAKE

10 mins prep plus 15 mins baking time | serves 4

I love to make a batch of this on a weekend morning, devouring it while it is warm and comforting or keeping it in the fridge for a quick weekday breakfast. This recipe is also a great way to introduce millet into your diet. This little grain is nutrient rich and drought tolerant, making it an important food for the future. Although it is a traditional crop in many parts of the world, over the last 50 years it was often abandoned for crops like wheat, corn and rice. So, eating more millet is a small way you can increase diversity in your own diet and help this healthy grain make a comeback!

Ingredients

Coconut oil *(for greasing)*	
Frozen berries	1 cup
Hazelnuts *(roughly chopped)*	¼ cup
Maple syrup	1–2 tbsp
Millet flakes	½ cup
(or other flaked cereal)	
Quick oats	½ cup
Chia seeds or flaxseeds	2 tbsp
LSA mix	2 tbsp
(ground linseed, sunflower and almonds) (optional)	
Desiccated coconut	⅓ cup
(or ground hazelnuts)	
Oat milk	1 cup
(Or other milk of your choice)	

Method

1. Preheat oven to 200°C.
2. Drizzle a little coconut oil in the bottom of the baking dish and use this to grease the bottom, sides and corners of the dish.
3. Pour 1 cup frozen berries into the baking dish (add a few more if needed to cover the base of the dish).
4. Scatter the chopped hazelnuts on top of the berries.
5. Drizzle the maple syrup evenly over the berry/hazelnut mixture.
6. In a medium mixing bowl, combine the millet flakes, quick oats, chia seeds, LSA and desiccated coconut. Mix until combined.
7. Pour in oat milk. Stir until combined and leave to sit for a couple of minutes.
8. Spoon the oat mix on top of the berry mixture in the baking dish. Press down gently with the back of the spoon until the mixture covers the berries.
9. Bake for approximately 15 minutes.

TWO FANCY OATMEALS

5 mins prep plus 5 mins cooking time | *serves 2*

These oatmeal options are a great way to make a breakfast staple more exciting. I like to make two portions, one to eat straight away and one to save for breakfast the next day. Just put it into a glass jar with a lid and after it has cooled a little place in the fridge. It makes a great grab-and-go breakfast treat.

BREAKFAST

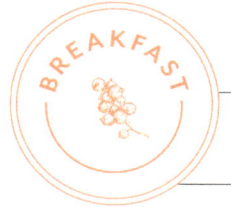

(V) (DF)

CARROT CAKE OATMEAL

Ingredients

Carrot (*grated finely*)	1
Quick oats	¼ cup
Millet flakes	¼ cup
Desiccated coconut	2 tbsp
Pumpkin or sunflower seeds	2 tbsp
Sultanas or raisins	handful
Cinnamon	1 tsp
Nutmeg	¼ tsp
Turmeric	¼ tsp
Milk (*I use oat*)	1 cup
Coconut oil or ghee (*optional*)	1 tsp
Orange or blood orange juice	¼ cup

Optional toppings include nut butter, nuts or seeds, coconut shavings or yoghurt.

Method

1. Place all ingredients (except the orange juice) into a medium saucepan. Place on low to medium heat. Stir all ingredients to combine well. Keep stirring intermittently to avoid mixture sticking to base of pan.

2. When the mixture is creamy, but just before it starts to boil, remove from the heat. Pour orange juice over the top and mix through with a spoon. If eating both serves immediately, distribute across two bowls. Put on any additional toppings you would like.

BLUSHING OATMEAL

Ingredients

Quick oats	½ cup
Frozen berries of your choice	handful
Desiccated or shaved coconut	3 tbsp
Milk (*I use oat*)	1 cup
Coconut oil or ghee (*optional*)	1 tsp

Optional toppings include fruit compote, nut butter, nuts and seeds and yoghurt.

Method

1. Place all ingredients into a saucepan. Place on low to medium heat. Stir all ingredients to combine well. Keep stirring intermittently to avoid mixture sticking to base of pan.

2. When the mixture is creamy, but just before it starts to boil, remove from the heat. If eating both serves immediately, distribute across two bowls. Put on any additional toppings you would like.

The Great Full

ROOIBOS APRICOT AND MAPLE GRANOLA

🕐 1 hr | ✋ 2 ½ cups

This granola is a tribute to the wonderful flavours of South Africa. On frequent work trips to this beautiful country, I've had the chance to drink litres of rooibos tea and learn about this indigenous plant, its health properties and the challenges facing its production. Rooibos tea is a slightly sweet, red herbal tea that is naturally caffeine free, making it popular in its native South Africa. But rooibos production is linked to a number of social, cultural and historical struggles. In the region where it grows, descendants of the Khoisan (the First People of South Africa) mostly live on the economic fringes. However, they have an immense traditional knowledge of rooibos and how to cultivate it, as they have used the plant for medicinal purposes for centuries. Some local organizations, like the Heiveld Co-operative, are taking action. This fully producer-owned and managed co-operative brings together 74 small-scale producers from the area to produce, process, package and export organic and fair trade certified rooibos tea. Thirty per cent of the co-op's profits are distributed to disadvantaged people or groups in the community, with the remaining profit divided among the members. The co-operative also actively engages with researchers, NGOs and international organizations to support research and knowledge sharing on environmental and social sustainability of the rooibos sector. Something to think about when you source the rooibos for this delicious granola!

Ingredients

Boiling water	½ cup
Rooibos teabags	4
Dried apricots, *finely chopped*	100g
Sunflower seeds	3 heaped tbsp
Quick oats	½ cup
Ground almonds or hazelnuts	½ cup
Sesame seeds	3 heaped tbsp
Pecans (*roughly chopped*)	½ cup
Ground cinnamon	½ tsp
Maple syrup	3 tbsp
Coconut oil (*melted*)	1½ tbsp

(V) (DF)

Method

1. Preheat oven to 160°C.

2. In a small mixing bowl, add the 4 teabags to the boiling water and leave to infuse a few minutes. Then add the finely chopped dried apricots and the sunflower seeds and leave them to soak in this tea mix for around 30 minutes or longer (e.g. overnight) if possible. Leave the teabags in during this time to help the flavour infuse.

3. Line a baking tray with a sheet of baking paper. Place the oats, ground almonds and sesame seeds on the tray. Mix around with your fingers or a wooden spoon until well combined. Place on the top row of the oven for 15 mins. Remember to put the timer on so you don't burn the ingredients.

4. When the oat mixture is ready, remove from the oven and pour it into a medium sized mixing bowl. Hold onto the baking paper because you will use it again.

5. Spoon the soaked apricot and sunflower seed mixture into the mixing bowl with the oats, including some of the liquid.

6. Add the chopped pecans, cinnamon, maple syrup melted coconut oil. Mix through until everything is well combined.

7. Transfer the mixture back onto the baking tray lined with baking paper. Use a wooden spoon or spatula to spread out the mixture until it is evenly distributed.

8. Return to the oven and bake at 160° C for 20–30 minutes. Twenty minutes will give you a softer, chewier granola and 30 minutes a very crunchy granola. Take it out when it is how you prefer it, just remember that it will always look a little less cooked in the oven than it will cooled.

9. Leave the tray on the bench to cool. When cool, place in an airtight container and store in the cupboard. Can be kept in the cupboard for several weeks, and up to 3 months in the freezer.

BREAKFAST

PART TWO | *Breakfast*

VEGAN PANCAKES

10 mins prep plus 20 mins cooking | *10 medium pancakes*

These pancakes are a weekend staple in our house. After many attempts to make the perfect vegan pancakes, we now have the procedure down to an efficient production line. I make the batter, leave it to sit for a bit, then my husband takes over the cooking and flipping. I have tried to share everything we have learned in the process in the instructions below, with the hope that you can also master vegan pancakes, but without so many disasters along the way! I highly recommend trying the savoury version once; it's a great way to get some vegetables into the start of your day.

Ingredients

Spelt flour	1 cup
Buckwheat flour	1 cup
Baking powder	2 tsp
A few pinches of salt	
Apple sauce	1 cup
Apple cider vinegar	2 tsp
Milk *(I use oat)*	1½ cups
Coconut oil	

(or if you are not vegan you could use ghee instead; both have the higher smoke point needed here)

V | DF

Optional add-ins:
1 banana, thinly sliced, handful of berries,
¼ cup dark chocolate (chopped)

Example Sweet Toppings:
Fruit compote, yoghurt,
nut or seed butter, maple syrup

Example Savoury toppings:
Sautéed mushrooms, hummus, spinach,
artichoke hearts, fresh herbs, salt and pepper

Method

1. Preheat oven to 160° C. Place all dry pancake ingredients (flours, baking powder, salt) in a mixing bowl. Make a well in the middle.

2. Pour in the apple sauce, apple cider vinegar and milk.

3. Use a whisk to mix ingredients until combined. No need to over stir or insist on getting out every lump.

4. If you are using add-ins, add them in now! For example, mix through one thinly sliced banana and/or a small handful of dark chocolate chips for an indulgent pancake, or a handful of blueberries for a lighter alternative.

5. Set batter aside for around 5 mins.

6. Use this time to prepare the toppings of your choice.

7. Take a flat frying pan or skillet and use some coconut oil to evenly grease the surface. Place the pan on a medium heat and leave until it is warm (a drop of water should sizzle when it hits it). When it is warm, use a measuring cup to measure out ¼ cup of the pancake mix. Pour this into the middle of the pan. When the bubbles start to pop and form holes, it is time to flip.

8. When the first pancake is ready, put it in a heatproof dish and into the preheated oven. Continue to store these in the oven while you cook off the whole batch.

9. When all the pancakes are done, place on the table with all the different toppings and let everyone create their own masterpiece.

The Great Full

FRUIT COMPOTES

One of the challenges with seasonal eating is that you have huge quantities of certain things at the one time and then periods with a lot less, especially if you live somewhere with a serious winter. Last year the warm summer was good for apples and pears in Switzerland and my parents-in-law suddenly had kilos and kilos from their usually modest backyard harvest. So, I took a bunch of fruit and made compotes galore to share with everyone. This is a great way to extend the fruit harvest into the winter months. You can use them to jazz up your breakfast oatmeal, to spread on toast with nut butter or as a topping for pancakes. If you are feeding a crowd for breakfast, you can make a big batch of toast, oatmeal or pancakes and serve them with a topping bar, including different compotes, yoghurt, nut butters, fruit, nuts, seeds and any sweetener you like.

PART TWO | *Breakfast*

ORANGE CHIA COMPOTE

20 mins | *1 cup*

Ingredients

Oranges	2
(Peeled and chopped into chunks, seeds removed)	
Orange juice	2 tbsp
Honey or maple syrup	1 tbsp
Chia seeds	1 tbsp

Optional add-ins: a few sprinkles of cinnamon, cardamom or finely grated fresh ginger.

Method

1. Add in the oranges, juice, honey or maple syrup and any optional add-ins to a small saucepan. Put on medium heat and warm up, not letting the liquid boil.

2. When mixture is warmed, remove from heat and mix through the chia seeds (you may want to add more if the mixture looks really watery).

3. Set aside for 10-15 minutes while the chia seeds absorb the liquid and become the consistency of jam.

{V} {DF} {GF}

BERRY CHIA COMPOTE

20 mins | *1 cup*

Ingredients

Frozen or fresh berries	2 cups
Juice of ½ lemon	
Honey or maple syrup	1 tbsp
Chia seeds	1 tbsp

{V} {DF} {GF}

Method

1. Place a small saucepan on the stove on medium heat. Add in the berries, lemon juice and honey or maple syrup.

2. Put on low to medium heat and warm up, not letting the liquid boil. When mixture is warmed and you can break up the berries with the spoon, remove from heat and mix through the chia seeds (you may want to add more if the mixture looks really watery).

3. Set aside for 10-15 minutes while the chia seeds absorb the liquid and become the consistency of jam.

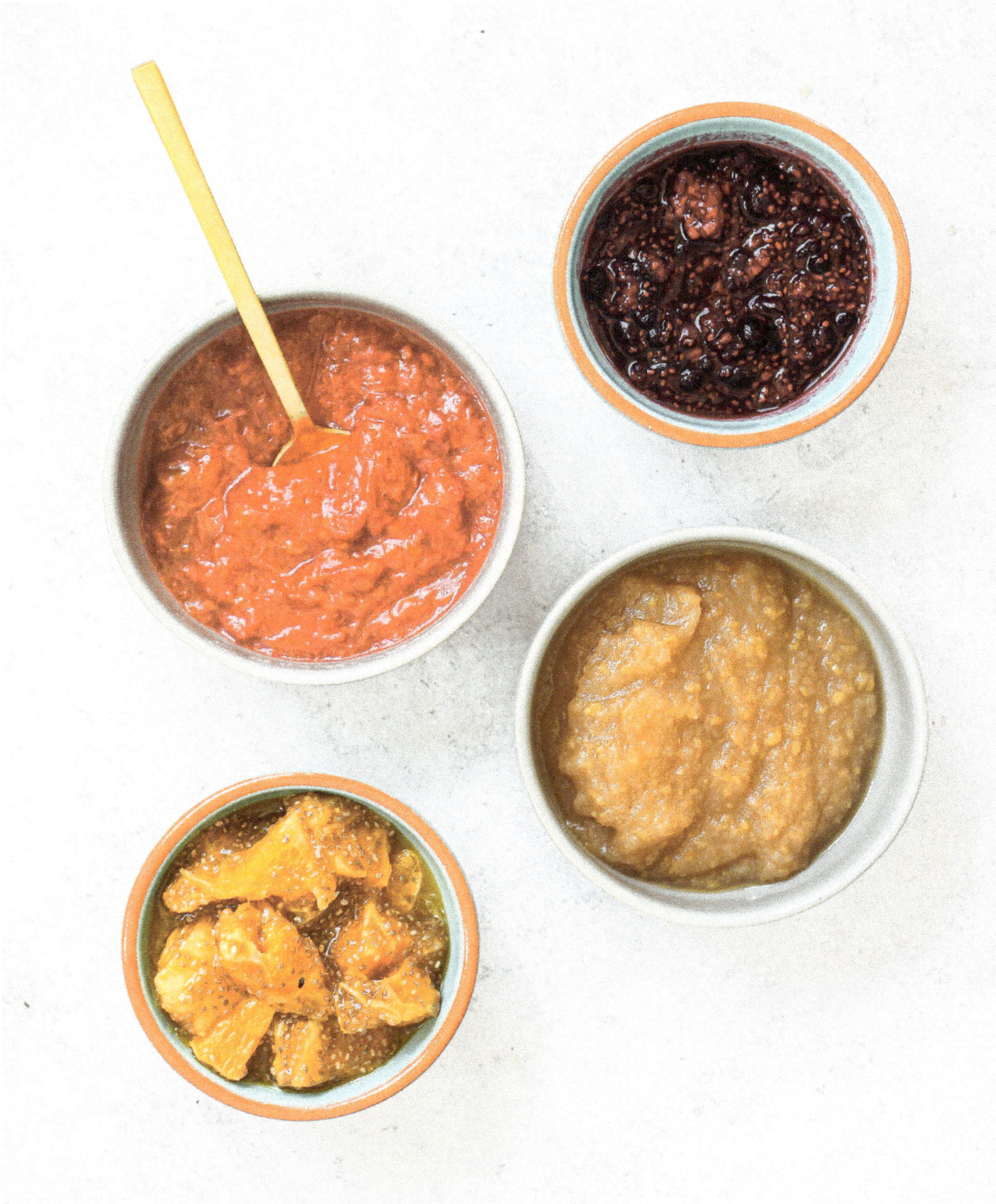

RHUBARB GINGER COMPOTE

20 mins / 1 cup

Ingredients

Coconut oil	½ tbsp
Rhubarb	250g
(Washed and cut into 1cm thick pieces)	
Frozen raspberries or strawberries	½ cup
(Optional)	
Fresh ginger *(grated)*	½ tsp
Honey or maple syrup	2 tbsp

V | DF | GF

Method

1. Place a large frying pan on medium heat.
2. When warm, add the coconut oil. Once the oil has melted add the chopped rhubarb. Stir for a few minutes.
3. Add grated ginger, stir then put the lid on and leave to steam (5–10 minutes) using the spoon to break up and stir the rhubarb occasionally.
4. Add the berries and mix through, breaking up the berries and rhubarb until all ingredients are cooked (the rhubarb is cooked when it becomes smooth).
5. Remove from heat and mix through honey or maple syrup to taste.

APPLE CINNAMON COMPOTE

30 mins / 3 cups

This also doubles as apple sauce in any recipe that calls for it.

Ingredients

Apples	6
Ground cinnamon	
Squeeze of lemon juice	

V | DF | GF

Method

1. Cut the apples into chunks, discarding the core. Place in a saucepan you have a lid for.
2. Fill with water until about ¾ of the height of the apples. Generously sprinkle some cinnamon over the top and add a squeeze of lemon juice.
3. Put the lid on the pot and bring to the boil, leaving to simmer about 20 minutes or until the fruit is soft. Remove from the heat and set aside to cool.
4. When cool, use an immersion mixer or blender to puree the compote. Put in jars and store in the fridge.

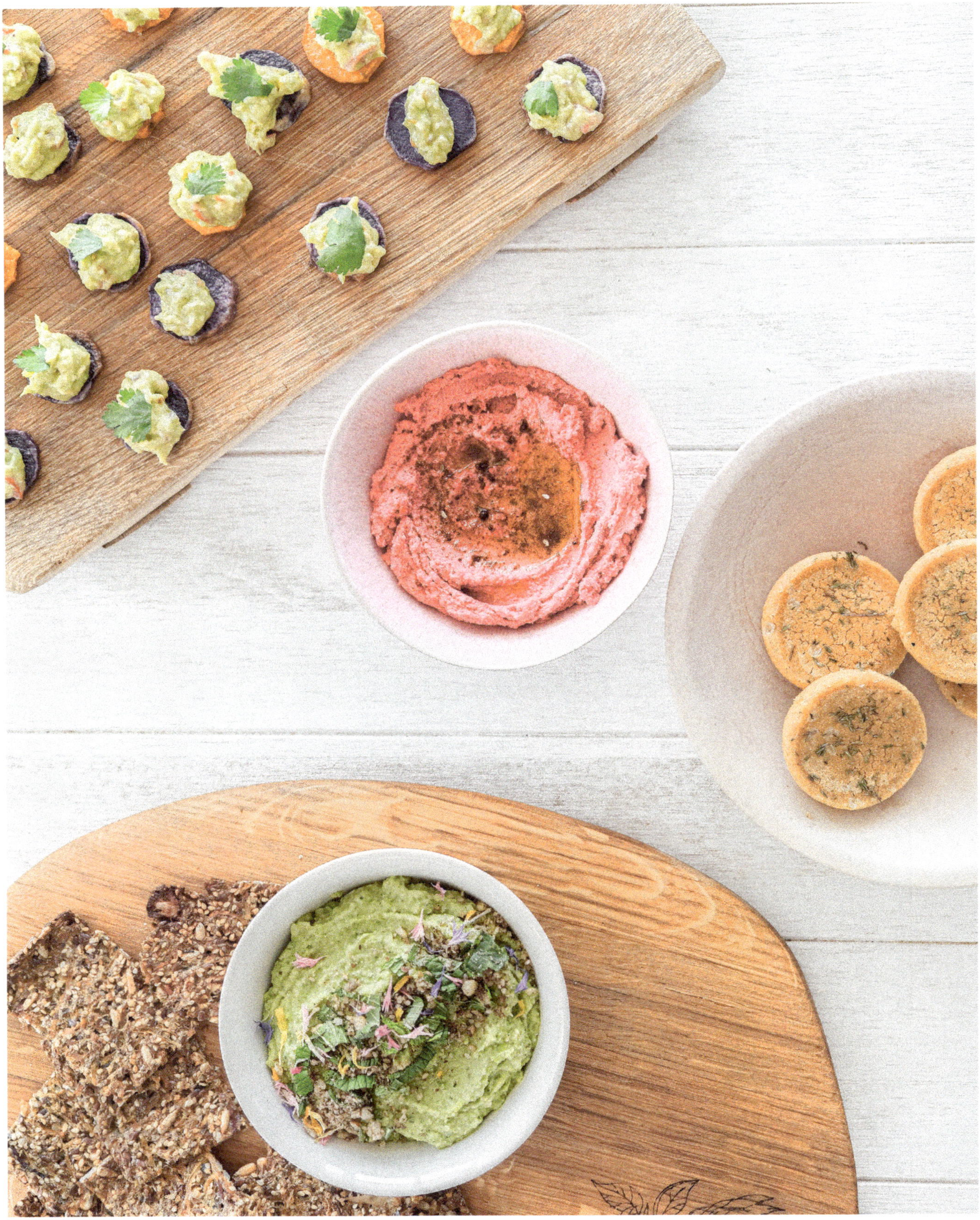

STARTERS

Tangy Salad Boats	117
Roasted Cauliflower with Mint Mousse and Hazelnut Sumac Dukkah	118
Easy (and Possibly Turkish) Bread	121
Shiitake Truffle and Mustard Crostini	123
Guacamole Potato Bites	125
Mini Millet Burgers	126

STARTERS

TANGY SALAD BOATS

10 mins / 4 as a starter

These tangy salad boats are my simple interpretation of a typical snack from Laos and Thailand called Mieng Kham ("one bite wrap"). I was reminded of them during a lunch meeting at a Thai restaurant in Berkeley a couple of years ago. Over a fascinating discussion about labour conditions in agriculture, a researcher from UC Berkeley and I devoured plates of Mieng Kham. This is my somewhat liberal adaptation of that dish. However, I don't take any ownership over this recipe – the inspiration came from a long line of people from a culture different to my own. I would like to honour these people and all those who openly share joyful and delicious food from their home country with others.

Ingredients

Salad Boats

Mini romaine lettuce or large spinach leaves	8–10
Desiccated or shredded coconut	2 tbsp
Salted cashews or peanuts *(roughly chopped)*	⅓ cup
Fresh ginger *(peeled and grated finely)*	1 heaped tsp
Red onion or shallots *(chopped finely)*	1 heaped tsp
Lime *(peeled then chopped into small chunks)*	½
Lemongrass *(chopped very finely)*	1 heaped tsp
Fresh mint leaves *(chopped finely)*	1 heaped tsp

Sauce

Tamarind paste	1 tbsp
Peanut butter	1 tbsp
Tamari	1 tbsp
Apple cider vinegar	1 tbsp

Method

1. Peel off the romaine lettuce leaves, trim the bottoms and wash each one. Shake off the excess water or dry with a paper towel or salad spinner and then arrange on a serving dish.

2. To make the filling, add the coconut, chopped nuts, grated ginger (including any juice produced when grating it), onions or shallots, lime chunks, lemongrass and fresh mint to a small mixing bowl. Mix with a spoon until all ingredients are evenly combined. Refrigerate until ready to serve then spoon into lettuce boats.

3. To make the sauce, place tamarind paste, peanut butter, tamari and apple cider vinegar into a small bowl and mix until well combined.

4. Just before serving, use a teaspoon to spoon the cooled filling into each of the lettuce boats.

5. Serve the salad boats with the sauce on the side or spooned on top of each one.

{V} {DF} {GF}

ROASTED CAULIFLOWER WITH MINT MOUSSE AND HAZELNUT SUMAC DUKKAH

10 mins prep plus 25 mins baking | 4 servings

This recipe is a testament to the wonders that salt, oil and lemon juice produce when combined. To use all three without abandon is something I learned at a one-week crash course in Italian cooking (and eating!) in Tuscany. Before that experience, I still had a bit of fear of salt and oil, thinking I had to be very measured with my use of both. I now use them very generously, often combined with an acid such as lemon juice. I have learned this is the secret behind most of the Italian dishes we all know and love.

Ingredients

Head of cauliflower	1
Olive oil	2 tbsp
Sumac	2 tsp
Ground turmeric	1 tsp
Salt and pepper to taste	

Mousse

Edamame beans or green peas, boiled until soft and drained	
(you could also use canned)	¾ cup
Avocado	1
Olive oil	2 tbsp
Lemon juice	2 tbsp
Ground coriander	¼ tsp
Small handful of fresh mint leaves	
(plus a few extra to use as garnish)	
Salt and pepper to taste	

Hazelnut dukkah

Hazelnuts	⅓ cup
Zaatar or sumac	1 tbsp
Sesame seeds	1 tbsp
Herb salt	½ tsp
Dried thyme	1 tsp

Method

1. Preheat oven to 200°C. Line an oven tray with baking paper.
2. Cut the cauliflower into smaller florets. Spread on the lined baking tray. Drizzle olive oil over the top and toss to coat. Sprinkle sumac, turmeric, salt and pepper on top then toss to coat evenly. Put in the oven for 25–30 mins.
3. Meanwhile, put all mousse ingredients in a food processor. Process until smooth, stopping and scraping down the sides intermittently. Taste and add anything you think is missing (more salt, pepper, lemon or oil if needed).
4. In a mortar and pestle or food processor, combine all ingredients for hazelnut dukkah. Crush or process until the ingredients are broken up into a chunky, crumbly spice powder.
5. To serve, spread the mousse on the bottom of the plate, using the back of the spoon. Place some cauliflower florets on top and sprinkle some dukkah over everything. Drizzle with a little olive oil and sprinkle with salt before serving with fresh mint leaves on top. Place any leftover dukkah in a jar in the pantry and keep it on hand to put on top of salads or soups.

STARTERS

EASY (AND POSSIBLY TURKISH) BREAD

5 mins prep plus 15 mins baking | 10 small pieces

When I was at university, one of my favourite restaurants was a cheap and cheerful Turkish restaurant. In the sweltering humidity of Brisbane, Australia, Turkey felt like an abstract concept, yet it was brought to life through tapestries and rugs strewn around the place. With every meal they served a delicious, cornbread-like chickpea bread. When I asked them for the recipe, I was delighted to discover it contained just two ingredients and took 15 minutes to make. The recipe below is my adaptation of this. It makes a great side to a soup or salad and is delicious as a starter served with dips or olive oil and dukkah. Right after I graduated, I headed to Turkey to backpack for a month. Despite traversing the country, to my disappointment I never found anything remotely similar to this bread. In fact, the closest I have found is socca, the chickpea flatbread from north Italy and France. Regardless of its origins, I think it is a great way to swap out a standard grain for a nutritious legume that is also helpful in fixing nitrogen in the soil.

Ingredients

Chickpea flour	2 cups
Bicarb soda	1 tsp
Garlic powder (*optional*)	½ tsp
Herb salt (*according to your taste*)	½–1 tsp
Sparkling mineral or soda water (*non-flavoured*)	2 cups
Sesame seeds	
Sumac and dried thyme	
Flaked salt	
Olive oil to grease	

* Use a muffin tray to make several small individual breads or a round baking tin to make one round loaf

Method

1. Preheat oven to 200° C. Grease a muffin tin or round baking tin.
2. Place the chickpea flour, bicarb soda, garlic powder and herb salt in a medium mixing bowl. Use a whisk to gently beat in the sparkling water to form a batter without any lumps.
3. If using a muffin tray pour about 2cm of batter in each muffin case. If using a round baking tin pour the entire batter in.
4. Sprinkle sesame seeds, sumac and thyme on top of the batter.
5. Place in the oven for approximately 10 minutes for the muffin tray or 15 minutes for the loaf tin.
6. Remove from oven and sprinkle with flaked salt before serving.

{V} {DF} {GF}

STARTERS

SHIITAKE TRUFFLE AND MUSTARD CROSTINI

15 mins | 10 pieces

Mushrooms are a great source of potassium, fibre, vitamin D and calcium. On top of that they are getting a lot of attention at the moment for the role they can play in a circular food economy. That's because you can grow mushrooms on material that is a waste product from other parts of food production. People now grow mushrooms on coffee grounds from cafes, from agricultural waste like straw and manure and processing waste like rice or wheat bran. After the mushrooms have grown, the substrate can be returned to the land and used as fertiliser. This is a great means of producing nutritious food in a way that closes a nutrient loop and makes the most of local resources. You can use mushrooms as delicious meaty ingredients in many vegetarian dishes, but this starter is one of my all-time favourites.

Ingredients

Mushrooms:

Shiitake mushrooms *(thinly sliced)*	100g
Butter or olive oil	1 tbsp
Clove garlic *(crushed)*	1
Tamari	1 tbsp
Apple balsamic vinegar	1 tbsp
Zaatar or sumac	¼ tsp

Honey Mustard:

Non-seeded mustard	2 tbsp
Honey	2 tsp
Truffle oil	2 tsp

One baguette or ciabatta loaf, sliced into approximately 10 small slices

Maldon salt or other flaked salt

Sprigs of fresh thyme

Method

1. Place a frying pan on medium heat. When warm, add the butter and garlic and sauté briefly. Add the mushrooms and sauté until they start to soften. Add the tamari and vinegar and continue to cook until the mixture starts to brown. Remove from heat and mix through the zaatar.

2. In a small bowl, mix together the mustard, honey and truffle oil.

3. Place the bread slices under a grill or in the oven for a few minutes to lightly toast.

4. Coat each piece of bread with a spoon full of the mustard, top with mushrooms then sprinkle some crushed flaked salt and fresh thyme over the top.

STARTERS

GUACAMOLE POTATO BITES

10 mins prep plus 20 mins baking | serves 4 as a starter (10–15 pieces)

Did you know there are over 4,000 varieties of potato in the world? Most of them are in the Andean countries, and the International Potato Centre in Peru keeps a gene bank containing the largest collection of potatoes in the world. This helps ensure they are conserved for the long-term while also being available to farmers, breeders and researchers to actually use. Here in Switzerland, a not-for-profit organisation called Pro Specie Rara works to preserve and expand the genetic diversity of local plants and animals, selling planting material for traditional Swiss varieties of crops, as well as labelling products that use these varieties. This includes a bright blue potato, the St Gallen Blue, which is just perfect for making this dish. What is interesting about this potato is that it is not exactly an old variety. It was bred 15 years ago, combining qualities from old varieties to get one that people would appreciate today. This is the first "new" variety Pro Specie Rara ever took into its range, and it was an important message: yes, old varieties are important, but so is developing them so they adapt to changing tastes, climate, pests and diseases when they show up. If you don't have blue potatoes, why not try an unusual variety in your area? This is also delicious with sweet potato.

Ingredients

Sweet potato *peeled and sliced into thin rounds*	1
Or	
Potatoes, *peeled and sliced into rounds*	4
Olive oil	
Herb salt	

Guacamole

Avocados	1½
Juice of lime	1
Red onion *(finely chopped)*	¼
Cherry tomatoes *(finely chopped)*	3
Chilli powder	1 pinch
Salt and pepper to taste *(be generous!)*	
Fresh coriander leaves to top	10

Method

1. Preheat the oven to 200° C. Line a baking tray. Place the sweet potato or potato rounds on the baking tray. Brush the potatoes with olive oil and sprinkle with herb salt. Put in the oven to cook for around 20 mins.

2. Make the guacamole by placing all ingredients in a small bowl and using a fork to mash together.

3. When the potato is ready remove from the oven and place the rounds on the serving dish. Place a spoonful of guacamole on top of each potato round. Top with one coriander leaf. Sprinkle with flaked salt before serving.

V DF GF

MINI MILLET BURGERS

25 min prep plus 30 min baking | *12–15 small patties*

This recipe comes from the lovely Daga Stojecka, who makes delicious little millet burgers for her plant-based catering business Green Daga. She does this alongside a fulltime job for the sheer love of sharing good, healthy food, and it comes across in everything she prepares. These mini burgers are great as part of a Buddha bowl, to use instead of falafel (see falafel and fries recipe page 178) or to just have in the fridge to snack on. As I was making them, I started to imagine a delicious little mini burger served on lettuce with a tangy garlic corn sauce, so I have added that to the recipe here. If cooking millet is something you have never done before, do not fear. Embrace the words of the magnificent Julia Childs: "Learn how to cook – try new recipes, learn from your mistakes, be fearless and above all, have fun!"

PART TWO | *Starters*

Ingredients

Mini-Burgers

Millet *(should yield 1 cup cooked)*	⅓ cup
Water	1 cup
Salt	
Olive oil	3 tbsp
Red onion *(finely diced)*	½
Mustard seeds or seeded mustard	½ tbsp
Large carrots *(peeled and finely grated)*	2
Sunflower seeds	¼ cup
Sunflower oil	2 tbsp
Non-seeded mustard	2 tsp
Chickpea flour	3 tbsp
Tamari	1½ tbsp
Maple syrup	½ tbsp
Fresh or dried thyme	½ tbsp
Few pinches of nutmeg	
Salt and pepper to taste	
Small lettuce leaves to serve	

Sauce

Plain soy yoghurt	150g
Sweet corn kernels	⅓ cup
Fresh dill	Small handful
Fresh chives	Small handful
Lime juice	2 tsp
Clove garlic *(crushed)*	½
Few sprinkles of paprika	
Salt and pepper to taste	

Method

1. Preheat oven to 200°C. Line a baking tray.

2. Rinse and drain millet. Place it in a small saucepan, add 1 cup water and some salt. Bring to the boil, then reduce the heat to low, put lid on and let it gently simmer 10–15 minutes, stirring as needed. Remove from heat and set aside with lid on until all the water is absorbed.

3. Place a frying pan on medium heat. When warm, add 3 tbsp of olive oil, the onion and mustard seeds. Sauté until onion is soft. Remove from heat.

4. Place cooked millet, carrot, sunflower seeds, sunflower oil, mustard, chickpea flour, tamari, maple syrup, thyme, nutmeg, salt and pepper into a mixing bowl. Add in the onion, mustard seed and oil mixture from the frying pan. Mix everything together with a wooden spoon until well combined. Use the back of the spoon to press down and break up any millet clumps.

5. Use a spoon to scoop out mixture and form a ball. Place it on the baking tray and press down with back of spoon to form patties. Fill the baking tray with 12–15 patties.

6. Place in the preheated oven on the top rack. Bake 25 min on one side then flip the patties and bake 5–7 min on the other side.

7. While the patties are baking, make the sauce by combining all ingredients in a mixing bowl.

8. When patties are ready, remove from oven and leave to cool a little. If serving as a starter, place each patty on a lettuce leaf and top with a dollop of sauce and a sprinkling of dill.

(V) (DF) (GF)

The Great Full

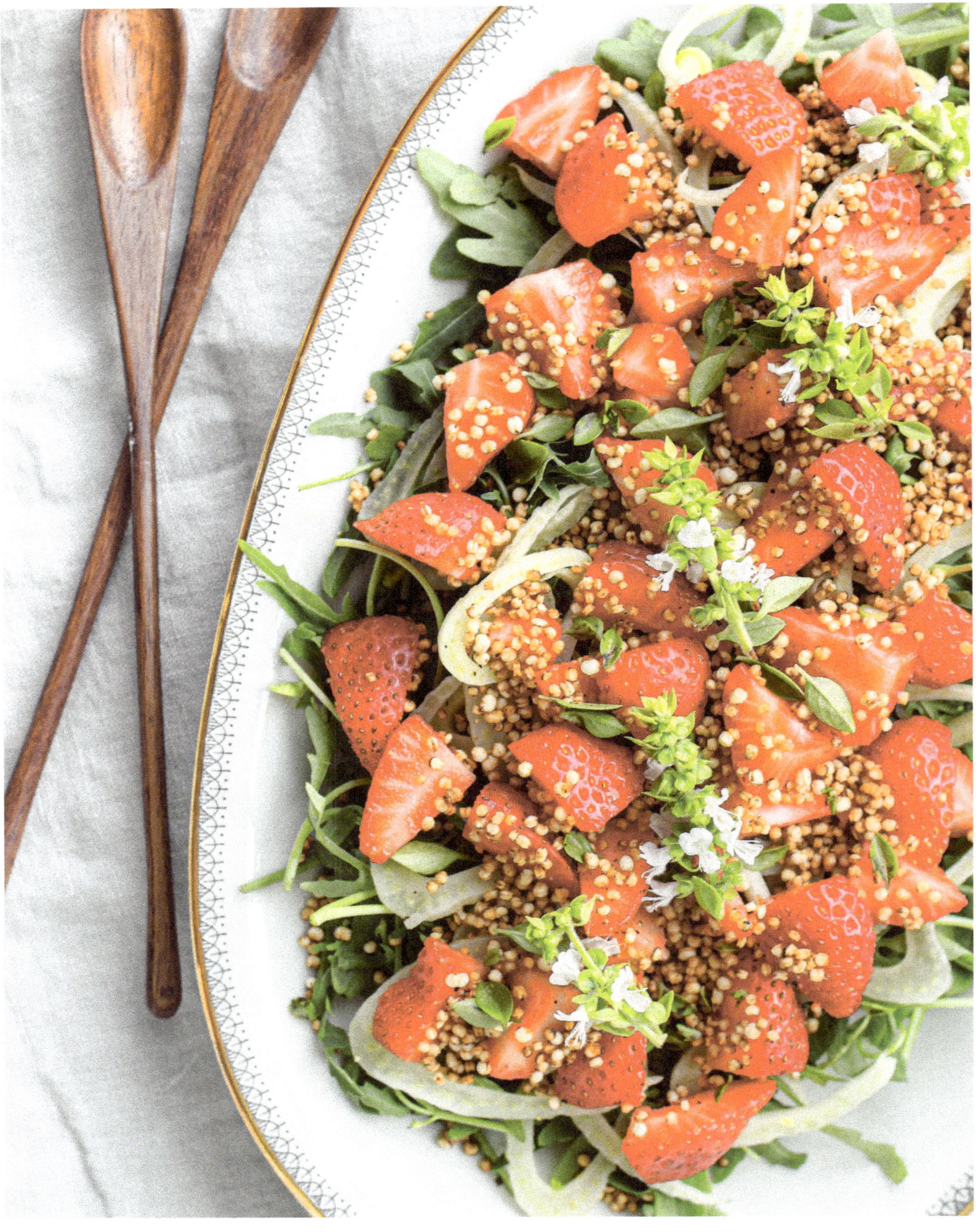

SALADS + SOUPS

Salad Basics	131
Soup Basics	133
Roasted Chickpea Zucchini and Pomegranate Salad	134
Tropical Soba Noodle Salad	137
Mediterranean Rice Salad	139
Strawberry Balsamic Salad with Roasted Puffed Grains	140
Summer Pea Salad	143
Refreshing Coconut Lime and Nut Slaw	145
Warm Winter Salad	147
Watermelon Gazpacho	149
Quick Vegan Ramen	151
Meditative Minestrone	152
Warming Vegetable and Corn Chowder	154
Creamy Roast Potato Lemon and Dill Soup	157
Spiced Harissa Carrot and Lentil Soup	159
Green Magic Soup	161

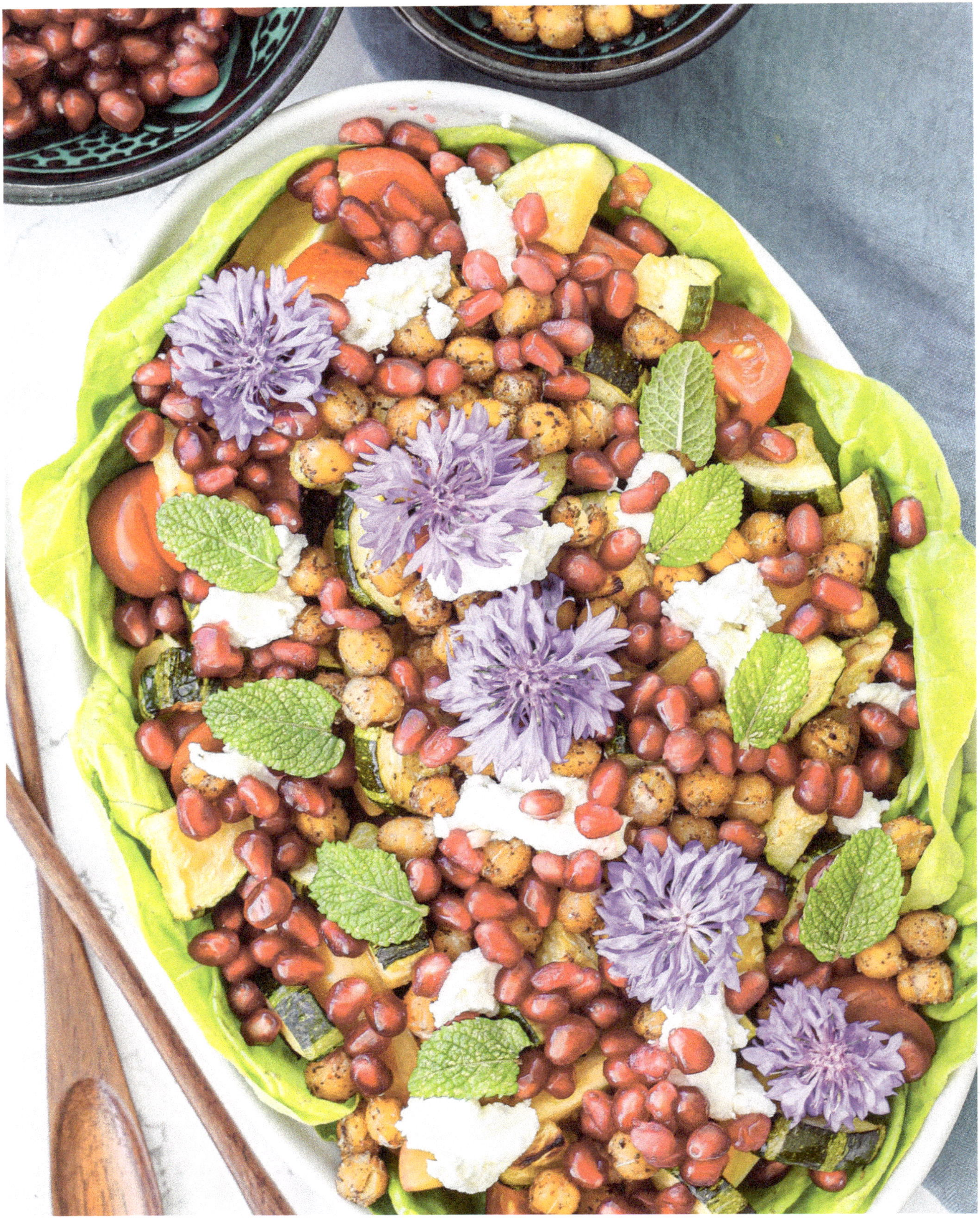

PART TWO | *Salads and Soups*

In winter, there is nothing better than a hearty vegetable soup to provide warmth, comfort and nourishment. In summer, a crispy, seasonal salad is the most delicious and refreshing meal you can find. Before I share a bunch of recipes for soups and salads I wanted to let you in on some tips and tricks to help you create your own recipes based on whatever you have on hand. This makes it easy to conjure a meal out of what may seem like an empty cupboard or fridge!

SALAD BASICS

My country of origin (Australia) and my country of residence (Switzerland) have many differences. Beaches vs mountains. Sun vs snow. But the one that I will never get used to is the different understanding of what constitutes a salad. In Australia, a salad is often a meal on its own, combining all kinds of weird and wonderful ingredients. In Switzerland, it is perfectly acceptable to serve green lettuce leaves with a dressing and call it a salad. Although I have come to appreciate the simplicity of a Swiss salad – perfectly crispy lettuce leaves with a delicious dressing – I still prefer one that is a meal on its own. When you have the basic components of a salad clear in your mind, it is easy to whip up something delicious in no time, making use of whatever you have on hand. Below are the key components I like to add to each salad to get something that is crispy, crunchy and full of flavour, colour and nutrients.

Base (Green or Grain or both!)
Lettuce, Spinach, Rocket, Kale (massage in a bit of olive oil, lemon juice and salt first), Black rice, Wild rice, Quinoa, Millet, Buckwheat, Couscous

Seasonal Vegetables
Tomatoes, Cucumber, Baked Vegetables, Asparagus, Mushrooms, Broccoli, Mushrooms

Seasonal Fruit (optional)
Strawberries, Melon, Watermelon, Grapes, Pomegranate, Figs, Pear, Apple

Legume or other protein
Black beans, Chickpeas, Lentils, Kidney beans, Sprouts

Seeds + Nuts
Sunflower seeds, Pumpkin Seeds, Hemp seeds, Sesame seeds, Soaked nuts, Dukkah

Tangy
Pickled vegetables, Capers, Preserved lemon, Olives

Creamy
Avocado, Goats' cheese, Haloumi, Cooked egg, Parmesan, Hummus (smear it on the bottom of the dish and put the salad on top)

Dressing
See list page 246, or just use some oil, vinegar, lemon juice and sprinkle some salt, pepper and fresh herbs

The Great Full | 131

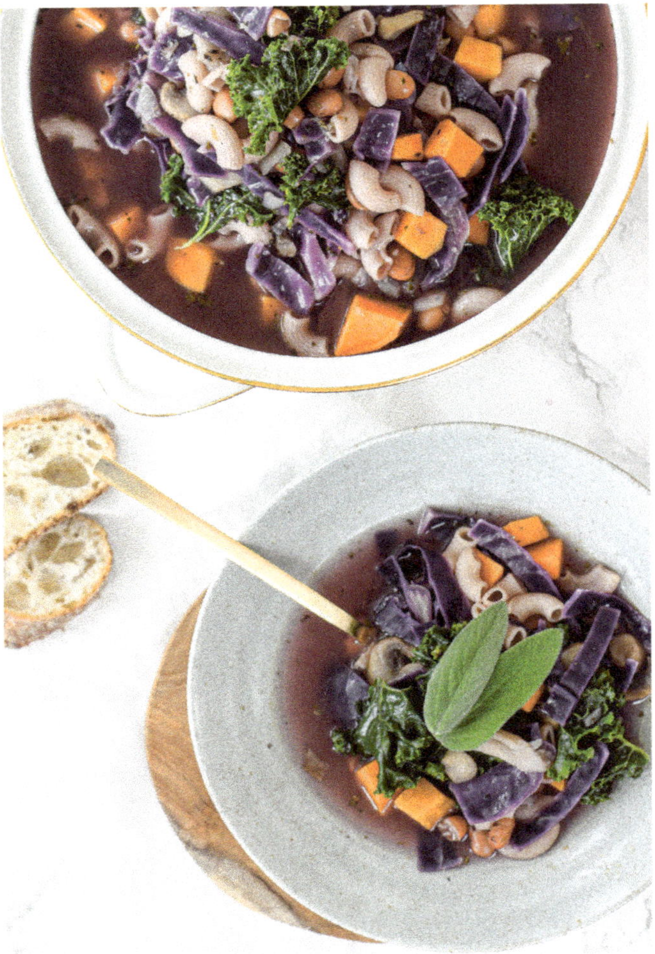
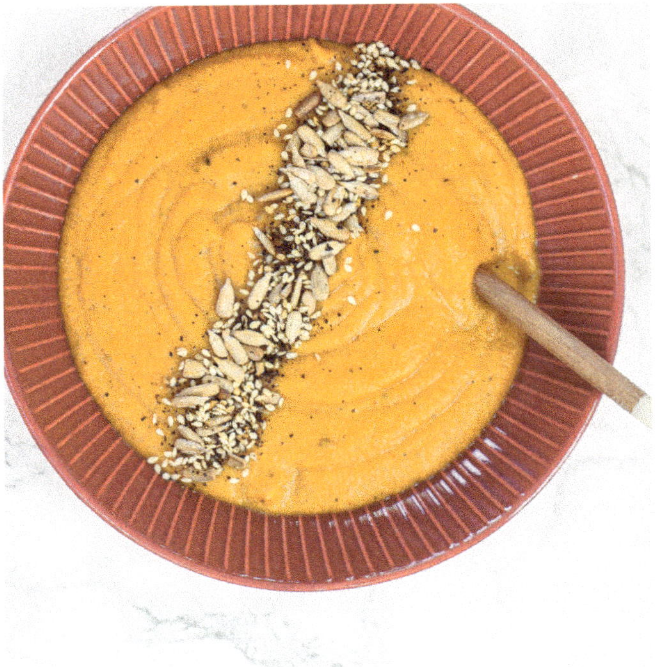
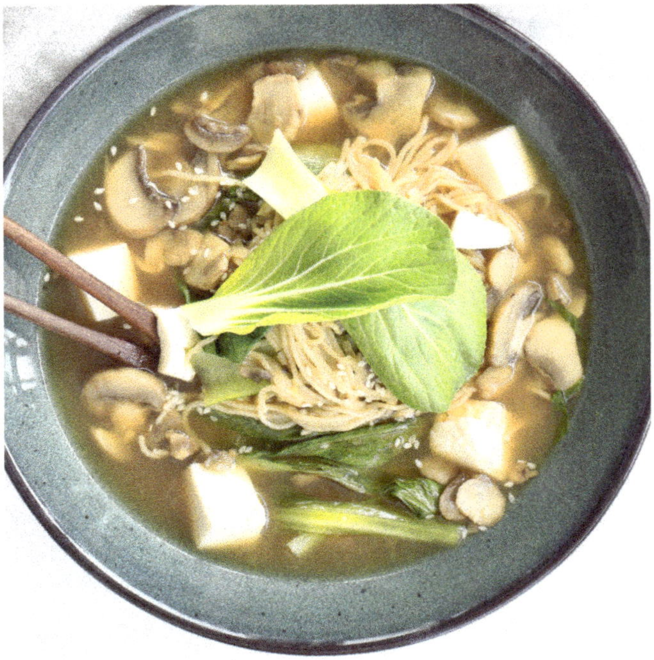
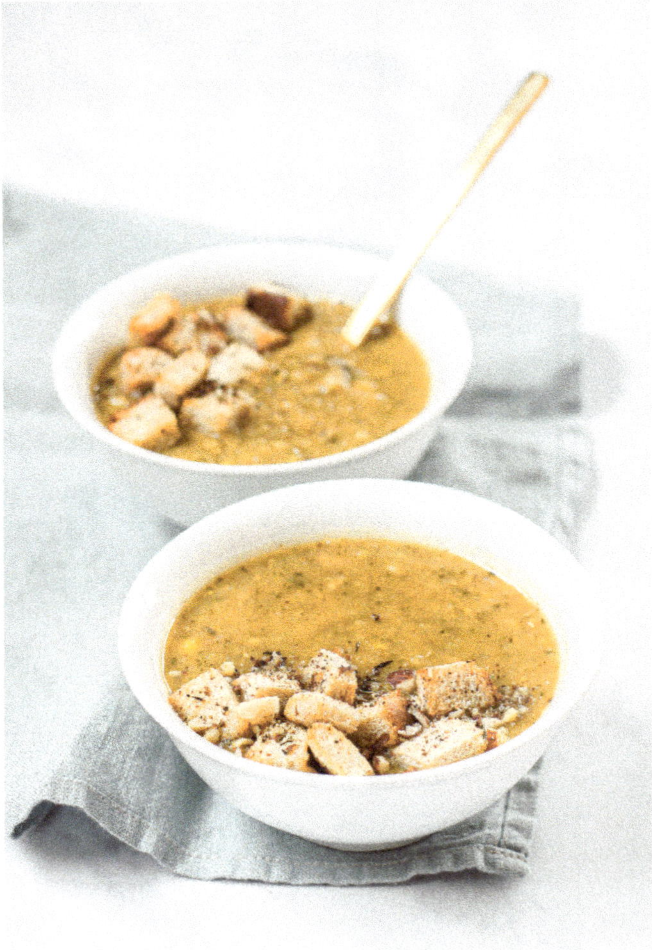

SOUP BASICS

I could easily have made an entire cookbook just with soup recipes. I love to make a big batch up on Sunday so that I have a simple and easy dinner ready to heat up after a long winter day. Many of my soups are just variations of the same thing, making use of the following key ingredients:

Fat	I like to use ghee for a richer, heartier soup, olive oil or sunflower oil for a lighter flavour or sesame or coconut oil for anything with Asian flavours.
Onions	You can use standard onions, red onions, leeks, scallions, spring onions or chives here, with the addition of garlic for an extra punch.
Stock	The stock is what will make or break your soup and it is the one non-negotiable ingredient. You can make up your own vegetable stock using vegetable scraps and onion skins. Just throw them in a bag in the freezer to store until you are ready to make the stock. There are many great recipes online, I really like the one from Dana at the Minimalist Baker blog (though I usually omit the tomato paste). If you don't make your own, you have two options – buy the readymade stock or buy stock powder or cubes. I prefer to buy the powder so I can quickly make up as much as I need by adding the required quantity of powder to boiling water. I tried about 5 different vegetable stock powders till I found one that I really like, and I play around with the suggested quantities, usually increasing the stock powder to water ratio a little.
Herbs	You can use fresh or dried herbs according to the flavour combination you are going for. For example, for Mediterranean flavoured soups, thyme, oregano, rosemary and sumac go well together.
Vegetables	I like to use hearty vegetables to make my soup a meal, though whatever vegetable is in peak season will make the most flavoursome soup. I like to roast the vegetables with some oil, salt and herbs before adding to the soup.
Protein	Cooked or canned beans as well as silken tofu make great additions to soups. They add some protein while also making the dish creamy and hearty.
Acid	This is the component most often forgotten by the home cook, but it is the final touch that makes the dish. You could use lemon, lime or a vinegar such as apple cider or white balsamic.
Toppings	Croutons are the quintessential soup topper. You can easily make them yourself – it is a great way to repurpose old bread. Alternatively, use a mix of crushed nuts, seeds, herbs and salt or some finely chopped chives.

Once you have these elements it is easy to make any soup: roast your vegetables; sauté onions and garlic in the fat or oil; add the stock; add the herbs; add any other vegetables or things that need to cook and simmer until tender; pour in roasted vegetables and cooked beans; leave to simmer a few minutes; remove from heat add few squeezes of acid; mix through. Then it is up to you – use an immersion blender to puree the soup or leave it chunky. Serve with any toppings you like!

ROASTED CHICKPEA ZUCCHINI AND POMEGRANATE SALAD

35 mins | serves 4 as a starter

I once heard a doctor speak about how he tries to get his family excited about eating lots of vegetables, something most people in the world don't do enough of. He had a simple little tool that is a hit with kids. On the fridge, he hung up a wheel with a rainbow of colours. At the end of the day, before dinner, everyone went around and thought about how many colours they ate during the day, with the aim to get as many different ones as possible. If you are a little low, then dinner is the chance to tick some more colours off the wheel. This salad can help with that – it is not only delicious but filled with colourful ingredients that will appeal to even the most hardened vegetable sceptic in your life!

Ingredients

Zucchini	400g
Olive oil *(for drizzling)*	
Herb salt	
Dried garlic powder	
Black pepper	
Can chickpeas	400g
Baby spinach *(or any greens)*	2 handfuls
Cherry or small heirloom tomatoes *(optional)*	2 handfuls
Pomegranate seeds	½ cup
Fresh mint leaves	10
Goats' cheese or feta	50g
Olive oil	
Herb salt	
Dried garlic powder	
Black pepper	

Spice mix

Zaatar mix or sumac	1 tsp
Dried garlic powder	½ tsp
Ground coriander	½ tsp
Chilli powder	¼ tsp
Herb salt	½ tsp
Ground turmeric	½ tsp

Dressing

Olive oil	2 tbsp
Apple cider vinegar	1 tbsp
Tahini	1 tbsp
Maple syrup	1 tbsp
Lemon juice	1 tbsp
Salt and pepper	

(GF)

Method

1. Preheat the oven to 200° C. Line two baking trays with baking paper.

2. Cut each zucchini in half lengthways then chop into semicircles, each around a ½ inch thick. Place chopped zucchini on one of the lined oven trays. Drizzle with olive oil, sprinkle with herb salt, dried garlic and cracked black pepper and set aside.

3. In a medium mixing bowl prepare the spice mix by combining the spices. Open the jar or can of chickpeas, then drain and rinse them. Pat them dry with a paper towel. Pour the chickpeas into the mixing bowl on top of the spice mix. Drizzle a little bit of olive oil over the chickpeas then use a spoon to mix the chickpeas until they are evenly coated. Pour the chickpea mixture onto the second lined baking tray and spread evenly.

4. Place the tray with the chickpeas and the tray with the zucchini in the oven. Roast for about 25 minutes until the zucchini starts to brown and the chickpeas are just starting to get crunchy. You may need to remove the chickpeas about 5 minutes earlier than the zucchini.

5. While the zucchini and chickpeas are cooking, take a serving dish or salad bowl and place the baby spinach on the bottom. Halve or quarter the tomatoes and place them on top (optional).

6. Remove the seeds from pomegranate, cut the mint leaves into strips, cut the feta or goats' cheese into small chunks.

7. Place all the dressing ingredients into a jar and shake to combine. Set aside and shake again just before dressing the salad.

8. When the zucchini and chickpeas are ready, remove them from the oven. Layer the zucchini on top of the greens in the serving dish. Sprinkle the goats' cheese or feta on top, followed by the chickpeas. Top with the pomegranate and mint leaves. Pour over the dressing just before serving.

SALADS + SOUPS

TROPICAL SOBA NOODLE SALAD

30 mins | serves 4

This is a recipe I made up while living in Australia, so it has a lot of ingredients that I don't have on hand in Switzerland. I like to make it whenever I go home, or as a treat for those times when I miss the flavours from closer to the equator. It is fresh and tangy and perfect for a warm summer day. It is also a great salad to pop in a jar to take to work. Just put the dressing in the bottom, follow with the noodles and then layer the other ingredients on top. Turn it upside down when you are ready to eat and you have a tasty salad that isn't soggy!

Ingredients

Mango (cubed)	1
Cucumber (cubed)	250g
Edamame beans (shelled) or snow peas (chopped)	1 cup
Red cabbage (shredded)	200g
Lemon juice	1 tsp
Salt	½ tsp
Red onion (finely chopped)	1
Macadamia nuts (roughly chopped)	⅓ cup
Hemp seeds (optional)	⅓ cup
Fresh coriander (roughly chopped)	handful
Fresh mint (roughly chopped)	handful
Soba or brown rice noodles	160g

Dressing

Sesame oil	¼ cup
Maple syrup	2 tbsp
Apple cider vinegar	3 tbsp
Lime juice	1 tbsp
Tamari	2 tbsp

Method

1. Cook the noodles according to instructions. Drain and run under cold water. Place the noodles in a large salad bowl.
2. Place the shredded cabbage in a small bowl, add lemon juice and salt. Wash hands and massage the cabbage with your fingers for a few minutes, until liquid starts to come out.
3. Put all the dressing ingredients in a jar. Put the lid on and shake until combined.
4. Place the cubed mango, cucumber and edamame on top of the noodles. Top with the cabbage, coriander, mint and finally the macadamias and hemp seeds. Pour the salad dressing on top just before serving.

V | DF | GF

SALADS + SOUPS

MEDITERRANEAN RICE SALAD

20 mins plus rice/lentil cooking time | serves 4–6

I love to make a big batch of this salad on the weekend as it rolls over very well into weekday lunches. Not only does it store well, it is full of fibre and nutrients and gives you the fuel you need to get through a long afternoon. If you want to roll it over, I recommend leaving the spinach out, adding it and the dressing, just before serving.

Ingredients

Brown rice or wild rice	1 cup
Black (beluga) lentils *salted after cooking*	1 cup
Zucchini, *cut in half rounds*	600g
Sundried tomatoes, *sliced*	1 cup
Artichoke hearts, sliced *(optional)*	1 cup
Capers	¼ cup
Walnuts, *roughly chopped*	½ cup
Kalamata olives, *pitted, sliced*	handful
Zaatar or sumac	1 tsp
Thyme *(dried or fresh)*	1 ½ tsp
Baby spinach	handful

Optional toppings

Fresh basil leaves	
Red onion, *finely diced*	½

Mustard dressing

Olive oil	¼ cup
Lemon juice	3 tbsp
Non-seeded mustard *(I use honey mustard)*	3 tbsp
Soy or dairy free cream	3 tbsp
Salt and pepper to taste	

Method

1. Cook the brown rice and the lentils. (You can do this in advance and store in the fridge until ready to make the salad.)

2. Preheat oven to 200°C. Line a baking tray. Spread out chopped zucchini on the tray, drizzle with olive oil and sprinkle with herb salt. Bake for 20 minutes.

3. Place the sundried tomatoes, artichoke hearts, capers, walnuts and olives in a large bowl and add the zaatar/sumac and thyme. Add the cooked brown rice, lentils and zucchini to the salad bowl. Mix everything with a spoon until well combined. Sprinkle on the zaatar and thyme and mix through. Add the baby spinach just before serving.

4. Place all the dressing ingredients in a jar, put the lid on and shake until combined.

5. Pour the dressing over the salad and mix through just before serving. Garnish with fresh basil leaves and red onion.

V DF GF

STRAWBERRY BALSAMIC SALAD WITH ROASTED PUFFED GRAINS

20 mins | 2 large / 4 small

Something I will never forget is standing in the middle of the Salinas Valley in California, where the strawberry fields stretched forever. I was there to see how a new piece of mechanization was improving conditions for workers by reducing the distance they had to walk up and down the rows. But they still had to be bent over picking strawberries in the sun and biting wind the whole day. Some of the strawberries would not make it to their pallets – they were too small or bruised to meet the standards of the buyer and were left on the field. When we asked the supervisor how the system could be made more equitable, he told us, "The consumer needs to pay more for the luxury of strawberries. The workers deserve more. This is incredibly hard work. And you should write to big companies like Driscolls Berries and tell them you don't need the most perfect looking strawberry. The over the top quality standards on size lead to so much unnecessary waste on the fields." So, when I make this salad, or whenever I buy strawberries, I always think about that advice.

PART TWO | *Salads and Soups*

SALADS + SOUPS {V} {DF} {GF}

Ingredients

Salad

Puffed quinoa or brown rice *(plain and unsweetened)*	⅓ cup
Apple cider vinegar	½ tbsp
Olive oil	½ tbsp
Salt and pepper to taste	
Rocket or baby spinach leaves	100g
Fennel *(thinly sliced, tops and bottom removed)*	1 bulb
Fresh strawberries *(sliced into quarters, tops removed)*	250g
Pecans *(optional)*	
Soft goats' cheese *(optional)*	
Fresh basil leaves, *to top*	

Dressing

Balsamic vinegar	1½ tbsp
Olive oil	1 tbsp
Lemon juice	½ tbsp
Maple syrup	½ tbsp
Herb salt	¼ tsp
Cracked black pepper to taste	

Method

1. Preheat the oven to 180° C. Line a baking tray with baking paper and set aside.

2. Place the quinoa or rice puffs in a small mixing bowl. Add in apple cider vinegar, olive oil, salt, cracked pepper and mix through with a spoon until well combined. Pour out onto the baking paper and spread with a spoon until well distributed across the tray.

3. Place tray on the top rack in the preheated oven and leave to cook for 10 minutes.

4. While the puffs are cooking, prepare the rest of the salad. Place the rocket or spinach on the bottom of a salad dish. Spread the thinly sliced fennel on top of the greens. Top with the sliced strawberries. If using nuts or goats' cheese sprinkle this on top of the strawberries.

5. When the grains are ready remove from oven and leave to cool. Place on top of the salad. Shred the basil leaves and sprinkle them on top of everything.

6. To make the dressing: place all ingredients in a small jar or salad mixer. Mix until combined. When ready to serve pour the dressing on top of salad.

The Great Full

SALADS + SOUPS

SUMMER PEA SALAD

30 mins | serves 2

This salad always marks the arrival of summer for me. The time of year when fresh peas in their pods start to appear at the farmers market. Paired with quick-pickled cabbage, nuts and quinoa, they make up this delicious and colourful salad.

Ingredients

Salad

Quinoa *(optional)*	½ cup
Small red cabbage *(thinly shredded)*	½
Sea salt	1 tsp
Lime or lemon juice	1 tsp
Fresh peas *(shelled)*	⅔ cup
Rocket	4 handfuls
Almonds *(slivered or chopped)*	2 handfuls

Lemon Mustard Tahini Dressing

Olive oil	2 tbsp
Lemon juice	1½ tbsp
Tamari	1 tbsp
Seeded mustard	2 tbsp
Tahini	1 tbsp
Maple syrup	½ tsp
Apple cider vinegar	1 tsp

Method

1. Cook quinoa.
2. Place the cabbage in a bowl with the salt and lemon/lime juice. Use your hands to massage into the cabbage for a few minutes. Leave it to sit on the countertop until salad is ready to compile. You can also make this in advance and store it in the fridge.
3. Shell the peas if they are still in their pods. Steam, blanch or parboil the peas for 2–5 minutes or until slightly tender. Remove from heat.
4. Shake or mix all dressing ingredients to combine.
5. To compile the salad, place rocket in serving bowl. Top with quinoa, red cabbage and peas. Sprinkle slivered almonds on the top. Pour dressing over the salad.

SALADS + SOUPS

PART TWO | *Salads and Soups*

REFRESHING COCONUT LIME AND NUT SLAW

20 mins | 6 as a starter or side

The vegetables I have used here are just a suggestion, but feel free to throw in anything you have lying around in the fridge that needs rescuing. I like to have a few basic recipes that I know are good for using up vegetable scraps or soon-to-rot produce. This is one of them, as are the soups, and the curry and risotto recipes in this book. I hope they help you save the lives of at least a few veggies!

Ingredients

Slaw

Apples	2
Fennel bulbs	2
Red cabbage	500g

Dressing

Coconut milk	¼ cup
Smooth peanut butter	¼ cup
Sesame oil	2 tbsp
Lime or lemon juice	1½ tbsp
Tamari	1½ tbsp
Fresh ginger	3cm
Small garlic clove	1
Maple syrup	1 tbsp
Salt and pepper to taste	

Optional Toppings

Salted peanuts, crushed
Fresh dill
Fresh coriander
Hemp seeds
Lime zest

Method

1. Slice the apple, fennel and red cabbage into thin shreds. (If you have a food processor, you can use the shredding attachment.) Place in a mixing bowl and add some lemon juice and a few pinches of salt. Set aside.

2. Place all the dressing ingredients in the blender. Blend until combined. Add salt and pepper to taste.

3. Pour the dressing on top of the slaw and mix through. Put in the serving bowl and top with crushed peanuts, fresh herbs, hemp seeds, and lime zest.

V | DF | GF

The Great Full

SALADS + SOUPS

WARM WINTER SALAD

🕐 *15 mins* | ✋ *4 as a starter*

I love this salad because it features the most successful crop on our balcony: cumquats! We have a tree that faithfully produces a harvest every year, a different story to some of our other farming experiments. Balcony farming is probably not the most resource efficient way to feed ourselves, but it is a great way to truly appreciate what it takes to get food on our plates. Growing our own produce allows our urban selves to experience, first-hand, the progress of our food from seed to harvest. To appreciate all the water, soil and toil that it takes to create our food.

Ingredients

Blood oranges *(peeled, cut into rounds and quartered)*	2
Cumquats *(cut in half, thinly sliced and deseeded)*	4
Pecans *(roughly chopped)*	½ cup
Ghee	2 tsp
Maple syrup	2 tbsp
A few pinches of flaked salt *(crushed)*	
Red cabbage *(thinly sliced)*	200g
Salt	
Lemon juice	
Kale, *stalks removed*	3 cups
Olive oil	1 tbsp
Fennel bulb, *thinly sliced*	1

Dressing

Olive oil	4 tbsp
Apple balsamic vinegar *(or any other light-coloured vinegar)*	2 tbsp
Honey mustard *(or use smooth mustard and add 1 tbsp honey)*	2 tbsp
Soy or other non-dairy cream	4 tbsp
Herb salt	1 tsp
Squeeze of lemon juice	

Method

1. Preheat oven to 200° C.
2. Place the orange segments, cumquat slices and chopped pecans on a lined baking tray. Drizzle melted ghee and maple syrup over the top. Sprinkle with salt and use a spoon to mix until all ingredients are well coated. Place in preheated oven and bake for 10–15 minutes. Remove when starting to brown but not burnt.
3. Place the sliced cabbage in a small mixing bowl. Sprinkle salt and lemon juice on top. Use fingers to massage the cabbage for a couple of minutes until liquid starts coming out from it. Set aside.
4. Place all dressing ingredients into a jar with a lid. Shake until well combined.
5. Rinse and dry the kale then roughly chop into large pieces. Put in a serving bowl, drizzle olive oil and lemon juice on top then sprinkle with salt. Use your hands to massage the kale until it is all well coated with oil and you feel it start to soften.
6. Place the cabbage on top of the kale. Arrange the thinly sliced fennel on top of the cabbage. Place the baked orange and nut mix on top of everything else.
7. Dress the salad at the time of serving.

{DF} {GF}

SALADS + SOUPS

WATERMELON GAZPACHO

15 mins | 6 servings as a starter

I came up with this recipe in the middle of a heatwave in Zurich. The scorching temperatures made me want to eat watermelon or salad for breakfast, lunch and dinner. So this soup is basically salad and watermelon in a blender and despite how that sounds it is delicious. If you are one to listen to scientists, then drinking pureed salad may be something you have to get used to. Researchers predict that due to climate change we are more likely to see weather extremes (including heat waves) in the future. This will have a lot of negative impacts on what and how we can produce food, including water shortages, crops wilting and people having to work in the extreme heat. This is a good reason to do what you can and eat as climate friendly as possible. Generally, that means more plants and way less meat and animal products on our plates.

Ingredients

Small watermelon *(approximately 1 kg with skin)*	½
Tomatoes, *roughly chopped*	300g
Cucumber, *peeled, roughly chopped*	250g
Small red onion *peeled, roughly chopped*	1
Fresh mild red chilli, *seeds removed* *(use dried if fresh not available)*	½
Lemon juice	2 tbsp
Apple cider vinegar	1 tbsp
Balsamic vinegar	½ tbsp
Olive oil	2 tbsp
Fresh basil	10g
Salt *to taste*	1 tsp
Cracked black pepper *to taste*	
Ice	2 handfuls

Method

1. Remove the skin from the watermelon and then roughly chop the flesh. Add to blender and pulse a few times until it has a liquid consistency.

2. Add chopped tomatoes, cucumber, red onion, chilli, lemon juice, vinegars, olive oil, basil and salt to the blender. Blend until all is well combined and has a soup-like consistency. You may need to add a few splashes of water to get the blender mixing properly. Taste it and add more salt, pepper, chilli, lemon juice, vinegar or oil if needed.

3. Pour into a jug and place in the refrigerator to cool for approximately 1 hour.

4. To serve, place some ice in the bottom of glasses or small bowls. Pour the gazpacho over the top. Garnish with some finely chopped watermelon, tomatoes, onion and basil. Top with cracked black pepper and salt to taste.

SALADS + SOUPS

QUICK VEGAN RAMEN

20 mins | serves 2

Everyone needs that "I am too tired to cook or think" meal. This is mine. I know I can whip it up in less time that it takes to get takeaway and it leaves me feeling warm, cosy and nourished. Feel free to throw in different vegetables depending on what you have on hand or in season. It is also a great way to use up those sad greens wilting in the back of the fridge!

Ingredients

Sesame oil	2 tbsp
Onion, *diced*	½
Fresh ginger, grated *(thumb-sized piece)*	15g
Mushrooms, sliced *(shiitake or a mix of different mushrooms)*	250g
Tamari *(or soy sauce)*	4 tbsp
Vegetable stock	1L
Brown or black rice ramen noodles *(or soba noodles)*	2 cakes
Baby spinach, *rinsed*	3 handfuls
Silken tofu, *cut into 1½cm cubes*	200g
Lemon or lime juice	2 tbsp
Handful of fresh coriander *(optional to serve)*	
Handful of chopped peanuts *(optional to serve)*	

V | DF | GF

Method

1. Put sesame oil in a pot (minimum capacity 3L), add onion and ginger and sauté on medium to high heat for a couple of minutes or until onion becomes transparent. Add mushrooms and stir until coated in oil mixture. Sauté for a few minutes until mushrooms start to brown.

2. Prepare stock. If using homemade or liquid stock, simply heat it up. If using powdered stock, boil 1L of water then add the stock powder in the amount indicated on the packet.

3. Add tamari to mushroom mixture and stir until combined.

4. Add the warm stock to the pot. Stir then leave for a few minutes until the broth starts to simmer.

5. Add the cakes of ramen into the simmering pot. Check on the packet how long the ramen needs to cook then put on the kitchen timer for that amount of time. When the ramen is cooked, turn the heat off but leave the pot on the hotplate so it stays warm (if you use gas, just turn it down very low).

6. Add the spinach to the pot and put the lid on, leaving it for a few moments until it wilts. Once it has wilted, remove the lid and add the tofu and lemon juice. Add salt and pepper to taste.

7. Serve in two soup bowls, topping with some chopped coriander and nuts (optional) before serving.

MEDITATIVE MINESTRONE

⏲ *30 mins* | ✋ *serves 4*

Sometimes I feel like I have to claw myself into the kitchen at the end of a long day. The temptation to buy something made by someone else and zone out in front of Netflix is so strong, even though I know these things are not the best choices for my health or happiness. After spending the day running around, sometimes finding the last drop of energy to take care of ourselves is the hardest. Recently I realized that each night I have a choice – either I can let cooking and cleaning up after dinner be a stress, or I can let the process be the path to rediscovering joy and balance inside myself. It is up to me to shift my mindset – from seeing this as a chore, to seeing it as a chance for mindfulness. When I remember, I use my time in the kitchen to relax my body and focus on my breath and simplicity in the task at hand. When I am chopping the vegetables, I am just chopping the vegetables, not trying to plan out the rest of my life in my head! My mind wanders back and forth, but each time I notice this I bring my awareness back to the breath, or to chopping vegetables. In this way we can train ourselves to have patience, to focus and be present. Good skills for outside of the kitchen as well, I would say.

PART TWO | *Salads and Soups*

SALADS + SOUPS (DF) (GF)

Ingredients

Onions, diced	150g
Kale, chard or spinach *(shredded)*	150g
Mushrooms *(sliced)*	250g
Sweet potato *(cut into cubes)*	400g
Red cabbage *(sliced)*	300g
Olive oil	1 tbsp
Ghee	1 tbsp
(or 1 tbsp coconut oil or olive oil)	
Dried Italian herb mix	1 tbsp
Fresh rosemary	4 sprigs
Fresh thyme	10 sprigs
Can borlotti beans	400g
(or any other beans)	
Vegetable stock	2L
Finely ground black pepper	1 tsp
Whole wheat, gluten free or lentil pasta	
(fusilli, penne, macaroni or shells work best)	1 cup
Juice ½ a lemon	
Fresh parmesan *(optional, for serving)*	
Salt and pepper to taste	

Method

1. Place olive oil, ghee and chopped onion in a cast iron cocotte or a soup pot. Turn heat to medium. Sauté onions until soft. Add dried Italian herb mix and stir.

2. Add sweet potato and mushroom. Mix well, place lid on and cook for 5 minutes, stirring occasionally to avoid sticking.

3. Meanwhile, make a posy from the fresh herbs by tying rosemary and thyme sprigs together in a bunch with string. This keeps the herb stalks together and saves you/your guests picking them out of their soup.

4. Add in 2L of stock, cabbage, fresh herb posy and black pepper. Put lid on, increase heat and simmer for 15 minutes.

5. Add pasta. Place lid on and continue to simmer for the cooking time indicated on the pasta packet.

6. Drain and rinse the can of beans.

7. When pasta is cooked, remove the lid from the soup pot. Add in the beans and mix through. Add kale/chard/spinach on the top, place the lid on and leave for around 2 minutes while the greens wilt (this will take longer for kale, less time for spinach).

8. Remove from heat. Squeeze in juice of half a lemon and mix through.

9. Serve with some grated parmesan and season with salt and pepper to taste.

The Great Full

WARMING VEGETABLE AND CORN CHOWDER

1 hour | serves 6

This soup has a special place in my heart for the story that brought it to life. Each year I spend 2 weeks running a course on sustainability and food systems for university students from around the world. I have done this in India, South Africa, Ivory Coast and several times in Switzerland. A few years ago, we were helping farmers harvest in order to understand the practical side of food production. We were all shocked when we had to leave seemingly good-looking zucchini in the field behind us. The farmers' acute eyes already said that the produce was "imperfect" in some way and would be rejected by the buyer. Rather than spend the time to harvest it, it was better to leave it in the field and turn it back into the soil as nutrients. Seeing food loss first-hand like this really felt strange. We asked if we could harvest the zucchini for our own meals over the week and ended up leaving with two huge crates. As we took them back to our guesthouse down the road, we bumped into the family living in the house next door. They were immigrants living in temporary housing while their refugee status was evaluated. We asked if they wanted some of the zucchini. They responded by running inside and gathering bags and hands to collect as much as they could. The language barrier made it hard to communicate with words, but their actions told us how much they valued this fresh produce. They lived just down the road from the farm where it would have rotted on the field. It highlighted to me the strange disconnect in our world between surplus and need. The zucchini I took home that day made their way into this soup – a delicious take on corn chowder, minus the cream, milk and butter.

Ingredients

Potatoes, *roughly chopped*	500g
Sweet potatoes	400g
Peeled and roughly chopped	
Medium or large zucchini	4
Roughly chopped	
Olive oil	
Herb salt	
Fresh sweet corn	2 ears
(Or 1 can, drained)	
Leek, sliced	200g
Olive oil	2 tbsp
Vegetable stock	1 ½ L
Juice of one lemon	
Parmesan or nutritional yeast *(optional)*	

Spice Mix

2 teaspoons each of dried thyme, oregano and sumac, mixed together

Method

1. Preheat oven to 200° C.

2. Put potatoes, sweet potatoes and zucchini on a lined baking tray. Drizzle with oil, sprinkle generously with herb salt and put in preheated oven for 35 minutes or until gold roasted.

3. If using fresh sweet corn, remove husk and place in salted boiling water for 5 minutes until cooked. Remove from pan and leave to cool. When cool, slice off the kernels and chop into small pieces.

4. As the vegetables are coming to end of roasting time, chop up leeks and put them in a soup pot with capacity of at least 4L. Drizzle with olive oil and stir-fry until leeks are soft.

5. Add vegetable stock. Sprinkle in the spice mix. Gently boil for a few minutes. When the vegetables are ready take them out of the oven and add them to the pot and simmer for 5 minutes.

6. Remove from heat and blend with an immersion blender. Add the chopped sweet corn, blend again for a few pulses, leaving some corn kernels whole. Add the lemon juice.

7. Serve, adding flaked salt and pepper to taste. Top with grated parmesan or, if you are vegan, nutritional yeast.

SALADS + SOUPS

CREAMY ROAST POTATO LEMON AND DILL SOUP

40 mins | serves 4–6

Just in case it has escaped your attention so far, I really love potatoes. Boiled, fried, baked, it doesn't really matter. This soup is basically an excuse to make a whole meal out of potatoes. It is hearty and delicious and exactly what you want from a comfort food on a cold day.

Ingredients

Potatoes, *peeled and diced*	1 kg
Leeks, *finely sliced*	350g
Olive oil	2 tbsp
Vegetable stock	1½ L
Can of cannellini beans, *drained and rinsed*	400g
Fresh dill, *finely chopped*	10g
Juice of 1 lemon, *more to taste*	
Herb salt and black pepper to taste	

Tip: If you need some more greens in your life, throw a few handfuls of spinach into the soup before blending!

Method

1. Preheat oven to 200°C. Line a baking tray with baking paper. Put peeled and cubed potatoes on the baking tray. Drizzle 1 tbsp olive oil over potatoes, season with herbed salt. Toss the potatoes until all coated in oil. Place in the oven and bake for 30 minutes.

2. While potatoes are baking, gently heat remaining 1 tbsp olive oil in a soup pot or cocotte, add the leeks and gently stir-fry until they are soft. Add the vegetable stock.

3. Drain and rinse the beans. Add to the pot. Bring to boil then remove pot from heat.

4. Add the lemon juice and dill. Season with salt and pepper to taste.

5. When potatoes are ready remove from oven and add to the pot.

6. Use a hand mixer to blend the soup into a smooth consistency.

7. To serve, sprinkle with dill, croutons, seeds or some crushed kale chips.

SALADS + SOUPS

SPICED HARISSA CARROT AND LENTIL SOUP

35 mins | serves 4–6

This soup is a great example of how combining salt, fat, acid, heat and just a touch of sweetness can get you a truly delectable dish. There is something about this combo that absolutely hits the spot on a winter evening in front of the fire. If I have any old bread lying around, I like to use it up by making croutons to sprinkle on top. You simply chop up the bread, coat it in some olive oil and herb salt and throw it in the oven until it starts to brown. Et voilà, old bread made new again.

Ingredients

Carrots *(peeled and chopped)*	400g
Pumpkin, sweet potato or apple *(peeled and chopped)*	400g
Cloves garlic *(peeled)*	4
Olive oil	2 tbsp
Honey or maple syrup	1 tbsp
Herb salt	½ tsp
Harissa spice mix	2 tsp
Onion, finely diced	1
Olive oil	1 tbsp
Ghee or olive oil	½ tbsp
Vegetable stock	1½ L
Red lentils	¾ cup
Apple cider vinegar	1 tbsp

Topping: mix together some sunflower seeds, sesame seeds, herb salt and zaatar

Method

1. Preheat oven to 200° C. Line a baking tray. Place the chopped carrots, pumpkin and whole garlic cloves on the tray. Drizzle olive oil and honey on top, sprinkle with herb salt and harissa spice mix. Use a spoon to mix and coat. Put in the oven to roast for approximately 30 minutes.

2. About 10 minutes before the vegetables are finished, place a cast iron pot or soup pot on medium heat. When heated add the olive oil, ghee and onion. Stir to sauté onion until translucent. Pour in 1½L vegetable stock followed by the red lentils. Allow to simmer for around 8 minutes.

3. Remove from heat. Add the roasted vegetables and garlic to the pot, along with the apple cider vinegar. Use an immersion blender or food processor to puree the soup. Add salt and pepper to taste.

4. Sprinkle with seed mixture before serving.

{DF} {GF}

SALADS + SOUPS

GREEN MAGIC SOUP

35 mins | serves 4–6

It is funny the things you remember from childhood. I distinctly recall being at daycare, aged about 3, and being told that we would be eating "Martian soup" for lunch. I think the staff thought that rebranding the green soup as something from outer space would make us excited, but it had exactly the opposite effect. I can still see the table full of crying toddlers refusing to eat the green soup in front of them. To be honest, I have seen similar expressions from adults when I put this soup in front of them. It seems that the last thing anyone wants, at any age, is a bowl of green soup. But please give it a chance. It is actually delicious and perfect after a few days, weeks or years of overindulgence. It fills you up with warmth, greens and veggies in a surprisingly satisfying way. No wonder the Martians like it.

Ingredients

Potatoes, *peeled and diced*	500g
Olive oil to drizzle	
Herb salt	
Olive oil	4 tbsp
Cloves garlic	3
Leeks	200g
Broccoli, *cut into florets*	1 head
Vegetable stock	1L
Kale or spinach *(About 3 large handfuls)*	60g
Silken tofu	200g
Juice of a lemon	1
Chilli flakes	½ tsp
Fresh ginger *(grated)*	1 tsp
Salt, pepper and sumac to taste	

Method

1. Preheat oven to 200° C. Line a baking tray. Put the potatoes on the tray. Drizzle olive oil over them, sprinkle with herb salt and toss with your hands till coated. Place in the oven and roast for 30 minutes.

2. Warm the soup pot on medium heat. Add the olive oil, garlic and leek and sauté a few minutes until soft.

3. Add the broccoli and stir to coat in oil. Pour in the vegetable stock. Put the lid on, bring to the boil and simmer for 5 minutes, or until the broccoli is tender but not mushy.

4. Add the spinach or kale and put the lid on until it wilts.

5. Remove pot from heat. Add the roasted potatoes, along with the silken tofu, lemon juice, chilli flakes and ginger. Blend into a smooth soup. Add salt, pepper and sumac to taste. Top with spices, nuts, seeds or croutons to serve.

{V} {DF} {GF}

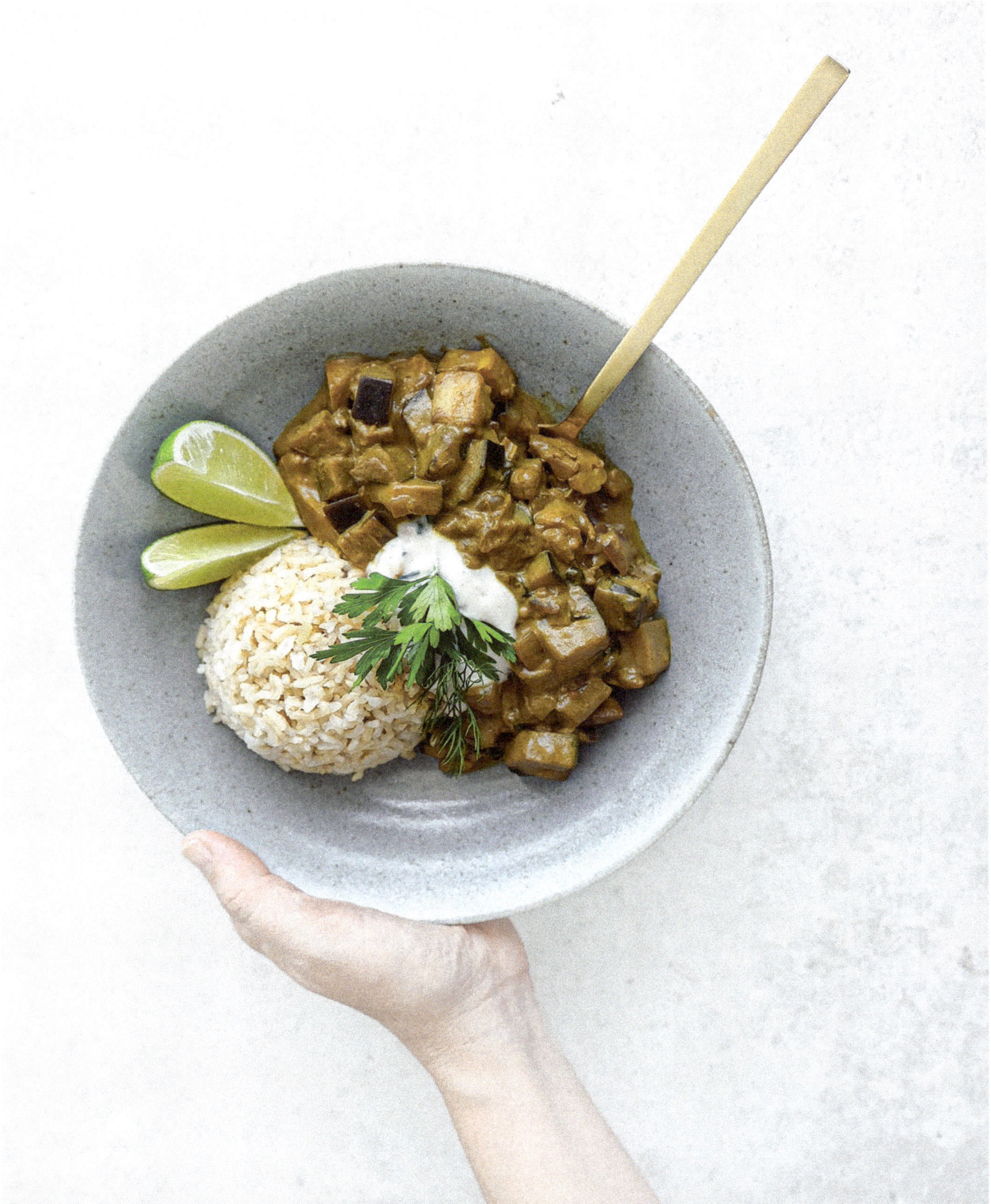

MAINS

Warm Pumpkin Spinach and Quinoa Salad	164
Aubergine Napoletana Pasta	166
Sweet Potato Burrito Bowls	168
Easy Mac and Sundried Tomato Sauce	170
Sweet Potato Noodle Pad Thai	171
Dominican Black Beans and Rice	172
Lasakopita	175
Creamy Beetroot Sweet Potato and Feta Layered Bake	176
Falafel and Fries	178
Sri Lankan Jackfruit Curry	180
Roasted Tofu and Greens Noodle Bowl	182
Artichoke and Easy Green Pesto Pasta	185
World's Easiest Risotto	187
Sunshine Buddha Bowl	189

WARM PUMPKIN SPINACH AND QUINOA SALAD

35 mins | serves 4 small/2 large

This recipe features quinoa, one of the world's favourite health foods. It is gluten free, high in fibre, protein, vitamins and minerals, making it an excellent contributor to a plant-based diet. However, it has come under scrutiny for the impact it has on the Andean regions where it is mostly grown. Recent reports show that when quinoa prices are high and stable, growing this crop has a positive impact on the livelihoods and wellbeing of the Peruvian smallholders, who are some of the poorest people in the country. That changes when demand and prices drop, or new producers move into the market. But the international interest in this pseudo-grain is pretty focussed on the white, light varieties. This has led growers in the Andes to concentrate on only a few improved varieties of quinoa, though there are 120 known varieties. We are starting to see a bit more diversity show up in the market, with red, black and yellow quinoa now available. Some come from more diverse, smallholder farms that cultivate based on agroecological principles. It is worth seeking these out if you want to help support production systems that are more resilient in the face of shocks like climate change.

MAINS

(V) (DF) (GF)

Ingredients

Pumpkin	700g
Quinoa	1 cup
Olive oil	2 tbsp
Clove of garlic, finely chopped	1
Fresh rosemary	1 tbsp
remove leaves from stalk and finely chop	
Baby spinach	2 handfuls
(or shredded kale, massaged with some olive oil)	
Almonds or hazelnuts	small handful
finely chopped (to garnish)	

Spice seasoning mix

Herb salt	½ tsp
Ground cumin	½ tsp
Ground coriander	1 tsp
Finely ground black pepper	½ tsp
Ground cinnamon	¼ tsp
Chilli powder	1 pinch

Dressing

Lemon juice	1½ tbsp
Tahini	1 tbsp
Tamari	2 tbsp
Olive or sesame oil	1 tbsp
Apple cider vinegar *(optional)*	1 tbsp

Method

1. Peel the pumpkin and cut the flesh into small cubes (approximately 1cm). Set aside.

2. Make the seasoning mix. Combine the salt, cumin, coriander, black pepper, cinnamon and chilli in a small bowl and set aside.

3. Rinse 1 cup of dried quinoa thoroughly in a sieve. Cook according to instructions on the packet.

4. While the quinoa is cooking, place olive oil in a deep saucepan, wok or cast iron pot (one that you have a lid for) on medium heat. When the oil is warm, add the garlic and rosemary. When garlic starts to soften, place the pumpkin in the pan and mix until coated in oil.

5. Place a lid on the saucepan. Keep checking the pumpkin mixture every minute or so, stirring it and reducing the heat slightly if needed.

6. When the pumpkin starts to brown, stir the seasoning mix through until the pumpkin is well coated. Place the lid on again, stirring the pumpkin every few minutes. If it sticks, add a small splash of water to the pan.

7. When the pumpkin is cooked (it will be soft), add the spinach leaves and put the lid back on to let them steam for about a minute. Once the spinach is steamed, remove the lid and mix the pumpkin and spinach together. Remove from heat.

8. To make the dressing, place all ingredients in a small jar and shake to combine.

9. To serve, place the quinoa in a bowl. Top with pumpkin and spinach mixture. Pour the dressing over then top with the chopped nuts.

AUBERGINE NAPOLETANA PASTA

⏱ *35 mins* | ✋ *serves 2*

I like to make a lot of my food from scratch, but I am not a fundamentalist about this. Sometimes I lean on a few ready-made things in the cupboard to make the process of cooking easier, especially on those days when the energy or time can't be found. I always have a few good jars of "as close to homemade as possible" tomato-based pasta sauce in the cupboard. This can quickly be combined with any vegetables you have to make a healthy pasta sauce. Throw it on top of some lentil or chickpea pasta, or spiralled zucchini, and you have yourself a pretty healthy meal in no time. Here I add aubergine to give a meaty texture and flavour that makes this meal very satisfying. This sauce also improves with time, so put any leftovers back into the pasta sauce jar and store it in the fridge to use another day.

PART TWO | Mains

MAINS

(V) (DF) (GF)

Ingredients

Sauce

Large aubergine, *peeled*	1
Olive oil	3 tbsp
Clove garlic, *peeled and crushed*	1
Onion, *finely diced*	½
Jar of napoletana or puttanesca sauce	300g
Fresh basil	handful
Herb salt	
Black pepper	

Zucchini noodles

Large zucchini	4
Garlic powder	
Squeeze of lemon juice	

(Alternatively, use a whole grain, gluten free or legume spaghetti of your choice)

Method

1. Peel and dice the aubergine into small cubes, removing the stem. Transfer to a paper towel. Sprinkle with salt. Set aside.

2. If making zucchini noodles, use the spiralizer to spiralize the zucchini. Place zucchini noodles in a bowl and squeeze lemon juice over the top. Set aside.

3. If making spaghetti or pasta, cook according to instructions.

4. Heat olive oil in a saucepan over a medium heat. Add the crushed garlic and onion, sauté until they start to soften. Pat the aubergine dry using the paper towel, then add it to the saucepan. Sauté, stirring regularly so that it browns evenly. When aubergine is brown and soft, add the napoletana sauce and herb salt and black pepper to taste. Turn off the heat but leave the frying pan on the heat element (or turn the gas down to the lowest setting) so the sauce stays warm. Stir occasionally.

5. In a wok or deep-frying pan, warm ½ tbsp olive oil. Add the zucchini noodles and use tongs to turn the noodles so that they are lightly coated in oil. Sprinkle some powdered garlic over the noodles and turn to mix through. Keep turning the noodles in the pan with the tongs until they soften. This will only take a couple of minutes. You don't want to leave the noodles too long as this will make them too soggy. If in doubt, take them out earlier rather than later.

6. When zucchini noodles (or other spaghetti) are ready, use tongs to divide them into two portions in pasta bowls. Top with sauce. Sprinkle with fresh basil before serving.

The Great Full

SWEET POTATO BURRITO BOWLS

🕐 *35 mins* | ✋ *serves 4*

These delicious burrito bowls are the ultimate comfort food – soft roasted sweet potatoes stuffed full of Mexican inspired toppings. This combination of ingredients makes it a super nutrient-dense meal while also being tasty, colourful and a lot of fun to share with friends. Sweet potatoes have had their time in the spotlight over the last years, being used to make brownies, toast and even noodles. But they are a fascinating food for another reason – they are being used as a tool to tackle malnutrition in parts of the world where vitamin A deficiency is a big problem. The orange-flesh sweet potatoes (OFSP) are naturally high in vitamin A and are being bred, through traditional means, to have even higher levels of vitamin A. This means that just one handful of OFSP can meet a child's daily vitamin A needs. Harvest Plus, an international research organisation, worked with governments in Mozambique and Uganda to introduce the vitamin A varieties to farmers and communities for free. This involved some unconventional approaches, like hosting concerts and plays to highlight the health benefits of growing and eating this particular type of sweet potato. OFSPs are an example of bio-fortification, growing or breeding a crop to increase its nutritional value so that it can directly reach rural populations in developing regions, where micronutrient deficiencies can be a major health challenge. Some food for thought while you enjoy this nutrient-dense dish yourself!

MAINS

Ingredients

Medium sweet potatoes	4
Quinoa	1 cup

Bean mix

Adzuki, kidney beans or black beans	400g
Olive oil	1 tbsp
Clove garlic, *thinly sliced*	1
Red onion, *finely chopped*	¼
Ground paprika	1 tsp
Ground coriander	1 tsp
Tamari	2 tsp
Maple syrup	1 tsp
Herb salt and pepper to taste	

Guacamole

Avocados	1½
Juice of lime, *more to taste*	1
Red onion, *finely chopped*	¼
Cherry tomatoes, *finely chopped*	3
Chilli powder	1 pinch
Salt and pepper *to taste*	
Fresh coriander, *finely chopped*	1 tbsp

Red cabbage pickle

Red cabbage, thinly shredded	400g
(Approximately ½ medium cabbage)	
Salt	1 tsp
Lime or lemon juice	1 tbsp

To serve

Salt and pepper	
Fresh coriander	handful
Lime, *cut into wedges*	1

{V} {DF} {GF}

Method

1. Wash the sweet potatoes. Prick around the outsides with a fork several times. Place on a baking rack lined with baking paper. (Slide a baking tray underneath to catch any drips while cooking.) Place the sweet potatoes in the oven then turn it on to 230° C. Set the timer for 45 minutes. When the timer goes off, turn the oven off but let the sweet potatoes sit in there for another 30 minutes. While the sweet potatoes are in the oven prepare all the filling ingredients (see below).

2. Quinoa: rinse and strain 1 cup dry quinoa then cook according to instructions on packet.

3. Bean Mix: drain the beans and rinse thoroughly under water. Place a saucepan on medium heat. Add the olive oil, garlic and onion. Fry until onion starts to soften. Add the beans and all other ingredients. Lower heat to a minimum and stir for a few minutes. Remove from heat and set the saucepan aside until ready to serve.

4. Guacamole: add all ingredients to a bowl and mash with a fork until well combined.

5. Red cabbage pickle: slice the cabbage very thinly. Place in a bowl. Add salt and lemon/lime juice. Use your hands to massage the cabbage for a few minutes. Leave to sit until all the other ingredients are ready.

6. To compile, remove the sweet potatoes from the oven and place them on a large serving plate or one on each individual plate. With a sharp knife, gently cut a slit through the middle of the sweet potato. Open up the slit as much as you can to make room for the filling. Arrange the filling as you like: for example, first place a scoop of quinoa in the middle, a scoop of the beans on one side and a scoop of cabbage on the other. Top with large dollop of guacamole and some fresh coriander. Add any other condiments you may already have (salsa verde, tomato salsa) and enjoy! You could also place all the fillings in separate bowls and let your guests fill the sweet potato however they wish.

(If you have left overs, cut open the sweet potato and place it in a container with a combination of the other ingredients for a delicious ready-to-go lunch or dinner.)

EASY MAC AND SUNDRIED TOMATO SAUCE

🕐 20 mins | ✋ serves 4

I like to take quintessential comfort foods, like macaroni and cheese, and give them a healthier twist. Here I have added sweet potatoes and sundried tomatoes as the base of the sauce, which delivers the creamy deliciousness you expect from mac and cheese, with a few more vitamins. This dish is so easy and satisfying that I can convince myself to make it even when I am uninspired to cook. Its always good to have a few such recipes to help you out in such times!

Ingredients

Sweet potato, *peeled, chopped*	300g
Sundried tomatoes, *drain off the oil*	½ cup
Milk *(I use oat)*	⅓ cup
Olive oil	2 tbsp
Apple cider vinegar	2 tbsp
Salt and pepper to taste	
Pasta	350g

(I like to use lentil pasta spirals or macaroni)

Optional add-ins:
Capers
Fresh baby spinach or micro-greens

Method

1. Place the sweet potatoes in saucepan, just cover with water and put on medium heat with the lid on. Steam for 7–10 minutes, until soft. Drain.

2. Place steamed sweet potato, sundried tomatoes, milk, olive oil and apple cider vinegar in a food processor. Process until smooth. Add salt and pepper to taste. Pulse to combine.

3. Cook the pasta according to instructions.

4. Drain the pasta, return to the pot and mix through the sweet potato sauce along with any add-ins you want to use. Serve with some flaked salt sprinkled on top.

Note: this sauce is also great for potato salad. Just boil some potatoes in salt water, drain them, mix the sauce through and add some spinach or micro-greens, capers, chopped gherkins and salt and pepper.

{V} {DF} {GF}

PART TWO | Mains

SWEET POTATO NOODLE PAD THAI

30 mins | serves 2

I am a huge fan of spiralizing vegetables and fruit. For the uninitiated, this involves using a nifty little machine to transform your standard produce into new and exciting forms. You can make noodles, spirals, shavings and all kinds of other things. The real magic trick of this machine is taking parts of the vegetable you don't normally use – like the stem of broccoli – and turning it into a fun format to throw into your dish. Here I have used sweet potatoes to make noodles, but you could swap that out with all kinds of other vegetables.

Ingredients

Medium sweet potato	1
Onion	1
Sesame oil	4 tbsp
Garlic powder	
Brown rice noodles	150–200g
(I use brown rice soba noodles)	
Lemon juice	3 tbsp
Tamari	4 tbsp
Tamarind paste	4 tbsp
Peanut butter	4 tbsp
(ideally one made only from peanuts)	
Eggs	2
Mung bean sprouts	2 handfuls
Squeeze of lemon juice	
Peanuts or macadamia nuts, *chopped*	handful
(to garnish)	
Fresh coriander *(to garnish)*	handful
Salt and pepper to taste	

(V) (DF) (GF)

Method

1. Place a small saucepan of water on the stove and bring to the boil.

2. Spiralize the sweet potato into noodles and set aside.

3. Finely chop the onion. Add sesame oil and onion to the wok, stir-fry until soft, then add the spiralized sweet potato noodles. Sprinkle with a little garlic powder. Fry for another 5–7 minutes until the noodles are soft, using tongs turn them regularly.

4. While the sweet potato is cooking, place the brown rice noodles in the saucepan with boiling water. Cook according to instructions. When cooked drain and set aside.

5. Make the pad thai paste: in a glass or small bowl, combine the lemon juice, tamari, tamarind paste and peanut butter. Mix together to make a paste.

6. When the sweet potato is cooked, push it over to one side of the wok. Crack the eggs into the space you created and use the spatula to stir and break them up until just cooked.

7. Add in the sprouts, the paste and the strained brown rice noodles. Mix together until all combined (don't worry it will be a little sticky!). Season with salt and pepper to taste.

8. Divide the pad thai into bowls to serve. Squeeze some lemon juice on top. Top with a handful of fresh coriander and chopped nuts.

The Great Full

DOMINICAN BLACK BEANS AND RICE

1 hr 30 mins (plus overnight soaking time for the beans) | serves 6

This recipe comes courtesy of Shana Sturla, a colleague and friend who is a professor of toxicology. This is an adaptation of one of the recipes from her Dominican family. She shared it with me to accompany an interview I did with her when the World Health Organisation announced that it was classifying red and processed meat as carcinogens, meaning that higher consumption of these foods was linked to higher rates of certain types of cancer. We sat together and chatted about what consumers should take away from this. It was a similar message we hear over and over: reduce consumption of red meat as much as possible and eat processed meat only occasionally, if at all (that includes bacon!). This is a meat-free meal she uses in her family as a weeknight staple. What I love about it is that you can make a big batch on the weekend and cook up some different seasonal vegetables in parallel. Mix and match them and you have a few delicious and healthy meals sorted out for the week.

MAINS

V | *DF* | *GF*

Ingredients

Brown rice	2 cups

Beans

Dried black beans	1 cup
(rinsed and soaked in cold water overnight)	
Vegetable stock	2 cups
Cloves garlic, *minced*	2
Ground cumin	1 heaped tsp
Dried oregano	1 heaped tsp

Sofrito

Olive oil	1 tbsp
Small onion	1
Cloves garlic, *minced*	2
Spring onions, *chopped*	2
Bell pepper, *coarsely chopped*	½
Spanish olives, *sliced*	2 tbsp

Sauce

Maple syrup or honey	1 tbsp
Lime juice	2 tbsp
Red wine vinegar or red wine	1 tbsp
Tomato paste	2 tbsp
Salt and black pepper	

Handful of fresh coriander leaves to garnish.

Method

1. Drain and rinse the rice. Cook in a rice cooker or in a pot on the stove.

2. While the rice is cooking, drain and rinse the beans. Place the beans in a saucepan and add stock, garlic, cumin and oregano. Bring to a boil over high heat. Skim any foam that rises to the surface. Reduce heat to medium-low and gently simmer with the lid off. Keep simmering, stirring occasionally, for 45 minutes to 1 hour until the beans are tender. Add water as necessary to keep the beans just submerged.

3. While the beans are cooking make the sofrito by heating oil in a frying pan over medium heat. Add the onion, spring onions and garlic and cook over medium heat for a few minutes. Add the bell pepper and cook a couple of additional minutes. Add the olives. Cook a couple more minutes. Turn off the heat and leave to sit until the beans are fully cooked. When the beans are cooked, drain them and then add the sofrito to the bean mixture.

4. Add the sauce ingredients to the bean mixture. Cover and simmer for 15 minutes or until the beans are very soft. Add water and additional seasoning (cumin, salt, pepper, oregano) if needed.

5. To serve spoon the beans over the rice and add a handful of fresh coriander and a wedge of lime. If you wish, you can add some vegetables, greens or sliced avocado.

MAINS

LASAKOPITA

20 min prep plus 30 min baking | serves 4 small/2 large

Italy and Greece are two of my favourite places to visit in Europe. The food and hospitality in both countries carves out a special place in my heart and makes me want to go back year after year. This recipe combines two dishes that I love from each country – cannelloni and spanakopita – into some sort of mashup that is delicious and easy to share with loved ones. It has a flavour that reminds me of special nights out with my mum as a kid in Australia, when we would go to a little Italian restaurant at the beach for a treat. Isn't it amazing how the flavour of food can transport us to times, places and people far away? This dish somehow manages to simultaneously transport me to Italy, Greece and Australia.

Ingredients

Lasagne sheets *(I use gluten free)*	5
Swiss chard *washed, dried and finely shredded*	350g
Fresh dill, *finely chopped*	10g
Feta *crumbled or finely chopped*	200g
Ground nutmeg	2 x ¼ tsp
Finely ground pepper	2 x ¼ tsp
Aubergine, *very thinly sliced into rounds*	150g
Tomato pasta sauce	340g jar
Red pesto	1 heaped tbsp
Herb salt	
Olive oil to drizzle and grease	

GF

Method

1. Preheat oven to 200°C.
2. Grease a loaf tin with olive oil and top with a splash of water.
3. Place one layer of lasagne sheets on the bottom of the tin. (You may need to break them up to make them fit and to minimize the overlap.)
4. Spread 2 handfuls of shredded chard on top of lasagne sheets. Gently press down. Sprinkle half of the fresh dill on top of the chard.
5. Place half of the crumbled feta on top of the greens. Sprinkle with ¼ tsp nutmeg and ¼ teaspoon pepper.
6. Make a layer of aubergine rounds. Sprinkle with herb salt. Top with ½ the jar of tomato pasta sauce.
7. Repeat steps 3 to 6. You may need to press down occasionally to make enough space in the tin (it will cook down in the oven as the chard wilts). Reserve around 3 tablespoons of the pasta sauce for the top.
8. Place the final lasagne sheets on top as the last layer. Take the jar with the remaining pasta sauce, mix in the red pesto and a drizzle of olive oil. Stir or shake until combined. Spoon across the top of the last lasagne sheet.
9. Put in the oven to cook for 30 minutes.
   (Cooking time may vary depending on the lasagne sheets you use.)

CREAMY BEETROOT SWEET POTATO AND FETA LAYERED BAKE

◷ 1 hour | ✋ serves 4

Silver Island is a little gem in the Aegean Sea where I have the great pleasure to teach a yoga retreat once a year. The owners have a deep commitment to nature, sustainability and creating nourishing experiences for their guests, including an abundance of delicious vegetarian food. Last time I visited, Lissa, one of the owners, had created a simple but delicious sweet potato and beetroot bake. As they were able to cook with some sort of island magic, which evaded me as soon as I got home, I had to add a few ingredients and steps to get the same effect. What resulted was this delicious dish that was a winner with everyone I have served it to. Silver Island Yoga also has a cookbook, in case you also want to be inspired by more of their delicious food!

Ingredients

Beetroots	3
Peeled and sliced into rounds	
Sweet potatoes	2
Peeled and sliced into rounds	
Can of cannellini beans	400g
Feta	200g
Fresh basil *(a handful)*	20g
Small red onion, *roughly chopped*	1
Olive oil *(plus extra for drizzling)*	3 tbsp
Herb salt	¼ tsp
Hazelnuts, *roughly chopped*	⅓ cup
Zaatar	1½ tsp
Extra herb salt	

GF

Method

1. Preheat oven to 200° C.
2. Place sliced beetroot and sweet potato on two lined baking trays. Drizzle with olive oil and place in the preheated oven (place the tray with beetroot in the top of the oven). Bake for 15–20 mins until the vegetables start to soften.
3. In a food processor, combine cannellini beans, feta, basil, onion, olive oil and herb salt. Process until the mixture forms a smooth hummus-like consistency, but don't stress if there are still some lumps.
4. Grease a square baking dish (approximately 20cm wide x 5cm deep) with olive oil.
5. When the beetroot and sweet potato are finished, remove them from the oven but leave the oven on.
6. Assemble the layered bake. In the greased baking dish, place a layer of beetroot rounds to cover the bottom of the dish. You may need to cut up some of the rounds so they fill the gaps. Top with a layer of bean/feta mix – use about 1/3 of the mixture for this. Place a layer of sweet potato rounds to create the next layer. Top with a layer of bean/feta mix. Place another layer of sweet potato and then bean/feta mix, then a final layer of beetroot rounds. Drizzle olive oil on top of the final beetroot layer.
7. Sprinkle hazelnuts, zaatar and some herb salt on top.
8. Place in the oven for 20–30 minutes until the vegetables are cooked, the filling is bubbling and the top is just starting to brown.

FALAFEL AND FRIES

10 mins prep plus 30 mins cooking | *serves 2*

Fluffy pita bread filled with falafel and a side of hand-cut fries is my kind of happy meal. This is a problem sometimes. You see, the bus stop I wait at to get home each evening is directly across the road from a falafel shop. When I am tired and weak it holds a lot of power. So, I decided to come up with a healthier alternative that I could make at home quickly, sans deep-frying and take-away plastic. It uses a few pre-prepared ingredients which are sometimes just necessary because, well, life. That said, if you develop the skills and make the time to make your own pita bread and falafel you would win my deepest respect. This recipe is a great example of where you can mix and match flavours and ingredients depending on your mood and tastes. I especially recommend playing with different root vegetables, like parsnip, for the chips!

MAINS

V optional   DF optional

Ingredients

Fries

Sweet potato	400g
(or potato, parsnip or any other root vegetable)	
Herb salt	½ tsp
Olive oil	2 glugs
Squeeze of lemon juice	

Falafel pita

Falafel balls *(I buy these pre-made)*	8
or make the mini millet burgers on page 126	
Small pita breads	2

Fillings

Choose your own adventure, for example: lettuce, red onion, feta, tomato, cucumber and hummus.

Dressing

Olive oil	2 tbsp
Apple balsamic vinegar	1 tbsp
(or any other light-coloured vinegar)	
Mustard *(I like a honey mustard)*	1 tbsp
Soy cream	2 tbsp
Ground paprika	½ tsp
Herb salt	½ tsp

Method

1. Preheat oven to 200° C. Line a baking tray.

2. Peel and cut the potatoes into fingers. Place on the baking tray. Drizzle over olive oil and lemon juice, then sprinkle with herb salt. Use your hands to mix everything together until fries are well coated. Here is a tip: line up the fries so they are not touching each other – it will help them cook better. Put in the preheated oven for 25–30 minutes.

3. While the fries are cooking, prepare the filling ingredients by chopping everything up. I like to put these out on a plate in the middle of the table for everyone to take what they like.

4. When there is 10 mins left for the fries, add the falafel balls to the oven (or earlier depending on cooking instructions).

5. Make the dressing by combining olive oil, vinegar, mustard, soy cream, paprika and salt in glass jar with a lid and shaking till combined.

6. Just before the fries are ready, heat the pita bread. You can do this by putting it in the oven for about 5 minutes – spray a little bit of water (3 sprays on each side) on the pockets beforehand to stop them drying out. Alternatively steam them – this gives the bread a texture like a bao bun.

7. Place the bread, falafel, fillings, dressing and fries on the table and let everyone make their own! Cut the pita bread half open. Put in the lettuce, vegetables, feta and falafel and drizzle the dressing on top of everything. Close it up and enjoy with a side of fries.

SRI LANKAN JACKFRUIT CURRY

35 mins | serves 4

One of the most beautiful work trips I have ever been on was to Sri Lanka. Ravi, the professor we were working with, was an incredible host to our group, taking us to see kitchen garden projects that were supporting local families. Namely, the projects aimed to improve livelihood and food and nutrition security through growing diverse crops for home consumption and sale. Our trip ended with a delicious home cooked feast at Ravi's house. The jackfruit curry is something that sticks in my mind to this day, and this is my humble attempt to recreate it. Jackfruit is a very interesting ingredient that grows abundantly across south and south-east Asia. It is nutritious and has a great meaty consistency, but is also drought resistant and survives high temperatures, making it an important crop in the face of climate change. This recipe is a special tribute to Professor Ravi, to his important work and his immense hospitality that the world sadly lost too soon.

MAINS

(V) (DF) (GF)

Ingredients

Brown basmati rice *(or rice of your choice)*	250g
Cauliflower, *cut into small florets*	300g
Kohlrabi, *cubed*	1
Zucchini, *cubed*	1
Aubergine, *cubed*	250g
Sesame oil	¼ cup
Onion, *finely diced*	1
Lemongrass, *finely chopped*	1 stick
Fresh ginger, *finely grated*	1 tsp
Sri Lankan Curry Powder*	
Can of coconut milk	400 ml
Tamari or soy sauce	2 tbsp
Tamarind paste	3 tbsp
Herb salt	1 ½ tsp
Can of jackfruit	400g
Greens *(spinach, chard or kale), washed and chopped*	2 handfuls
Corn starch *(optional)*	1 tsp
Salt and black pepper to taste	
Fresh coriander, plain coconut yoghurt and lime wedges to serve	

* Sri Lankan Curry Powder

Combine the following spices: 2 tsp turmeric, 1 tsp cumin, 1 tsp coriander, 1 tsp paprika, ½ tsp cinnamon, 1 tsp mustard seeds

Method

1. Put the rice on to cook, in a rice cooker or on the stove.
2. Sprinkle some salt on the chopped vegetables and set them aside.
3. Heat a heavy saucepan, wok or cast iron pan on medium to high heat. Add the sesame oil, onion, lemongrass, fresh ginger and Sri Lankan curry powder. Stir-fry until the onion is translucent.
4. Add the cauliflower, kohlrabi, zucchini and aubergine and stir until coated. Keep sautéing and stirring for a few minutes. Add a few splashes of water if needed to stop anything sticking on the bottom of the pan.
5. Add coconut milk, tamari or soy sauce, tamarind paste and herb salt. Cook with the lid on until the vegetables are tender, around 15 minutes.
6. Add jackfruit and greens and cook for a few more minutes, using the wooden spoon to break the jackfruit up a little. If the curry has too much liquid, add a teaspoon of corn starch and mix it through to thicken the sauce.
7. Add salt and black pepper to taste before serving on a bed of rice with some fresh coriander, plain coconut yoghurt and lime wedges.

ROASTED TOFU AND GREENS NOODLE BOWL

30 min | *serves 2*

Tofu has a pretty bad rap in many people's minds. Some think it is responsible for deforestation in the Amazon. Actually, although soy production is a major driver of deforestation in the Amazon, 80% of that soy is used for animal feed. Others think that it tastes like cardboard, even though there are so many delicious ways to prepare it. I hope this is one of the dishes that changes your mind about tofu, showing you it can be the basis of a quick, healthy and delicious meal.

Ingredients

Firm tofu,	200g
pressed down a few times on paper towel to release water, cut in to cubes	
Sesame oil	1½ tbsp
Tamari	1½ tbsp
Maple syrup	1 tbsp
Lemon or lime juice	1 tbsp
Sprinkle of chilli or cayenne pepper	
Broccoli *(cut into florets)* or	
broccoli rabe *(washed and roughly chopped)*	400g
Brown or black rice noodles or soba noodles	180g

Toppings

Sesame seeds or hemp seeds
Crushed peanuts
Fresh coriander

Fresh lime quarters	2

Dressing

Tamari	1½ tbsp
Natural peanut butter or tahini	1½ tbsp
Sesame oil	1 tbsp
Apple cider or rice vinegar	1 tbsp
Maple syrup or honey	½ tbsp

Method

1. Preheat oven to 200° C.

2. Place cubed tofu into a baking dish. Pour over the sesame oil, tamari, maple syrup and lemon/lime juice. Sprinkle chilli or cayenne on top. Use a spoon to coat the tofu evenly in the sauce. Place on the top rack of the preheated oven to bake for 10 minutes, remove and stir, return to oven for 15 more minutes. Remove when tofu is brown on the edges.

3. Fill a medium saucepan halfway with water and add a generous amount of salt. Bring to the boil. If using broccoli, add to the pot, place the lid on and steam for 3–5 mins. If using broccoli rabe, add to the pot and blanch for 2-3 minutes until crisp-tender. Strain and set aside.

4. Cook the rice noodles according to instructions on the packet. Drain noodles and place in the serving bowls.

5. Place all dressing ingredients in a small jar with a lid. Shake until combined.

6. Place the broccoli and tofu on top of the noodles. Sprinkle with sesame seeds or peanuts. Add a small handful of fresh coriander and a lime quarter. Pour the dressing over the top.

{V} {DF} {GF}

MAINS

ARTICHOKE AND EASY GREEN PESTO PASTA

🕐 30 mins / ✋ serves 2

My husband is Italian, which has had a huge impact on my ability to throw together a great pasta dinner in no time. With practice, I have learned that a great pasta comes down to just a few basic things – using the freshest, tastiest produce you can find, salting the pasta water generously, not being afraid of oil in large quantities, using fresh citrus and herbs and always adding a sprinkle of love.

Ingredients

Spaghetti of your choice	250g
Olive oil	1 tbsp
Clove garlic, *minced*	1
Large zucchini, *Halved lengthwise then cut into thin half moons*	1
Swiss chard, *washed and shredded or large handful of spinach*	3 stalks
Marinated artichoke hearts	150g
Capers	handful

Pesto

Mild red chilli, finely chopped	½
Olive oil	5 tbsp
Clove garlic, *minced or finely chopped*	1
Fresh basil, *finely chopped*	handful
Salt to taste	
Juice of one lemon	

To serve

Fresh basil
Lemon zest
Shaved parmesan or pecorino
Flaked salt

Method

1. First make the pesto. Add all pesto ingredients to a mortar and pestle and gently grind together. If you don't have a mortar and pestle just chop all the ingredients very finely, place in a small bowl and mix together with a fork, crushing the pieces against the bottom a little. Set pesto aside.

2. Fill a medium saucepan with water and salt it generously. Put it on medium heat. When boiling add the spaghetti and cook according to packet instructions.

3. Meanwhile, heat a frying pan on medium to high heat. Add olive oil, minced garlic and zucchini. Stir to sauté evenly. When zucchini is nearly cooked, add the Swiss chard, stir until wilted.

4. Add artichokes and capers and stir through.

5. Remove frying pan from heat and pour or spoon the pesto on top of the zucchini mix.

6. When the spaghetti is ready, drain it and add it to the frying pan with the zucchini pesto mix. Use tongs to mix well. Season with salt and pepper to taste. Add more oil or lemon juice if you think it needs it. Serve with any combination of toppings you like – fresh basil, lemon zest, parmesan or pecorino.

ⓥ *optional*

MAINS

WORLD'S EASIEST RISOTTO

⏱ 30 mins | ✋ serves 2-4

I notice that risotto is so often over complicated, with too much butter, cheese and milk added into the process. This version does away with all of that but still leaves you with a creamy result that satisfies even my Italian family members. Here I have offered you a basic recipe along with some ideas for what you could add to it – a couple of everyday options and one for a "fancy" version you can serve to guests.

Ingredients

Red onion, *finely diced*	1
Olive oil	3 tbsp
Risotto rice	1 cup
White wine	120ml
(or use 60ml apple cider vinegar, 60ml water)	
Vegetable stock	750ml
Lemon juice	1 tbsp
Salt and pepper to taste	

(V) (DF) (GF)

Method

1. Take a pot with a heavy base, like a cast iron pot or skillet, warm on medium heat. Add olive oil, diced onions and thyme. Stir until the onions are translucent. Add the rice and stir to coat it in oil.

2. Pour in the white wine (it should sizzle) and mix until absorbed. Start adding the stock, ½ a cup at a time. Stir regularly to make sure the rice doesn't stick to the bottom. Keep the heat on low to medium so the rice is gently simmering. Continue to add the stock each time the previous batch is absorbed. Keep the lid on the pot between stirring.

3. In parallel, prepare any add-ins you would like to use (see below).

4. Remove rice from heat. Add lemon juice, salt and pepper to taste. Mix through the add-ins.

Possible Add-Ins

Mushroom: Stir-fry 250g mushrooms with 1 tbsp of butter or olive oil and 1 crushed clove of garlic, when the mushrooms start to brown add 1 tbsp tamari and 1 tbsp balsamic vinegar and stir-fry until absorbed. Just before the risotto is finished cooking, mix through 2 handfuls of baby spinach or kale leaves (stalks removed and chopped). Remove the risotto pot from the heat and add the stir-fried mushrooms and ½ can borlotti beans (drained and rinsed).

Pumpkin: Roast a cup of cubed pumpkin with olive oil, rosemary and garlic and fold through the rice at the end.

Asparagus: For a fancier version, blanch some fresh asparagus (ends trimmed) in salted water then grill with a little olive oil. Remove from grill and sprinkle with flaked salt. Serve the basic risotto topped with the grilled asparagus along with some lemon zest, crushed pistachios, flaked salt and if you really feel fancy, some edible flowers!

MAINS

SUNSHINE BUDDHA BOWL

30 mins (plus overnight soaking time for the walnuts) | serves 2

My weeknight dinners are often some variation of a Buddha bowl. The elements are really simple, and once you start playing with it, the combinations are endless. Basically, you just need some vegetables, greens, a protein, a grain and a delicious dressing. It is a great way to use up any vegetables nearing the end of their lives, or to catch up on your nutrient intake in one hit. This is just one example of what you can throw together to get you started.

Ingredients

Small head cauliflower, *cut into florets*	1
Can of chickpeas, *drained*	400g
Olive oil	
Ground turmeric	
Sumac	
Herb salt	
Garlic powder *(optional)*	
Brown rice or soba noodles	180g
Baby spinach or kale *(stalks removed)*	2 handfuls
Lemon juice	

Garlic dressing

Walnuts *(soaked in water overnight)*	⅓ cup
Clove of garlic, *crushed*	1
Sunflower oil	3 tbsp
Apple cider vinegar	2 tbsp
Herb salt and pepper to taste	

Toppings: fresh herbs, nuts or seeds, sprouts

Method

1. Preheat the oven to 200° C. Line a baking tray.
2. Place the cauliflower florets and drained chickpeas on the baking tray. Drizzle some olive oil over both, then sprinkle with turmeric, sumac, herb salt and garlic powder. Place in the oven to cook for 20–25 minutes.
3. Cook the noodles according to packet instructions.
4. If using kale, place in a small bowl and drizzle some olive oil and lemon juice over the top. Sprinkle with a little herb salt. Massage the kale for a couple of minutes, working the oil and lemon juice into the leaves until they soften.
5. Place all the dressing ingredients into a food processor. Process until a smooth liquid forms.
6. When all the ingredients are ready, assemble into the bowls and top with any fresh herbs, nuts, seeds or sprouts you would like. Serve the dressing on the side for each person to add as much as they would like.

V | DF | GF

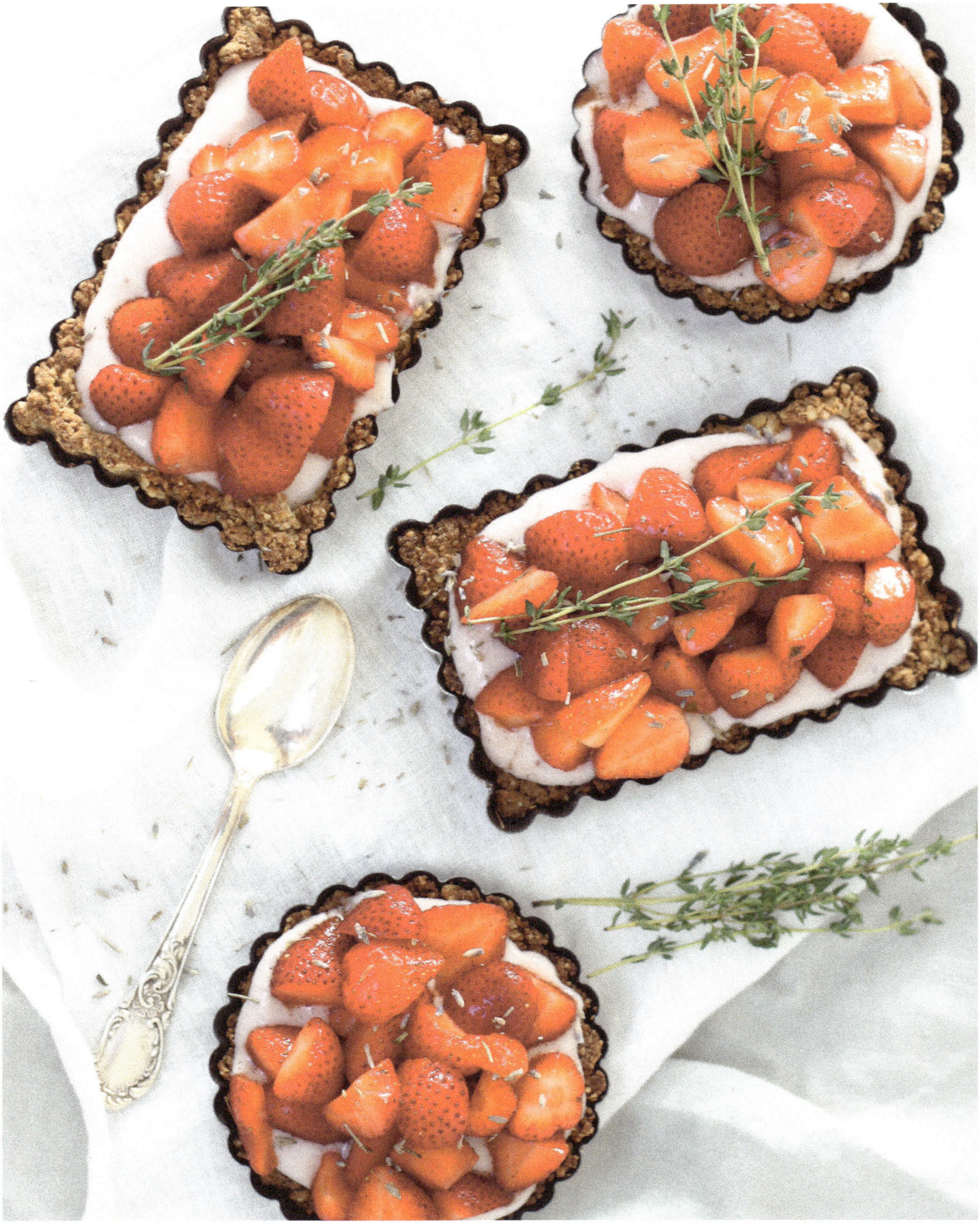

SWEET TREATS

Chocolate Cherry and Coconut Truffles	193
Date and Chestnut Banana Bread	194
Pineapple Ginger Carrot Cake	196
Chocolate Nut Rice Crackles	199
Summer Peach Tart	200
Sweet Potato Prune and Hazelnut Muffins	202
Raspberry Cherry Rose Chocolate Kisses	204
Vitamin Bites	207
Beetini Brownies	209
Make Your Own Chocolate – Three Ways	213
Spiced Orange Upside Down Cake	215
Chocolate Indulgence Tart	219
Lemon Tarts	221
Chocolate Stuffed Dates	223
Salted Cacao and Nut Butter Popsicles	225
Aprichoc Hazelnut Blondies	227
Berry Cherry Crumble Cake	229

SWEET TREATS

CHOCOLATE CHERRY AND COCONUT TRUFFLES

⏱ 15 mins | ✋ 10-15 balls

When I first made these truffles, it was at the height of the delicious Swiss cherry season. I first thought I would have to wait a whole year until cherries were in season again before I remade them. Then I made the delightful discovery that they work perfectly well with frozen cherries. That is the wonder of preservation methods like freezing, drying, pickling, fermenting or canning – it allows us to extend the time we can enjoy produce and helps us keep more diversity in our diet during the colder months. Sometimes, frozen fruit and vegetables get a bad rap because of the energy used to store them or the perceived reduction in nutrients. But in reality, most people don't eat the World Health Organisation recommended 5 portions of fruit and vegetables per day. Frozen options are convenient, cost-effective and still retain quite a lot of their nutrients, which makes them a helpful part of a diverse diet.

Ingredients

Fresh or frozen pitted cherries	¾ cup
Ground hazelnuts or almonds	⅔ cup
Pitted dates *(well packed)*	⅓ cup
Cacao powder	¼ cup
Coconut oil	1 tbsp
Desiccated coconut *(plus approximately 3 heaped tbsp, for rolling)*	⅓ cup

Method

1. Combine all the ingredients in a food processor, blending until everything is broken down and the mixture is well combined. You are aiming for a sticky consistency that will hold together well when you roll it into a ball. If you find the mixture is too wet, add a little more of the ground nuts, coconut or cacao and mix well.

2. Sprinkle some desiccated coconut onto a plate or a cutting board. Using a teaspoon, spoon out a scoop of the processed mixture and roll it into a ball in the palms of your hands. Roll the ball in the coconut to evenly coat it. Do this until you have no more mixture left.

3. Place the balls in the refrigerator for minimum 20 minutes to firm up. Store in the refrigerator for several days and enjoy having a sweet treat on hand whenever the craving strikes!

{V} {DF} {GF}

DATE AND CHESTNUT BANANA BREAD

20 mins prep plus 1 hour baking | *10 slices*

This is a vegan take on banana bread that I absolutely love. The chestnuts, dates and sunflower seeds give it a really earthy flavour that is hard to resist. I find it an excellent way to use up any bananas that have been forgotten in the fruit bowl, giving them a delightful second chance at life. This deliciousness was inspired by the date loaf in the wonderful My Darling Lemon Thyme cookbook by Emma Galloway.

Ingredients

Chia seeds	2 tbsp
Cold water	8 tbsp
Dates, *pitted and very finely chopped*	1 cup
Bicarb soda	1 tsp
Boiling water	2 tbsp
Mashed banana	1½ cups
(Approximately 3 large very ripe bananas, I am talking black-peel ripe!)	
Olive oil	½ cup
Maple syrup or honey *(optional)*	2 tbsp
Vanilla extract *(optional)*	1 tsp
Grated zest of ½ lemon	
Chestnut flour	1 cup
Spelt flour	1 cup
Baking powder	2 tsp
Pinch of salt	
Handful of sunflower seeds	

Method

1. Preheat the oven to 200° C. Use some olive oil to grease the loaf tin, then line it with a sheet of baking paper. Set aside.

2. Place the chia seeds in a cup then add the 8 tablespoons of cold water. Mix together then leave to sit until the chia seeds have absorbed all the water, usually 10–15 mins.

3. Place the chopped dates, bicarb soda and boiling water in a small bowl to soak.

4. Combine the mashed banana, olive oil, maple syrup, vanilla, lemon zest and chia mixture in a large bowl. Mix together until mixture is smooth. Sift in the chestnut flour, spelt flour, baking powder and pinch of salt. Mix together until well combined.

5. Add the dates to the above mixture, including any water that remains in the small bowl. Stir until well combined and evenly distributed. Break up any clumps where the dates are sticking together.

6. Using a spatula, scrape the mixture into the greased and lined loaf tin. Spread the mixture so it is evenly distributed. Sprinkle the mixture with sunflower seeds.

7. Place in the preheated oven and bake for approximately 1 hour. When ready, the top should be lightly browned, and a skewer should come out clean when inserted in the middle. Depending on your oven and your loaf tin you may need more or less time.

8. When ready, remove from oven and allow to cool before slicing and serving. Though honestly, if you are like me and can't wait, you can slice it hot and just deal with the fact that the slices are not so neat and clean. Up to you!

PINEAPPLE GINGER CARROT CAKE

25 mins prep plus 30 mins baking | *10 slices*

When I was a kid, I absolutely loved a pineapple carrot cake that a family friend used to make. Back then it was packed full of sugar, cream and oil, which ensured it not only tasted amazing but gave you a sugar high for a good number of hours! I was recently inspired to dig the recipe out and completely revamp it, so it was more aligned with how I like to eat now. So that is what you will find below – a new and improved carrot cake that still tastes fantastic but is much healthier. With pineapple to freshen it up, a bunch of spices and a lot of carroty goodness, it is the perfect, moist cake to enjoy with an afternoon cup of tea or a turmeric latte.

PART TWO | *Sweet Treats*

Ingredients

Cake Mixture

Spelt flour, sifted	1½ cups
Ground hazelnuts *(or almonds)*	½ cup
Baking powder	2 tsp
Ground cinnamon	2 tsp
Ground ginger	1½ tsp
Ground cardamom	1 tsp
Pinch of salt	
Desiccated coconut	½ cup
Eggs	4
Sunflower oil	½ cup
Maple syrup *(or liquid honey)*	⅓ cup
Vanilla essence	½ tsp
Unsweetened pineapple juice	⅓ cup
Canned pineapple pieces *finely chopped*	¾ cup
Carrot, *finely grated*	1½ cups
Walnuts, *finely chopped*	½ cup
Dates, *pitted and finely chopped*	⅓ cup

Icing

Almond butter	¼ cup
Coconut milk	¼ cup
Thick honey or rice syrup	2–3 tbps
Coconut oil	1 tsp
Apple cider vinegar	½ tsp

{DF}

Method

1. Preheat oven to 200°C. Grease a brownie pan or a loaf tin.

2. In a large mixing bowl, combine all dry ingredients: sifted flour, ground nuts, baking powder, cinnamon, ginger, cardamom, salt, coconut.

3. Make a well in the middle of the dry ingredients. Add the eggs, sunflower oil, maple syrup, vanilla, pineapple juice. Using a fork, whisk all the ingredients until well combined and there are no lumps.

4. Add the pineapple pieces, grated carrot, chopped walnuts and dates to the mixing bowl. Mix through with a wooden spoon until well combined and evenly distributed.

5. Pour mixture into the greased and lined pan. Place in the oven and bake for 30 minutes at 200°C. Check the cake at 25 minutes to see if it needs more or less time (press the middle and see if it bounces back). If you use a loaf tin, it will generally need more time to cook than a square brownie tin.

6. While the cake is cooking prepare the icing: place all ingredients in a bowl and use a fork to whisk until smooth. Place in the fridge for around 30 mins to thicken.

7. When the cake is ready remove from the oven and let it cool before icing it and decorating with edible flowers, nuts or other toppings of your choosing.

The Great Full | 197

SWEET TREATS

CHOCOLATE NUT RICE CRACKLES

5 mins | 15 small crackles

A couple of years ago I spent a month in Berkeley, California, where I stayed in an apartment with an unbelievably small and very old kitchen. I am talking cubicle sized. Like many things, what first appeared to be a frustration was actually an opportunity in disguise! This tiny kitchen led me to simplify and strip down my cooking, and these vegan chocolate nut rice crackles are one of the happy results. They take 5 minutes to throw together, need only 5 ingredients and are loved by adults and kids alike.

Ingredients

Coconut oil	1 tbsp
Smooth peanut butter	1 tbsp
Cacao powder	1½ tbsp
Maple syrup or honey	2 tbsp
Puffed brown rice	1 cup

(Or puffed quinoa or millet)

Method

1. Place the coconut oil, peanut butter, cacao powder and maple syrup into a small saucepan. Place the saucepan on a low heat.

2. Using a wooden spoon, continually stir the mixture, removing any lumps, until it is melted and combined. This should take 1–2 minutes only. Do not let the mixture boil.

3. When the mixture is runny, remove the saucepan from the heat. Add in the puffed rice and mix with a wooden spoon until all the rice puffs are coated in the chocolate mixture and it is evenly distributed.

4. Using a teaspoon, scoop out a heaped spoonful of the mixture at a time and place it into a small cupcake case. Gently press the mixture so it sticks together.

5. When the crackles are cool place them in the refrigerator for at least 20 minutes to set.

V DF GF

SUMMER PEACH TART

20 mins prep plus 20 mins cooking | *8 slices*

Cooking is my favourite creative outlet. I love to play with flavours, colours and ingredients and come up with new inventions, even if they don't ultimately work out. Take this tart for example – the fresh peaches from the Berkeley farmers market sent me down a creative rabbit hole that began with muffins, took a turn towards a galette and ended up as a tart. A few disappointments but eventually a winner. I wasn't always this way. In my early years of fending for myself, I had just a few simple meals I would make on rotation between eating out or getting takeaway. This slowly changed, and I have since become a confident cook simply through a willingness to experiment. Cooking is like any other creative process – it's an opportunity to let go of attachment to outcome, enjoy the process and have a go even if you "fail". These things hold us all back in life, not only in the kitchen. So, in our serious adult lives, why not make some room for creative play, trying out new things and moving out of the comfort zone? That is the space where you grow and innovate, and what starts in the kitchen may even spread into the rest of your life!

Ingredients

For the Base

Sunflower oil to grease pan	
Ground hazelnuts	¾ cup
Quick oats	¼ cup
Desiccated coconut	¼ cup
Brown rice flour,	½ cup
(or spelt flour or whole meal flour)	
Pinch of sea salt	
Cacao powder	2 tbsp
Coconut oil, *melted*	2 ½ tbsp
Maple syrup	3 tbsp

For the Filling

Peaches or other stone fruit *thinly sliced*	2
Maple syrup	2 tbsp
Fresh ginger, *grated*	1 tsp
Squeeze of lemon juice	
Plain or vanilla yoghurt	300g
(Soy, coconut or greek yoghurt, hard-set if available)	
Handful of fresh basil leaves	

{V} *optional*

{DF} *optional*

{GF} *optional*

Method

Note: make the crust first and leave enough time for it to cool (i.e. start at least 1 hour before intended serving time).

1. Preheat the oven to 180°C. Generously grease a tart pan or pie dish (use one with a diameter of around 25cm) and set aside.

2. To make the crust, combine the hazelnuts, oats, coconut, flour, salt and cacao powder in a mixing bowl. Add the melted coconut oil and maple syrup. Using a fork, combine until the mixture is moist but not sticky or clumping together.

3. Transfer mixture into the greased tart pan or pie dish and press into the base and up the sides using your fingertips until it is compact and evenly distributed. You only need about 1cm height up the sides.

4. Prick the bottom of the crust with a fork a few times. Place in the preheated oven and leave to bake for 20 minutes at 180°C. Remove from oven and set aside to cool for at least 30 minutes.

5. To make the filling, lightly grease a stovetop grill pan or frying pan with olive oil. Place the peaches in the pan and grill on one side until cooked through (they will become a little transparent). Note: this step is optional. You can also just slice the peaches and use them fresh.

6. While the peaches are cooking, place the maple syrup, grated ginger and a squeeze of lemon juice in a small saucepan on low heat. Warm the mixture, stirring regularly. Just before it starts to boil, remove from the heat and set aside.

7. When the base is cooled, pour the yoghurt inside, stopping when the filling is just under the rim of the crust.

8. Arrange the peaches on top of the yoghurt. Pour the maple-ginger mixture over the top, making sure it is evenly distributed. Tear up the basil leaves (or use individual leaves of miniature basil) and sprinkle them on top before serving.

9. This tart is best eaten right after it has been made. However, it will keep in the fridge for a couple of days, and I believe it even passes for breakfast the next day (if it lasts that long!).

SWEET POTATO PRUNE AND HAZELNUT MUFFINS

20 mins prep plus 25 mins baking | *8 muffins*

Sweet potatoes are one of the most nutritious root vegetables around and they taste fantastic, with a natural sweetness that works in both sweet and savoury dishes. Orange sweet potatoes are an excellent source of beta carotene, which the body converts to vitamin A, and also contain significant amounts of vitamin C and B. As I have done in this recipe, it's best to add a little fat (such as oil or butter) when you cook sweet potatoes as it can help vitamin A absorption. These muffins make a great treat for brunch, and you can use the remaining ones for breakfast or dessert for the rest of the week.

Ingredients

Wet Ingredients

Sweet potato *peeled and diced* (*approximately 1 sweet potato*)	1 cup
Butter	50g
Apple, *finely grated*	1
Milk (*almond, soy, oat or dairy*)	⅓ cup
Maple syrup	¼ cup
Egg	1

Dry ingredients

Brown rice flour	½ cup
Spelt flour (*Or whole wheat or gluten free flour*)	¼ cup
Ground hazelnuts	½ cup
Baking powder	1½ tsp
Ground ginger	½ tsp
Ground cinnamon	½ tsp

Additional ingredients

Prunes (*pitted*), *chopped finely*	½ cup
Pecans (*optional, to top*)	handful

{DF} {GF} *optional*

Method

1. Preheat oven to 200°C. Line a muffin tray with 8 cupcake cases.

2. Place the sweet potatoes in a pot and half cover with water. Place the pan on high heat on the stove with the lid on. When it comes to the boil leave to simmer for 15 minutes or until the sweet potato pieces are soft enough to mash with a fork.

3. While the sweet potatoes are steaming, finely chop the pitted prunes, being careful to remove any stones that may still be in the fruit. Set aside.

4. Sift the brown rice flour and spelt flour into a medium mixing bowl. Add the ground hazelnuts, baking powder, ginger and cinnamon. Use a wooden spoon to stir until well mixed.

5. When the sweet potatoes are ready, remove from the heat and strain. Empty all the liquid from the saucepan then put the strained sweet potatoes back into the saucepan. Add the butter and use a fork to thoroughly mash the butter and sweet potatoes. Add in the grated apple, milk and maple syrup and mix until well combined.

6. Crack the egg into a glass or small bowl and quickly whisk.

7. Add the wet mix from the saucepan to the dry mix in the mixing bowl. Add the whisked egg. Add the pitted prunes. Using a wooden spoon mix until all ingredients are well combined.

8. Using a tablespoon spoon the mixture into the cupcake cases.

9. Place the muffin tray on a wire rack in the preheated oven and bake for 20–25 minutes until the muffins brown on top. (You may need to bake a little longer depending on your oven.)

10. When ready remove from oven and allow to cool slightly before serving. If you like, place a pecan or other nuts of your choice on top before serving.

RASPBERRY CHERRY ROSE CHOCOLATE KISSES

20 mins plus 20 mins cooling time | *around 20 chocolates*

Whenever I make a recipe with chocolate in it, I use an unsweetened, organic, fair trade cacao powder. Yes, one with ALL the labels. Not because I am convinced labels are solving all our problems, but because I care a lot about the issues associated with chocolate and hope that by paying a premium for a labelled product, I am putting my money where my values are. When it comes to chocolate, there are a lot of things to think about. On the production side, there are challenges related to declining yields, pests and diseases destroying the crops, climate change, poor working conditions, child slavery and unequal distribution of value along the supply chain. On the consumption side, the product is linked, confusingly, to both health promoting properties like antioxidants and health damaging ones like cadmium exposure. That is why I try to enjoy chocolate with consideration, looking for ways to enjoy a healthier version of something that should still be a treat. These chocolates are a good place to start!

PART TWO | *Sweet Treats*

SWEET TREATS (V) (DF) (GF)

Ingredients

Chocolate

Cacao butter	6 tbsp
Cacao powder	4 tbsp
Maple syrup	2 tbsp

Or as an alternative to all of the above, 100g dark chocolate (melted)

Chia Jam Filling

Raspberries *(fresh or frozen)*	1 cup
Chia seeds	2 tbsp
Maple syrup	1½ tbsp
Water	1 tsp
Lemon juice	1 tsp
Rosewater	1 tsp

* This recipe requires silicone chocolate moulds, which you can find at specialty cooking stores or online.

Method

1. Combine the chia jam filling ingredients in a small pot. Place on the stove on a low heat. Use a wooden spoon to continuously stir the ingredients until the raspberries are completely broken down. This should take around 5 minutes. When the consistency is even and there are no large lumps remove from heat and set aside to cool.

2. If you are making the chocolate (rather than simply melting a pre-made block) place cacao butter in a heatproof bowl. Sit this bowl inside a saucepan that has been half filled with water. Warm on low heat until the cacao butter is fully melted. When the cacao butter has melted, remove heatproof bowl from bath. Mix in cacao powder and maple syrup, using a whisk to stir quickly and remove any lumps.

3. Using a teaspoon, half fill each chocolate mould with the melted chocolate. Add a small dollop of chia jam to each. Take the melted chocolate again and use a small spoon to pour a little on top of each dollop of jam, until every mould is filled to the top.

4. Place the moulds in the fridge for 20–30 minutes until they are fully set.

5. Remove the "kisses" from the moulds and serve. If you like you can place a dried rose petal on the top of each chocolate before serving to make them look a little special!

Sweet Treats

VITAMIN BITES

30 mins | 10-12 balls

These vitamin bites have helped me through long flights, road trips and work events when there is not much healthy food on offer. I first made them when I was running out the door to get on a flight to Kenya for work. I usually like to eat local food when I travel but I knew being in and out of the car visiting different projects in rural areas would mean we would mostly have oil- or sugar-laden snacks to choose from along the way. I made these in advance to share with my colleagues, making it a little more convenient to get some vegetables while we were on the go. Friends tell me they are also a great way to sneak some vegetables into your child's life!

Ingredients

Sweet potato *(peeled and cubed)*	½ cup
Carrots *(peeled and cubed)*	½ cup
Dried apricots	100g
(either the tangy variety or the sweet turkish variety. If you are sensitive to sulphur, get organic ones, which are also sulphur free)	
Ground almonds	¾ cup
(or any other ground nuts)	
Desiccated coconut	¼ cup
Hemp seeds	⅛ cup
Medjool dates, pitted	2
(or use normal dates, just use a couple more and soak for 15 mins in boiling water then drain before using)	
Coconut oil	1 tsp
Sesame seeds or desiccated coconut for coating	

Method

1. Steam sweet potato and carrots for 15–20 minutes, or until just tender. When ready, remove from heat and drain off any liquid.
2. Place the drained, steamed vegetables and all other ingredients in a food processor.
3. Mix and pulse until all ingredients are well combined and broken down. The final mixture should be slightly sticky and able to be formed into a ball easily. If it is too wet add a little extra coconut or nuts. If it is too dry add a few drops of water, nut/soya milk or orange juice.
4. Use a dessert spoon to scoop out portions of the mixture and roll it into balls with your clean hands.
5. Sprinkle shredded coconut or sesame seeds onto a baking sheet. Roll each ball in the mixture until it is coated. Place in an airtight container and store in the refrigerator or a cool dry place.

{V} {DF} {GF}

SWEET TREATS

PART TWO | *Sweet Treats*

BEETINI BROWNIES

30 mins | 10–12 brownies

These brownies are the perfect mix of sweetness, fatness and flavour that makes them hard to resist. The good news is they have enough goodness, in the form of tahini, beetroot and nuts that make one little square satisfying and filling. And if the mention of beetroot has you flipping the page over, hold up. I also don't love the flavour on its own. But combined with the other ingredients, it is imperceptible, simply adding the sweetness and texture that makes these brownies the best. Note – you can buy beetroot already cooked to save you some time – just make sure it is not in vinegar.

SWEET TREATS

BEETINI BROWNIES

(V) (DF)

Ingredients

Beetroot *(peeled and cooked)*	150g
Dark chocolate	100g
Tahini *(use smooth and runny tahini)*	⅓ cup
Coconut oil	3 tbsp
Spelt flour *(or brown rice or gluten free flour)*	½ cup
Corn starch	⅓ cup
Cacao powder	¼ cup
Baking powder	1 tsp
Walnuts, Brazil nuts or pecans, *roughly chopped*	½ cup
Dark chocolate chips *(or chopped dark chocolate)*	¼ cup
Pinch of salt	
Aquafaba *(the liquid from approximately 1 can of chickpeas)*	¾ cup
Maple syrup *(optional)*	2 tbsp
Sesame seeds or edible flowers to top	

Tahini Drizzle *(optional)*

Tahini	1 tbsp
Maple syrup	1 tbsp
Cacao powder	1 tbsp

Method

1. Preheat the oven to 200° C. Grease and line the brownie pan.
2. Put the cooked beetroot in the food processor. Blend until finely chopped. Alternatively, finely grate the beetroot. Take out 2/3 cup of the finely chopped beetroot and set aside.
3. Take a small mixing bowl and sit it inside a pot with some water in the bottom. Put on medium heat. Break up the block of dark chocolate into pieces and put it in the mixing bowl. Leave to melt slowly.
4. Take another mixing bowl and combine the rice flour, corn starch, cacao powder, baking powder, walnuts and salt.
5. When the chocolate has melted, take the bowl off the heat and add the tahini and coconut oil. Mix to combine.
6. Add the chocolate, tahini, coconut oil mix into the dry ingredients. Add the beetroot and chocolate chips. Use a spatula to mix lightly until combined.
7. Place the aquafaba in a small bowl and whisk it until it becomes foamy. Pour the aquafaba into the brownie mix and mix with a spatula or fork until combined.
8. Pour brownie mixture into the greased and lined pan.
9. Put the pan in the preheated oven and bake for around 15 minutes, depending on your oven.
10. While baking, use the bowl where you melted the chocolate to mix together the tahini drizzle ingredients. Put the bowl back in the pot of water and gently heat the mixture.
11. When the brownies are ready, remove from the oven and leave to cool on the bench. As soon as they are no longer piping hot you can pour on the drizzle then place them in the refrigerator to let them get fudgy. Top with sesame seeds or edible flowers before serving.

SWEET TREATS

PART TWO | *Sweet Treats*

MAKE YOUR OWN CHOCOLATE – THREE WAYS

10 mins prep plus 20 mins cooling | serves 2–4 depending how much you like chocolate!

Not to be dramatic or anything, but learning how easy it is to make your own chocolate kind of changed my life. Specifically, it gave me a way to make a healthier version of my most craved food. Now, except for some emergency situations, I mostly make my own chocolate or buy from an organization that is doing something cool and different in the chocolate space. My favourite one of these is Choba Choba, a chocolate company that calls what they do a "chocolate revolution". The founders, Christoph Inauen and Eric Garnier, spent 10 years working on sustainability in the chocolate industry. They decided that real change needed a new model entirely. So, they partnered with 36 organic cacao farmers from the Alto Huayabamba Valley in Peru and founded a chocolate company where farmers are not just raw material suppliers but are co-owners who have a direct stake in the company and benefit from its success. The farmers define the price of their cacao, benefit from profits as shareholders and are represented in the board of the company. A chocolate revolution indeed. And a delicious one at that.

Ingredients

Basic Chocolate

Cacao butter	6 tbsp
Cacao powder	4 tbsp
Maple syrup	2 tbsp
Chilli powder	2 pinches

Toppings

Goji berries	1 tbsp
Cacao nibs	½ tbsp
Or	
Sprinkle of edible lavender	
Sprinkle of crushed salt flakes	
Cacao nibs	½ tbsp
Or	
Dried cranberries	1 tbsp
Flaked almonds	1 tbsp
Cacao nibs	½ tbsp

Method

1. Line a baking tray with baking paper. The size doesn't matter, it just needs to fit in your fridge. Alternatively, you can use a loaf tin or a chocolate mould to make a block of chocolate.

2. Place the cacao butter in a heatproof bowl. Sit this bowl inside a saucepan half filled with water. Place saucepan on low heat until cacao butter is fully melted.

3. Remove the bowl from the bath. Mix in cacao powder and maple syrup, using a whisk to stir it quickly to remove any lumps.

4. Pour the mixture onto baking paper, using a wooden spoon to smooth it out. The mixture should be evenly distributed in a thin layer.

5. Sprinkle two small pinches of chilli powder over the top, making sure it is evenly spread across the surface.

6. Sprinkle toppings of your choice on top.

7. Place the tray in the fridge and allow to cool, around 20–30 minutes.

{V} {DF} {GF}

SWEET TREATS

SPICED ORANGE UPSIDE DOWN CAKE

25 mins prep plus 30 min baking | serves 8

This cake is a wonderful way to showcase whatever fruit is in season. I love to use blood oranges when they are at the peak of their deliciousness, but it would work well with other fruit too. You can try it out with plums, apricots, apples, nectarines or cherries (just make sure you remove the pip!) or whatever is in season. The spices and fluffiness of the cake are the perfect vehicle for the beautifully baked and caramelized fruit. My husband boldly proclaimed this was the best cake he had ever eaten. I'll leave it up to you to decide for yourself.

SWEET TREATS

SPICED ORANGE UPSIDE DOWN CAKE (DF) (GF)

Ingredients

Ghee or coconut oil, *melted* *(ghee will give a more caramel-like result)*	4 tsp
Honey or coconut sugar	4 tbsp
Blood oranges *peeled and sliced into rounds*	4
Brown rice flour	1 cup
Hazelnut meal	1 cup
Bicarb soda	1 tsp
Baking powder	1½ tsp
Ground cinnamon	1½ tsp
Ground cardamom	1½ tsp
Ground nutmeg	½ tsp
Apple sauce	½ cup
Maple syrup	100 ml
Eggs	2
Milk *(I used oat)*	150 ml
Squeeze of orange juice	

Method

1. Preheat the oven to 200° C.
2. Grease a round baking tin (approximately 25cm diameter) and line with baking paper, covering bottom and sides of the tin. Cut off any excess paper.
3. Place ghee in a small dish and sit it in the oven until it melts. Remove.
4. Peel the oranges and slice into rounds.
5. Pour the melted ghee into the base of the lined cake tin. Drizzle honey or sprinkle coconut sugar evenly on top. Layer the oranges on top of this, trying to cover as much of the pan base as possible. You may need to cut the orange into smaller segments to fill the gaps.
6. In a mixing bowl, combine the brown rice flour, hazelnut meal, bicarb soda, baking powder, cinnamon, cardamom and nutmeg. Make a well in the middle of the bowl.
7. Add the wet ingredients (apple sauce, maple syrup, eggs, milk and orange juice) to the well. Whisk all ingredients until well combined.
8. Pour the cake batter into the cake tin, on top of the layer of oranges.
9. Put the cake in the preheated oven. Bake for 25–30 minutes or until cooked. Use a skewer to check that the inside of the cake is no longer batter.
10. When cooked remove cake from oven and leave to cool.
11. When ready to serve, place a serving plate on top of the tin. Using one hand on each side to keep the contact between the tin and the plate, turn it upside down in one quick movement.

SWEET TREATS

CHOCOLATE INDULGENCE TART

15 mins prep plus 20 mins baking plus 1 hr cooling time | serves 8

There are a few cookbooks that have helped me immensely in developing my cooking skills. One of them is At Home in the Whole Foods Kitchen by the amazing Amy Chaplin. She has a whole section on tarts that taught me the basics that I now use to whip up all types of sweet and savoury variations. This is one tart that was inspired by her book. I love it because it is very easy but also great for when you have guests who are vegan or dairy free. I call it an indulgence tart because although it is healthier than many other chocolate desserts, it still has two blocks of dark chocolate in it. I think we need to remember that chocolate is a luxury product, something we should enjoy in moderation and of the best quality we can manage. And then every now and then, eating something like this to remember: all things in moderation, including moderation!

Ingredients

Tart base

Ground hazelnuts	¾ cup
Quick oats	¼ cup
Desiccated coconut	¼ cup
Spelt flour	½ cup
Pinch of salt	
Coconut oil, melted	2 ½ tbsp
Maple syrup	3 tbsp
Sunflower oil to grease tart pan	

Filling

Soy milk	1 cup

(important, you need to use soy milk for this to work)

Dark chocolate, roughly chopped	200g
Chilli powder	2 pinches

Topping

Sliced seasonal fruit such as blood oranges, cherries, berries, persimmon, passionfruit

Method

1. Preheat the oven to 180° C. Grease and line a tart pan or pie dish (use one with a diameter of max 25cm) and set aside.

2. Combine the hazelnuts, oats, coconut, flour, and salt in a mixing bowl. Add the melted coconut oil and maple syrup. Using a fork, combine until the mixture is moist but not sticky or clumping together.

3. Pour the mixture into the greased tart pan or pie dish and press into the base and up the sides using your fingertips until it is compact and evenly distributed. You only need about 1cm height up the sides.

4. Prick the bottom of the crust with a fork a few times. Place in the preheated oven and leave to bake for 20 mins. When cooked remove from the oven and set aside.

5. To make the filling, place soy milk in a small saucepan (one you have a lid for) and bring to the boil. Just before it boils, remove from heat. Add the chopped dark chocolate and put the lid on. Leave to sit for a couple of minutes. Remove the lid and use a whisk to combine the chocolate and milk until a smooth and uniform consistency.

6. Pour the chocolate filling into the tart base. Sprinkle the chilli powder evenly on top.

7. Place in the fridge to cool. It usually needs at least an hour to set.

SWEET TREATS

PART TWO | *Sweet Treats*

LEMON TARTS

30 mins prep plus 25 mins baking | *4 tarts or 8 slices*

These tarts make for a lovely refreshing dessert. They are great on their own or can be topped with fresh seasonal fruit or dried lavender to jazz them up a little. I usually serve them as individual tarts, but you can also make it into a slice to feed a hungry family. For the tarts you need individual tart tins, approximately 10cm in diameter. For the slice you can use a brownie or loaf pan.

Ingredients

Tart base

Quick oats	½ cup
Almond or hazelnut meal	½ cup
Brown rice, spelt or wholemeal flour	½ cup
Pinch of salt	
Maple syrup	2 tbsp
Coconut oil *(plus extra for greasing)*	2 tbsp

Lemon Curd Filling

Coconut milk	200 ml
Lemon juice	100 ml
Turmeric powder	⅛ tsp
Honey or maple syrup	2–3 tbsp
Corn starch	2 tbsp

To Top *(optional)*

Fresh seasonal fruit or berries

Or

Dried edible lavender

{V} {DF} {GF} *optional*

Method

1. Preheat the oven to 200° C.
2. Grease 4 individual tart tins or the slice tin with coconut oil.
3. In a mixing bowl, combine all the tart base ingredients. Mix with a fork until well combined.
4. Press mixture into tart cases, pressing up the sides so there is approximately 1cm height on the edges. Alternatively, press the mixture into the base of the slice tin, compacting it with your fingertips.
5. Place in the preheated oven for approximately 10 minutes until cooked but not brown.
6. Meanwhile, make the lemon curd filling. Place the coconut milk, lemon juice, turmeric powder, honey and corn starch into a small saucepan. Place on low to medium heat and whisk ingredients together. Keep whisking intermittently until it thickens (this usually takes around 6 minutes).
7. Remove the tart bases from the oven. Pour lemon curd filling into each one until it reaches just below the edge of the crust. If you are making it as a slice, pour all the filling on top of the base.
8. Place in the refrigerator until set (usually around 30 minutes). Serve with fresh berries on top or with edible lavender flowers.
9. Save any extra lemon curd in a jar in the fridge. It makes a great topping on oatmeal or a dessert with some berries on top.

The Great Full

SWEET TREATS

PART TWO | *Sweet Treats*

CHOCOLATE STUFFED DATES

5 mins prep plus 20 mins cooling | *8 stuffed dates*

People were already enjoying stuffed dates back in the Roman Empire, so I am not inventing anything here. But every time I take these along to friends, they love them so much and want the recipe, so I decided to include it anyway. As Devils on Horseback proved in the 80s, you can stuff dates and wrap them in just about anything! For example, cut them open and spread with a soft goats' cheese, top with a sprinkle of pistachios then drizzle with balsamic vinegar glaze. For a sweet version, try out the recipe below for a treat ready in no time.

Ingredients

Dates *(medjool dates work best)*	8
Nut butter *(I like crunchy peanut butter the best)*	4 tbsp
Few pinches of flaked salt	
Dark chocolate or dark chocolate chips	100g
Dried edible flowers *(optional, for decoration)*	

Method

1. Take the dates and make a cut along the top of each one and remove the pit. Do not cut all the way through as you want them to hold together.
2. Fill the space where the pit was with nut butter. Be generous!
3. Sprinkle with flaked salt.
4. Melt the chocolate then drizzle it over the top of the dates. Alternatively, you can dunk the whole thing in there and coat them for a more intense version.
5. Sprinkle some rose petals on top (optional) and place in the fridge to set.

V | DF | GF

SWEET TREATS

SALTED CACAO AND NUT BUTTER POPSICLES

5 mins prep plus 3 hrs to freeze | *4–6 popsicles depending on size of mould*

There is nothing better than arriving home on a hot summers day and remembering you made popsicles the night before. These ones are creamy and delicious yet much healthier than your usual ice-cream. You can whip them up in 5 mins and throw them in the freezer as a great treat for adults and kids alike!

Ingredients

Milk *(I use oat milk)*	1¼ cup
Smooth nut butter *(I use peanut butter)*	½ cup
Medjool dates *(or normal dates, soaked in boiling water 15 mins, drained)*	5
Cacao powder	2 tbsp
Salt flakes, *crushed (I use maldon)*	¼ tsp

Method

1. Place all ingredients in a blender. Blend until smooth.
2. Pour mixture into popsicle moulds. Place in the freezer for at least 3 hours or overnight to freeze.

V | DF | GF

SWEET TREATS

APRICHOC HAZELNUT BLONDIES

10 mins prep plus 25 mins to bake | 12 blondies

These Blondies have chickpeas as an unexpected ingredient. Don't worry, you won't even notice. They just make them the perfect doughy consistency while adding some protein and nutrients to help you feel satisfied after just one square. I combined the chickpeas with some flavours that always remind me of South Australia, where I was born. There, apricots from the Riverland area are rolled and coated in dark chocolate to produce something called Aprichocs, a match made in heaven if there ever was one. Whenever I taste these ingredients together, I also remember my mother's stories about cutting and sun-drying apricots during her summer holidays as a teenager. It is a nice way to be reminded of all the effort behind any ingredient in our food.

Ingredients

Milk (*I use oat milk*)	⅓ cup
Cooked or canned chickpeas	1 cup
Hazelnut meal or flour	½ cup
Spelt flour	½ cup
Coconut oil	2 tbsp
Maple syrup	3 tbsp
Baking powder	1 tsp
Walnuts, Brazil nuts or hazelnuts, *chopped*	⅓ cup
Dried apricots, *chopped into small chunks* (I like the tangy ones that are dried in halves)	⅓ cup
Dark chocolate, *chopped into small chunks*	¼ cup
Apricot jam (*optional, to top*)	4 tbsp

Method

1. Preheat oven to 200° C. Grease a square brownie tin with olive oil or sunflower oil being sure to coat all edges and corners.

2. Place the milk, chickpeas, hazelnut meal, spelt flour, coconut oil, maple syrup and baking powder into a food processor. Process until a smooth, batter-like consistency.

3. Transfer the mixture from the food processor into a bowl. Pour in the chopped nuts, dried apricots and dark chocolate. Use a spatula to mix everything through.

4. Pour the batter into the greased brownie tin. Spread out with the spatula until evenly distributed in the pan then smooth the top down.

5. Spoon the apricot jam on top and use the back of the spoon to spread it evenly.

6. Place in a preheated oven and bake for 20–25 minutes. The blondies are ready when the edges are just starting to brown and the jam is nice and bubbly.

SWEET TREATS

BERRY CHERRY CRUMBLE CAKE

⏲ *10 min prep plus 25–30 min baking* | ✋ *10 slices*

This is another recipe that comes via Daga Stojecka from Green Daga. She delivers lunches to the Birdhaus in Zurich, a wonderful women's co-working space where I set up camp to write this book. Having delicious home cooked food delivered to the door each lunch has been such a luxury. Like this delicious crumble cake, each meal always includes a little sweet treat to help you through the afternoon. This is quick and easy to make and goes perfectly with some tea and a chat with a friend.

Ingredients

Dough

Spelt flour	1 cup
Brown rice flour	½ cup
Baking powder	1 tsp
Ground cinnamon	½ tsp
Ground turmeric	½ tsp
Pinch of salt	
Sunflower oil	½ cup
Milk (*I use oat*)	½ cup
Maple syrup	⅓ cup
Mixed berries or pitted cherries	1 ½ cup
(*Fresh or frozen*)	

I like to mix half berries and half cherries. You can also use sliced seasonal fruit, such as plum, apple or apricot.

Crumble

Coconut oil	1 tbsp
Brown sugar or coconut sugar	¼ cup
Spelt or brown rice flour	¼ cup
Ground cinnamon	1 tsp

Method

1. Preheat oven to 200° C. Grease and line a round cake tin, approximately 24cm in diameter.

2. Place the flours, baking powder, cinnamon, turmeric and salt in a mixing bowl. Make a well in the middle. Add the oil, milk, and maple syrup. Stir together with a whisk until well combined.

3. Place all the ingredients for the crumble in a small mixing bowl. Use your fingers to rub the ingredients together until small crumbs form.

4. Put the dough into the lined tin, using a spoon to spread it evenly. Arrange the fruit on top, then sprinkle with the crumble mixture. Place in preheated oven and bake for 25–30 min until cooked in the middle (use a skewer to test).

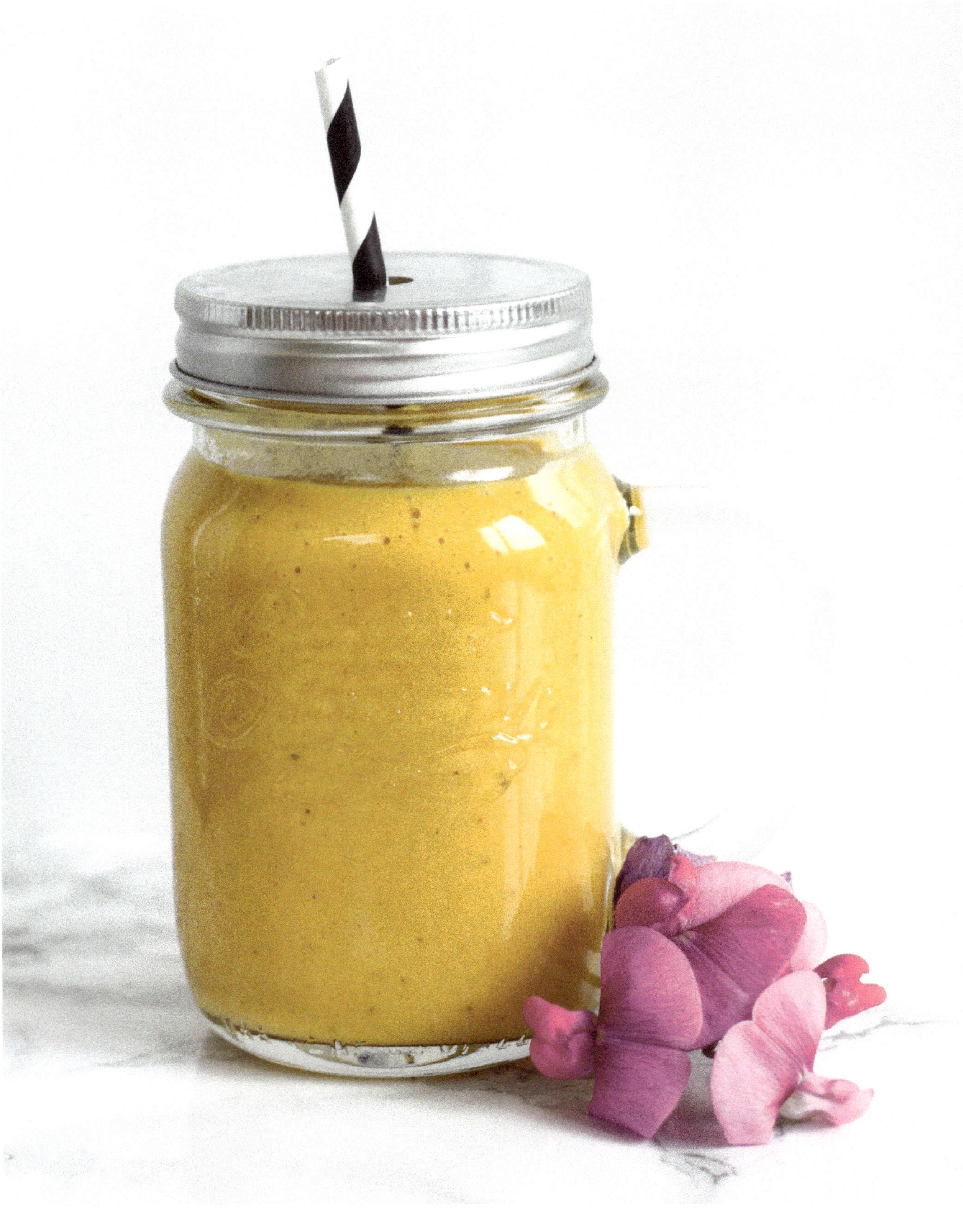

DRINKS

Syrian Lemon Mint Polo	233
Go to Green Smoothie	235
Turmeric Mango Smoothie or Popsicles	237
Green Elixir	238
Apfelshorle	239
Chia Fresca	241
Blood Orange Raspberry and Buckwheat Smoothie	243

DRINKS

SYRIAN LEMON MINT POLO

5 mins | 4–6 glasses

It was over this incredibly refreshing summer drink that I got to meet a delightful Syrian couple in Berlin. One sip of this lemon mint polo, they said, immediately took them back to balmy nights chatting with friends in Damascus. Back to times when life felt a little simpler than now. They each had a different, yet equally heart-wrenching, story of leaving Syria and settling in Berlin. Within a short period of time, but with a lot of hard work and determination, they spoke beautifully fluent German and took up their studies at university. Now, despite their busy schedules and uncertain future, they donate time to scaling the new wall that divides Berlin: the distinction between "newcomers" and "natives". They are a part of an organization called Über den Tellerrand ("Beyond the Plate"), which inspires encounters across cultures. Over cooking courses, people with and without a migrant experience share their culture, food and perspectives face to face. This offers an invitation to us all: why not use food as an entry point to better understand the migration crisis and what that means for people living in our own community? You could join a cooking class or dinner with people who have lived a migrant experience. Or why not seek out a café in your area that supports refugees to join the workforce? You could start an open conversation over your coffee. Through such exchanges, you will certainly meet inspiring people. And perhaps it will remind you, as it did me, that diversity is strength and difference is our teacher. And that food is not just a way of feeding our bodies, but a gateway to our culture, history and soul.

Ingredients

Ice	3 cups
Fresh mint *(approximately 20 leaves)*	handful
Lemon juice	2 tbsp
Maple syrup	2 tbsp
Pistachios, *chopped*	handful

Method

1. Place the ice, mint, lemon juice and maple syrup in the blender. Add a little cold water and turn the blender on. Keep adding water until the blender can mix easily. Add more water if you would like the drink more fluid, less if you would like to have more of a slushy or granita consistency.

2. Pour the mixture into small serving cups. Top with the chopped pistachios before serving.

{V} {DF} {GF}

DRINKS

GO TO GREEN SMOOTHIE

⏲ 5 mins | ✋ 1 glass

Here is my trusty recipe for when I need to get more greens in my life. It follows a pretty basic green smoothie formula that you can experiment with: a handful of greens, ¾ cup of liquid (such as a nut or grain milk, coconut milk or water), a handful of frozen fruit, a squeeze of lemon and any spices or powders you want to add. With that in mind you can get creative and try all kinds of different combinations based on what you have on hand. The best way to have a "smoothie-ready" kitchen is to have a selection of frozen fruit and berries on hand at all times. Frozen fruit also makes a great base for ice-cream and is an excellent way to avoid wasting overripe produce. Just make sure you let the fruit ripen then cut it up before freezing it to make it easy to throw in the blender.

Ingredients

Frozen banana	1
Baby spinach	1 handful
Fresh mint leaves	5
Oat milk *(or any other milk of your choice)*	¾ cup
Fresh ginger *(grated)*	⅓ tsp
Squeeze of lemon juice	

Method

Place all ingredients in a blender. Blend on high speed until smooth.

V DF GF

DRINKS

TURMERIC MANGO SMOOTHIE OR POPSICLES

5 mins | 2 glasses or 4 popsicles

I spent most of my high school years living in the tropical north of Australia, a magical part of the world where you could buy whole trays of mangoes and pineapples on the side of the road on the way home from school. I completely took this for granted at the time. When I first moved to Switzerland, I suddenly appreciated it. I still remember the first time I saw a mango here – it was in a high-end department store, displayed in a perfect pile of produce and costing as much as 3 full trays of mangoes had cost at home. That is why I started using mango puree as an alternative when cooking, as it stores longer, and you need less. But if you have access to fresh mangoes, by all means use them here! And enjoy them for me as well...

Ingredients

Milk *(I use oat or soy)*	1 cup
Dates, *pitted*	2
Mango puree*	75 ml
Turmeric spice mix	1 tsp
(See page 250, alternatively just add 1 tsp powdered turmeric)	
Frozen banana	1
(Make sure it's ripe before freezing)	
Ice cubes	2
Squeeze of lime or lemon juice	

*Note: choose a mango puree that does not have any added sugar and contains only pureed mango. Alternatively, you can make this yourself by blending up the flesh of a ripe mango.

Optional toppings for the popsicles

Dark chocolate, *melted*	50g
Coconut flakes	2 tbsp

Method

Place all ingredients in the blender. Blend on high speed until smooth. You can drink this as a smoothie or pour the mixture into popsicle moulds and freeze overnight. If doing the latter, dip the frozen popsicle in dark chocolate and sprinkle with coconut flakes, returning to the freezer for a few minutes to refreeze before serving.

GREEN ELIXIR

5 mins | 4 small glasses

You just need to take one look at this drink to know it is going to be good for you. But it is tastier than it looks, I promise! I like to make up a batch of it and keep it in the fridge for a couple of days, pouring a glass each morning for a refreshing start to the day. The vibrant colour is thanks to spirulina, which is actually the powdered biomass of a blue-green microalga. It has impressive nutritional properties, being high in protein (up to 70%), essential fatty acids, vitamins, minerals and pigments like chlorophyll. For generations, the women of the Kanembu tribe in Chad have been harvesting wild spirulina, drying it and cooking it into a sauce that they eat each day. It was here that French explorers discovered this alga, researching it further before starting to produce it commercially in the 70s. The interest in microalgae continues today. The United Nations promotes spirulina in development projects. Researchers have created a bioreactor that allows chlorella to grow while filtering carbon dioxide from the air and releasing oxygen. This was recently installed in the International Space Station to provide food for long space missions, and one day, maybe even life on Mars. In the meantime, us earthlings can also expect to see more algae-based food products on the shelves soon. As it requires no arable land to produce, generates high yields and can be grown where it is consumed, it is an exciting food of the future.

Ingredients

Apple *(cored and roughly chopped)*	1
Cucumber *(about half lebanese cucumber)*	½ cup
Spinach, *washed*	handful
Fresh ginger, *peeled and chopped*	3cm
Lemon juice	2 tsp
Apple cider vinegar	2 tsp
Water	½ cup
Spirulina powder	2 tsp

Method

Place all ingredients in a blender. Blend until combined. Drink immediately or put in a glass jar in the fridge and enjoy a glass each morning.

V | DF | GF

APFELSHORLE

⏱ 2 mins | ✋ 1 glass

My Swiss and German friends will be seriously questioning why this is in a recipe book. It is a drink you can find anywhere in this part of the world. But I don't see it in many other places and think that is a massive pity. It is the most delicious, simple and refreshing drink and makes a great substitute for soda, and even, I'm going to be bold here, beer. In Switzerland you can buy the most delicious apple juice I have ever tasted at farmers markets or direct from farms. In true Swiss fashion, you can even find it for sale in honesty boxes on the side of the road in the countryside. All the products just sit in there and people take what they want and pay into a little box. No one monitors it; it simply works on values of community and trust.

Ingredients

Apple juice ½ cup
Sparkling water ½ cup
Ice, mint leaves, lemon slices (optional)

Method

Combine apple juice and sparkling water. Add ice, mint and lemon if you want to make it fancier!

{V} {DF} {GF}

DRINKS

CHIA FRESCA

5 mins | 1 jug

This is a super simple and refreshing drink for a hot summer day.

Ingredients

Sparkling or still water	1L
Frozen blueberries	handful
(or other berries, cherries or pomegranate seeds)	
Chia seeds	2 tsp
Fresh mint leaves	handful
Squeeze of lemon juice	

Method

Combine all ingredients in a jug. Place in the fridge until ready to serve. You can keep refilling with water then when done you can eat the fattened berries!

V | DF | GF

DRINKS

PART TWO | *Drinks*

BLOOD ORANGE RASPBERRY AND BUCKWHEAT SMOOTHIE

Soak buckwheat overnight plus 5 mins prep | *2 glasses*

You may have noticed that I cook with buckwheat quite a lot. I like to use the flour for baking, the noodles for meals and the groats (the small whole seeds) in salads, soups and smoothies. I work with a scientist who has spent years researching buckwheat, so I asked him what he thinks people should know about this crop. He enthusiastically replied that he could talk for hours about buckwheat, but if he had to narrow it down, he would like you to know a few things. Firstly, buckwheat is gluten free, low GI and high in minerals and antioxidants, making it a nutritious choice. It is high in the amino acid lysine, which is often lacking in plant proteins, so it is a good choice for vegans and vegetarians. Thankfully, it is also easy to make something delicious with buckwheat – as an ancient crop it is linked to culinary traditions in many parts of the world – from galette in France to soba noodles in Japan. However, buckwheat has been a little neglected in recent decades, as it has lower yields compared to other crops and not much research has been done to change that. But that is starting to change, with more attention being given to how buckwheat can be grown as an intercrop (in rotation with other crops), thereby promoting soil health, suppressing weeds and bringing additional income to farmers. It can also improve biodiversity, not only by reviving an ancient crop but because bees looooove buckwheat. If you visit a field of buckwheat you will see it for yourself – a field full of happy little pollinators at work. It has a little bit of a special nutty taste that you may need to get used to, but many people then end up loving it. Just like the bees!

Ingredients

Blood orange, *peeled, seeds removed*	1
Frozen raspberries	1 cup
Juice of ½ lime	
Fresh ginger	2cm
Fresh basil	6 leaves
Buckwheat groats	¼ cup
Soaked in water in the fridge overnight, drained and rinsed before use	
Milk *(I use oat)*	½ cup
Splash maple syrup *(optional)*	

Method

Place all ingredients in a blender.
Blend until well combined.

{V} {DF} {GF}

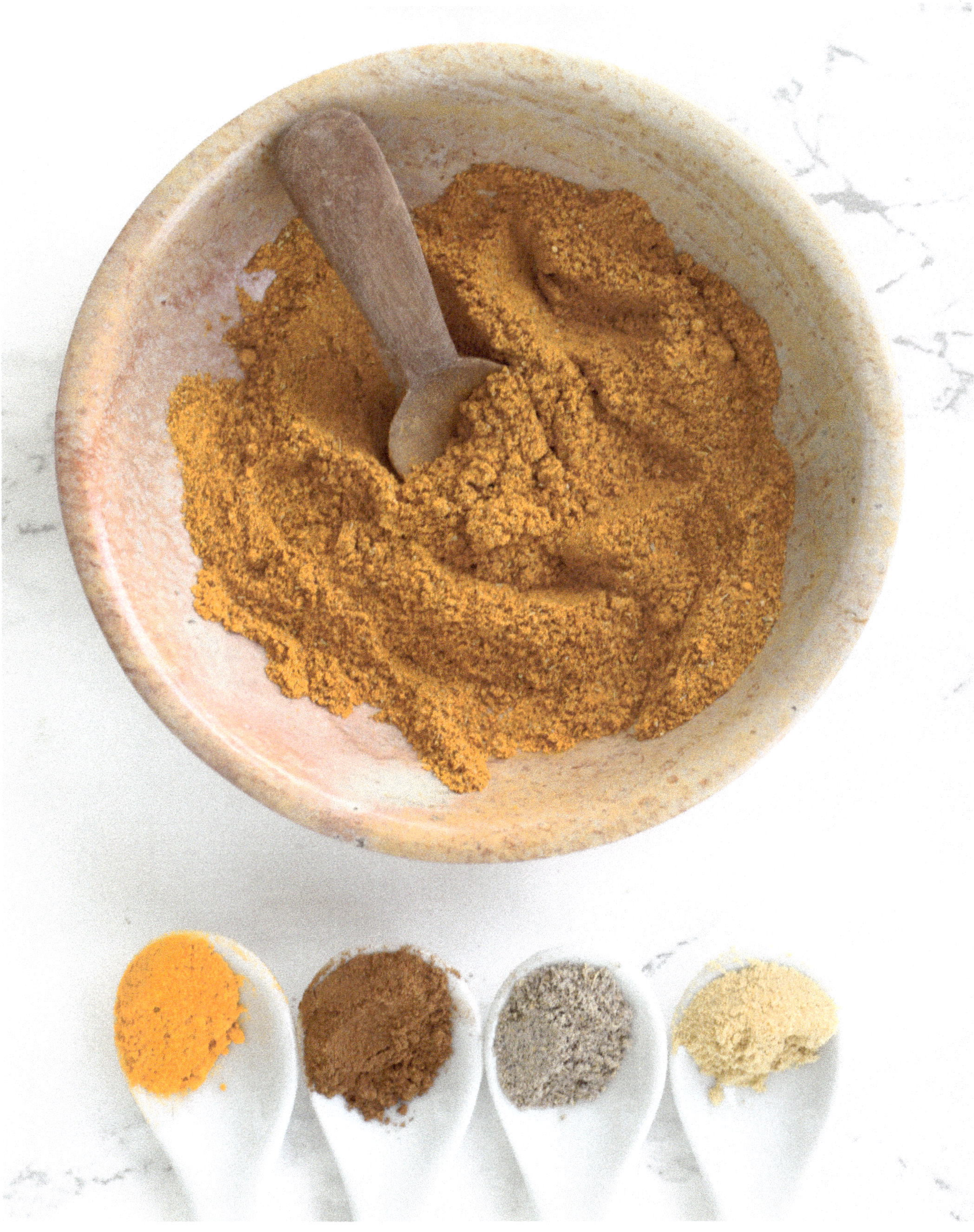

SAUCES + SPICES + TOPPINGS

Creamy Honey Mustard	246
Sesame Vinaigrette	246
Tahini Honey Lemon	247
Peanut Sesame Tamari	247
Garlic Dressing	247
Sundried Tomato Harissa Dip	248
Zaatar Hazelnut Dukkah	249
Turmeric Latte Spice Mix	250
Turmeric Latte	251

If you are looking to integrate more plant-based meals into your life, then the best thing you can do is learn a few simple sauces and dressings. They are the secret to making almost any meal appetizing and can transform an uninspiring plate of vegetables into a scrumptious meal. Here are some of my favourites.

5 mins | dresses 4 servings of salad

CREAMY HONEY MUSTARD

Ingredients

Olive oil	4 tbsp
Apple balsamic vinegar	2 tbsp
(or any other light coloured vinegar)	
Honey mustard	2 tbsp
(or use non-seeded mustard and add 1 tbsp honey)	
Soy or other non-dairy cream	4 tbsp
Squeeze of lemon juice	
Herb salt	1 tsp

Method

Place all ingredients in a jar, put the lid on and shake until combined.

{DF} {GF}

SESAME VINAIGRETTE

Ingredients

Sesame oil	¼ cup
Maple syrup	2 tbsp
Apple cider vinegar	3 tbsp
Lime juice	1 tbsp
Tamari	2 tbsp

Method

Place all ingredients in a jar, put the lid on and shake until combined.

{V} {DF} {GF}

PART TWO | *Sauces, Spices, Toppings*

TAHINI HONEY LEMON

Ingredients

Olive oil	6 tbsp
Tahini or almond butter	3 tbsp
Tamari	3 tbsp
Lemon juice or apple cider vinegar	3 tbsp
Honey	1 tbsp

Method

Place all ingredients in a jar, put the lid on and shake until combined.

(DF) (GF)

PEANUT SESAME TAMARI

Ingredients

Tamari	3 tbsp
Natural peanut butter or tahini	3 tbsp
Sesame oil	2 tbsp
Apple cider or rice vinegar	2 tbsp
Maple syrup or honey	1 tbsp

Method

Place all ingredients in a jar, put the lid on and shake until combined.

(V) (DF) (GF)

GARLIC DRESSING

Ingredients

Walnuts *(soaked overnight)*	⅓ cup
Small clove garlic *(crushed)*	1
Sunflower oil	3 tbsp
Apple cider vinegar	2 tbsp
Herb salt and peppe, *to taste*	

Method

Place all ingredients into a food processor and blitz to a smooth liquid.

(V) (DF) (GF)

The Great Full

SUNDRIED TOMATO HARISSA DIP

10 mins | approximately 1 cup

This is a great little dish that you can use as a topping on crackers or vegetable sticks, as a side for a serve of roasted vegetables or even as a pesto-like sauce for pasta.

Ingredients

Walnuts	½ cup
soaked in water at least 2 hrs or overnight	
Sundried tomatoes, *oil drained off*	100g
Apple cider vinegar	1 tbsp
Olive oil	2 tbsp
Tahini	2 tbsp
Harissa spice mix	1 ½ tsp
Dried thyme	1 tsp
Ground cumin	1 tsp
Oat milk	¾ cup
Squeeze of lemon juice	
Salt and pepper to taste	

Method

1. Place all ingredients in the food processor and process until quite smooth. It is a good idea to stop the processor periodically and scrape down the edges with a spatula to make sure everything is combined.

2. When finished remove from food processor. Serve immediately or place in a container in the fridge.

{V} {DF} {GF}

ZAATAR HAZELNUT DUKKAH

⏱ *5 mins* | ✋ *1/3 cup*

This dukkah is great as a salad topping or to simply dip some bread into. I usually make up a portion of it and have it in a jar in the cupboard to sprinkle on things as needed.

Ingredients

Hazelnuts	1/3 cup
Zaatar or sumac	1 tbsp
Sesame seeds	1 tbsp
Herb salt	1/2 tsp
Dried thyme	1 tsp

Method

Place all the ingredients in a mortar and pound with pestle until the nuts are coarsely crushed. Alternatively, you can use a food processor or spice grinder. Place dukkah in a glass jar and store in the cupboard until you need it.

V | DF | GF

TURMERIC LATTE SPICE MIX

🕐 5 mins | ✋ 5–6 turmeric lattes

Turmeric is the undisputed champion of spices. It has been used for centuries in Ayurvedic and Chinese medicine, has been the subject of thousands of research papers and is featured on every healthy food blog you will come across. And this is all for good reason! Turmeric has some amazing health promoting properties, like being anti-inflammatory. This turmeric spice mix will help you easily integrate some golden goodness into your diet. You can use it to make turmeric lattes or a whole range of other thing such as dressings, smoothies, dips or energy balls.

Ingredients

Ground turmeric	4 tsp
Ground cinnamon	2 tsp
Ground ginger	2 tsp
Ground cardamom	1 tsp
Ground nutmeg	½ tsp
Finely ground black pepper	6 pinches

Method

Mix all ingredients together. Store in a small glass jar or airtight container somewhere cool and dry.

Note: if you don't have all the spices don't worry, just add what you have. (Except the turmeric, that one you do need!) The black pepper is added because it helps your body take up the benefits of turmeric.

{V} {DF} {GF}

PART TWO | *Sauces, Spices, Toppings*

TURMERIC LATTE

5 mins | *serves 1 mug*

Ingredients

Turmeric spice mix	1 tsp
Milk *(I use oat or soy)*	1 cup
Maple syrup or honey to taste	

V | DF | GF

Method

1. Pour the milk into a stainless-steel saucepan. *(Note: turmeric will stain anything white or lightly coloured so best to use a metal pot.)* Add 1 teaspoon of the turmeric spice mix and gently whisk together with a metal whisk. Place on a medium heat until the mix starts to boil.

2. Reduce the heat and allow to simmer for at least 5 minutes, whisking intermittently. Just before it is ready, add maple syrup or honey to taste and whisk through. If you have a hand-held milk foamer, you can also use this at the end to create a nice foamy layer on top of the latte.

3. When ready remove from heat and pour into a mug.

The Great Full

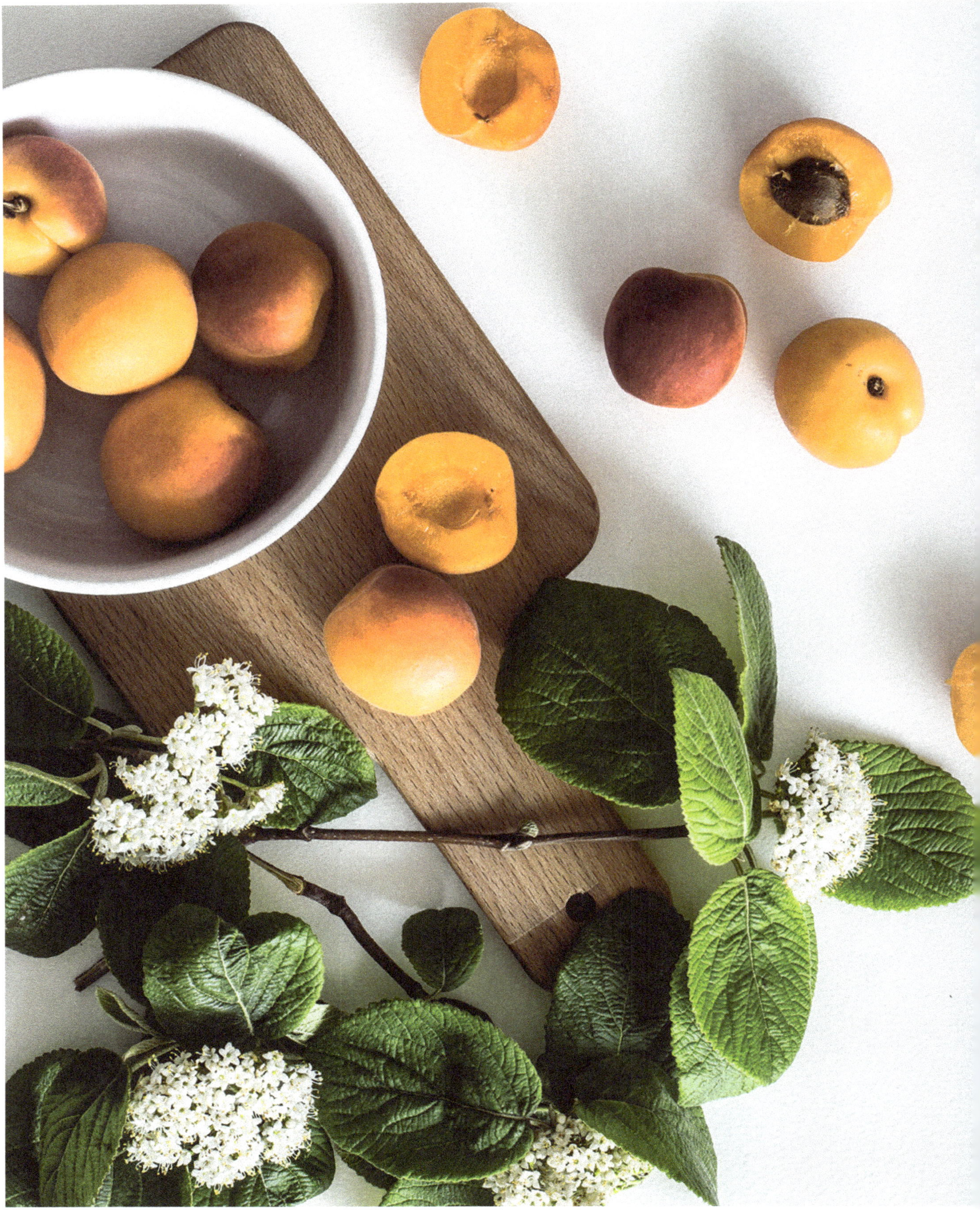

With Gratitude

No one can bring a book into the world on their own. It takes a long line of people offering their support in countless ways.

The first person who helped bring this book to life was the same person who gave me life. Mum, thanks for teaching me how to eat healthily no matter how tight the budget and for introducing me to the joy of good food. Your continual love and support mean so much to me. Pete, thanks for being there for me and echoing words of encouragement whenever needed.

A heartfelt thanks to my colleagues and faculty at the World Food System Centre at ETH Zurich. It was a pleasure to work on these topics with you over the years. Your disciplinary and personal perspectives give me the chance to constantly learn. A special thanks: to Aimee Shreck, who really broadened my thinking on food and social issues, always sending through compelling food for thought, connecting me with interesting networks and projects and always being willing to talk about the deeper, stickier issues; to Shana Sturla, for the interesting discussions and sharing her family recipe; to Jo Six, Adrian Müller and to the members of the Sustainable Food Processing Lab for discussing your research and fact checking text.

To all of the students from around the world I have had the pleasure to work with in the World Food System Summer School – thank you for the questions, bright ideas, concern about the world and motivation to be the change. It is always an inspiration to me.

To the wonderful Michelle, Ana, and all the Birdhaus ladies, thank you for creating a comfortable and inspiring space with likeminded women to write uninterrupted and supported. A special thanks to Janna, Virginie and CJ for fellow writer advice and encouragement. And the lovely Daga for her delicious and nourishing food and kindly sharing a couple of those recipes with me.

Thanks to mindset mastermind Erin Foley who helped me see the way forward in times of doubt.

Thanks to the lovely Palina for her photo editing genius and photography support.

To friends, family and readers who kindly tested recipes and supported me from the beginning of the blog – a huge thanks for your encouragement and feedback, it meant so much to me.

To the wonderful Katia Ariel, thank you for being exactly the editor this book needed. It was a pleasure to work with you.

To Kirsty, Clare and the wonderful ladies at Of Note Designs, thank you for your ability to make this book beautiful and bring it to life. I loved collaborating with you.

My final words go to my husband, Massimo. You bring a smile to my face every single day and it is a privilege to walk this life with you. There is nothing that brings me more joy than sharing a meal with you. Thank you for your boundless love and support.

Endnotes

1. BMI – Body Mass Index – is the primary measure of overweight or obesity. You can calculate your BMI by taking your weight in kilograms and dividing it by the square of your height in meters (kg/m2). Based on a number of epidemiological and observational studies, BMI was correlated with risk of mortality and morbidity and from this weight status classifications were linked to BMI ranges. BMI is, however, a rather crude measurement of body fatness. You can have a high BMI, perhaps due to high muscle and bone mass, and be perfectly healthy, or you can have a low BMI and suffer from chronic disease. Despite this, it remains the best measure that we can apply to a larger group of people without expensive or invasive tests in order to determine their risk of chronic disease. Using this as a measurement can have important implications. For example, in 1998 the US revised its classification of obesity by reducing the cut off BMI from 27 to 25. As a result, millions of Americans became classified as obese overnight without gaining any weight or changing in their lives or health. Some argue this is a part of medicalization of this epidemic, that it creates a market for the sale of associated medication. For more on this topic see the book Weighing In by Julie Guthman.

2. FAO, IFAD, UNICEF, WFP and WHO. 2018. The State of Food Security and Nutrition in the World 2018. Building climate resilience for food security and nutrition. Rome, FAO.

3. For simplicity, all figures were adjusted on the same proportion basis for a global population of 7 billion in order to make the illustration of the scale of the problem simpler. Actual figures: Global Population 7.6 billion (UN, 2017); Childhood Overweight and Obesity 38 million (State of Food Security and Nutrition in the World Report, 2018); Adult Overweight and Obesity 2.10 billion ((Global Nutrition Report, 2018); Undernourishment 821 million (State of Food Security and Nutrition in the World Report, 2018); Hidden Hunger >2billion (The global burden of chronic and hidden hunger: Trends and determinants, Global Food Security,Volume 17, 2018).

4. WHO (2015) Global Nutrition Targets 2025: Stunting Policy Brief. Retrieved: https://www.who.int/nutrition/topics/globaltargets_stunting_policybrief.pdf

5. Development Initiatives (2018). 2018 Global Nutrition Report: Shining a light to spur action on nutrition. Bristol, UK: Development Initiatives.

6. FAO, IFAD, UNICEF, WFP and WHO (2018) The State of Food Security and Nutrition in the World 2018. Building climate resilience for food security and nutrition. Rome, FAO. Retrieved: http://www.fao.org/3/I9553EN/i9553en.pdf

7. Black RE., Victora CG., Walker SP.,et al. (2013) Maternal and child undernutrition and overweight in low-income and middle-Income countries.Lancet. 2013; 6: 15-39

8. Cassidy, ES. West, PC., Gerber, JS., Foley, J. (2013) Redefining agricultural yields: from tonnes to people nourished per hectare. Environ. Res. Lett. 8 (2013) 034015 (8pp)

9. FAO (2019) Key facts on food loss and waste you should know! SAVE FOOD Global Initiative on Food Loss and Waste Reduction. Retrieved: http://www.fao.org/save-food/resources/keyfindings/en/

10. Food Security Information Network. (2018) Global Report on Food Crisis 2018. Retrieved: https://www1.wfp.org/publications/global-report-food-crises-2018

11. World Food Program (2018) World Food Programme Overview. Retrieved: https://www1.wfp.org/overview

12. The Economist (2014) Giving Generously. The Economist. Retrieved: https://www.economist.com/free-exchange/2014/03/03/giving-generously

13. Meds and Foods for Kids (2019) The Problem. Retrieved: https://mfkhaiti.org/the-problem/

14. Meds and Foods for Kids (2019) The Solution. Retrieved: https://mfkhaiti.org/the-solution/

15. Pingali PL. (2012) Green revolution: impacts, limits and the path ahead. Proceedings of the National Academy of Sciences of the United States of America, 109(31), 12302-12308. Retrieved: https://www.ncbi.nlm.nih.gov/pmc/articles/PMC3411969/

16. International Food Policy Research Institute. (2014) Global Hunger Index Chapter 3 Addressing the Challenge of Hidden Hunger. Retrieved: https://www.ifpri.org/sites/default/files/ghi/2014/feature_1818.html

17. Pingali PL. (2012) Green revolution: impacts, limits and the path ahead. Proceedings of the National Academy of Sciences of the United States of America, 109(31), 12302-12308. Retrieved: https://www.ncbi.nlm.nih.gov/pmc/articles/PMC3411969/

18. International Food Policy Research Institute. (2016) Hidden hunger: approaches to tackling micronutrient deficiencies. Retrieved: http://www.ifpri.org/publication/hidden-hunger-approaches-tackling-micronutrient-deficiencies

19. Welt Hunger Hilfe, International Food Policy Research Institute, Concern Worldwide. (2014) Global Hunger Index: The Challenge of Hidden Hunger. Retrieved: https://www.ifpri.org/sites/default/files/ghi/2014/feature_1818.html

20. Mensink G.B.M. et al. (2013) Mapping low intake of micronutrients across Europe. British Journal of Nutrition, October 2013

21. Ceylon Tobacco Company (2014) Sustainability. Retrieved: http://www.ceylontobaccocompany.com/group/sites/SRL_9PMJN9.nsf/vwPagesWebLive/DO9PMKL5

22. Thamilini, J., Wekumbura, C., Mohotti, J., Kumara, A., Kudagammana, T., Silva, R., Frossard, E. (2019) Organized homegardens contribute to micronutrient intakes and dietary diversity of rural households in Sri Lanka. Submitted to Frontiers in Plant Sciences (in revision)

23. UK Government. (2007) Tackling obesities: future choices. Retrieved: https://www.gov.uk/government/collections/tackling-obesities-future-choices

24. American Psychological Association (2019) Mind Body Health: Obesity. Retrieved: https://www.apa.org/helpcenter/obesity

25. Gafoor R., Booth H. P., Gulliford M. C. (2018) Antidepressant utilisation and incidence of weight gain during 10 years' follow-up: population based cohort study BMJ 2018; 361 :k1951. Retrieved: https://www.bmj.com/content/361/bmj.k1951

26. Time (2018) People around the world experienced record levels of stress and pain in 2017 study says. Retrieved: https://time.com/5393646/2017-gallup-global-emotions/

27. Daubenmier, J., Kristeller, J., Hecht, F., et. al. (2011) Mindfulness intervention for stress eating to reduce cortisol and abdominal fat among overweight and obese women. An exploratory randomized controlled study. Journal of Obesity, Volume 2011, Article ID 651936, 13 pages.

28. Hu F. B. (2013). Resolved: there is sufficient scientific evidence that decreasing sugar-sweetened beverage consumption will reduce the prevalence of obesity and obesity-related diseases. Obesity reviews : an official journal of the International Association for the Study of Obesity, 14(8), 606–619. doi:10.1111/obr.12040

29. Falbe, J., Thompson, H. R., Becker, C. M., Rojas, N., McCulloch, C. E., and Madsen, K. A. (2016). Impact of the Berkeley Excise Tax on Sugar-Sweetened Beverage Consumption. American journal of public health, 106(10), 1865–1871. doi:10.2105/AJPH.2016.303362

30. Roache, S. A., and Gostin, L. O. (2017). The Untapped Power of Soda Taxes: Incentivizing Consumers, Generating Revenue, and Altering Corporate Behavior. International journal of health policy and management, 6(9), 489–493. doi:10.15171/ijhpm.2017.69

31. Nakhimovsky, S. S., Feigl, A. B., Avila, C., O'Sullivan, G., Macgregor-Skinner, E., and Spranca, M. (2016). Taxes on Sugar-Sweetened Beverages to Reduce Overweight and Obesity in Middle-Income Countries: A Systematic Review. PLoS one, 11(9), e0163358. doi:10.1371/journal.pone.0163358

32. Guthman, J. (2011). Weighing in: Obesity, food justice, and the limits of capitalism. Berkeley: University of California Press.

33. Romieu, I., Dossus, L., Barquera, S., Blottière, H. M., Franks, P. W., Gunter, M., Hwalla, N., Hursting, S. D., Leitzmann, M., Margetts, B., Nishida, C., Potischman, N., Seidell, J., Stepien, M., Wang, Y., Westerterp,

K., Winichagoon, P., Wiseman, M., Willett, W. C., IARC working group on Energy Balance and Obesity (2017). Energy balance and obesity: what are the main drivers? Cancer causes and control : CCC, 28(3), 247-258. Accessed: https://www.ncbi.nlm.nih.gov/pmc/articles/PMC5325830/

34. Le Magueresse-Battistoni, B., Labaronne, E., Vidal, H., and Naville, D. (2017). Endocrine disrupting chemicals in mixture and obesity, diabetes and related metabolic disorders. World journal of biological chemistry, 8(2), 108–119. doi:10.4331/wjbc.v8.i2.108

35. Davis C. D. (2016). The Gut Microbiome and Its Role in Obesity. Nutrition today, 51(4), 167–174.

36. World Health Organization (2019) Global Health Observatory Data. Overweight and Obesity. Retrieved: https://www.who.int/gho/ncd/risk_factors/overweight/en/

37. NPR (2019) How Doctors Can Stop Stigmatizing — And Start Helping — Kids With Obesity. Retrieved: https://www.npr.org/sections/health-shots/2019/06/05/728812078/how-doctors-can-stop-stigmatizing-and-start-helping-kids-with-obesity?t=1560171149711andt=1561128157628

38. Tommy Tomlinson (2019) The weight I carry. What it is like to be too big in America. The Atlantic. Retrieved: https://www.theatlantic.com/health/archive/2019/01/weight-loss-essay-tomlinson/579832/. Permission to republish granted by the author via email correspondence.

39. The Lancet. (2019). Globally, one in five deaths are associated with poor diet. ScienceDaily. Retrieved: www.sciencedaily.com/releases/2019/04/190403193702.htm

40. ibid.

41. International Labour Organization (2019) Agriculture, plantations and other rural sectors. Retrieved:https://www.ilo.org/global/industries-and-sectors/agriculture-plantations-other-rural-sectors/lang--en/index.htm

42. World Bank (2019) Employment in Agriculture. Retrieved: https://data.worldbank.org/indicator/SL.AGR.EMPL.ZS?end=2018andstart=2008

43. International Labour Organization (2019) Agriculture, plantations and other rural sectors. Retrieved:https://www.ilo.org/global/industries-and-sectors/agriculture-plantations-other-rural-sectors/lang--en/index.htm

44. International Labor Organization (2019) Agriculture: hazardous work. Retrieved: https://www.ilo.org/safework/areasofwork/hazardous-work/WCMS_110188/lang--en/index.htm

45. UNHCR (2018) Agricultural workers are among the world's hungriest. Retrieved: https://www.ohchr.org/en/NewsEvents/Pages/DisplayNews.aspx?NewsID=23754andLangID=E

46. International Labor Organization (2019) Agriculture: hazardous work. Retrieved: https://www.ilo.org/safework/areasofwork/hazardous-work/WCMS_110188/lang--en/index.htm

47. International Labor Organization (2019) Agriculture: hazardous work. Retrieved: https://www.ilo.org/safework/areasofwork/hazardous-work/WCMS_110188/lang--en/index.htm

48. Belluz, J. (2019) The disturbing hypothesis for the sudden uptick in chronic kidney disease. Vox – Future Perfect. Retrieved: https://www.vox.com/future-perfect/2019/2/15/18213988/chronic-kidney-disease-climate-change

49. Roelofs, C., and Wegman, D. (2014). Workers: the climate canaries. American journal of public health, 104(10), 1799–1801. doi:10.2105/AJPH.2014.302145. Retrieved: https://www.ncbi.nlm.nih.gov/pmc/articles/PMC4167120/

50. Belluz, J. (2019) The disturbing hypothesis for the sudden uptick in chronic kidney disease. Vox – Future Perfect. Retrieved: https://www.vox.com/future-perfect/2019/2/15/18213988/chronic-kidney-disease-climate-change

51. Alianza Nacional de Campesinas (2017)700,000 Female Farmworkers Say They Stand With Hollywood Actors Against Sexual Assault. TIME Magazine. Retrieved: http://time.com/5018813/farmworkers-solidarity-hollywood-sexual-assault/

52. Tondo, L., Kelly, A. (2018) Sicilian police charge 5 men over trafficking of women in Ragusa. The Guardian. Retrieved: https://www.theguardian.com/global-development/2018/jun/07/sicilian-police-charge-five-men-over-trafficking-of-women-in-ragusa

53. Global Slavery Index. (2018) Country Case Studies: Italy. Retrieved: https://www.globalslaveryindex.org/2018/findings/country-studies/italy/

54. Food Chain Workers Alliance and Solidarity Research Cooperative (2016) No Piece of the Pie: US Food Workers in 2016. Los Angeles. Food Chain Workers Alliance. Retrieved: http://foodchainworkers.org/wp-content/uploads/2011/05/FCWA_NoPieceOfThePie_P.pdf

55. Dearing, P., (2016) The Fair Food Program. The Bridgespan Group. Retrieved: https://www.bridgespan.org/fair-food-program

56. Burkhalter, H., (2012) Fair Food Program helps end the use of slavery in the tomato fields. Washington Post. Opinions. Retrieved: https://www.washingtonpost.com/opinions/fair-food-program-helps-end-the-use-of-slavery-in-the-tomato-fields/2012

57. Marshall, A., (2011) From Vietnam's Forced-Labor Camps: 'Blood Cashews'. TIME. Retrieved: http://content.time.com/time/world/article/0,8599,2092004,00.html

58. ProFound (2014) Trade structure and channels for cashew nut kernels. CBI Dutch Ministry of Foreign Affairs. Retrieved: www.cbi.eu

59. Evans, R., Mariwah, S., Antwi, K.(2014) 'Cashew Cultivation, Access to Land and Food Security in BrongAhafo Region, Ghana: Preventing the intergenerational transmission of poverty', Research Note 6, Walker Institute for Climate System Research, University of Reading, July 2014, Retrieved: www.walkerinstitute.ac.uk/publications/research_notes/WalkerInResNote6.pdf

60. Interviews conducted with Mirjam Traoré-Arnold, Responsible for Agriculture and Certification Development, gebana Burkina Faso and Tom Von Euw, CEO Pakka Switzerland.

61. Willett, W., Rockström, J., Loken, B., et al. (2019) Food in the Anthropocene: the EAT–Lancet Commission on healthy diets from sustainable food systems. Lancet; 393: 447-492

62. Liu, R., Hooker, N. Parasidis, E., Simons, C. (2017) A Natural Experiment: Using Immersive Technologies to Study the Impact of "All Natural" Labeling on Perceived Food Quality, Nutritional Content, and Liking. Journal of Food Science 82:3

63. Standage, T. (2009). An Edible History of Humanity. Atlantic Books, London.

64. Willett, W., Rockström, J., Loken, B., et al. (2019) Food in the Anthropocene: the EAT–Lancet Commission on healthy diets from sustainable food systems. Lancet; 393: 447-492

65. Pingali PL. (2012) Green revolution: impacts, limits and the path ahead. Proceedings of the National Academy of Sciences of the United States of America, 109(31), 12302-12308. Retrieved: https://www.ncbi.nlm.nih.gov/pmc/articles/PMC3411969/

66. ibid.

67. Intergovernmental Science-Policy Platform on Biodiversity and Ecosystem Services (IPBES) (2019) Nature's Dangerous Decline 'Unprecedented' Species Extinction Rates 'Accelerating'. IPBES Media Released. Retrieved: https://www.ipbes.net/news/Media-Release-Global-Assessment

68. Sanchez-Bayo, F., Wyckhuys, K. (2019) Worldwide decline of the entomofauna: A review of its drivers. Biological Conservation, Vol. 232 pp 8-27. Retrieved: https://www.sciencedirect.com/science/article/pii/S0006320718313636

69. Jankielsohn, Astrid. (2018). The Importance of Insects in Agricultural Ecosystems. Advances in Entomology. 06. 62-73.

70. Sanchez-Bayo, F., Wyckhuys, K. (2019) Worldwide decline of the entomofauna: A review of its drivers. Biological Conservation, Vol. 232 pp 8-27. Retrieved: https://www.sciencedirect.com/science/article/pii/S0006320718313636

71. FAO (2001) What is happening to agrobiodiversity? Retrieved: http://www.fao.org/3/y5609e/y5609e02.htm

72. FAO (2019) Biodiversity reveals the treasures all around us. FAO. Retrieved http://www.fao.org/fao-stories/article/en/c/1133432/

73. Pimentel, D., Harvey, C., Resosudarmo, P., et. al. (1995) Environmental and economic costs of soil erosion and conservation benefits. Science, 267: 5201. Pp. 1117-1123. Retrieved: https://science.sciencemag.org/content/267/5201/1117

74. FAO (2015) Soils are degraded but the degradation can be rolled back. FAO News Article. Retrieved: http://www.fao.org/news/story/en/item/357059/icode/

75. Nkonya, E., Gerber, N., Baumgartner, P., et. al. (2011) The Economics of Desertification, Land Degradation, and Drought Toward an Integrated Global Assessment. ZEF Discussion Papers on Development Policy No. 150. Retrieved: https://ssrn.com/abstract=1890668

76. Mason, P., Lang, T. (2017) Sustainable Diets. Routledge

77. FAO (2015) Healthy soils for healthy life. FAO. Retrieved: http://www.fao.org/soils-2015/en/

78. Wild, B., Lieberherr, E., Okem, A., Six, J. (2019) Nitrified human urine as a sustainable and socially acceptable fertilizer: An analysis of consumer acceptance in Msunduzi, South Africa, Sustainability 11(9), 2456 https://doi.org/10.3390/su11092456

79. Vermeulen, SJ, Campbell, BM., Ingram JSI., (2012) Climate Change and Food Systems. Annual Review of Environment and Resources 2012 37:1, 195-222. Retrieved: https://www.annualreviews.org/doi/full/10.1146/annurev-environ-020411-130608

80. ibid.

81. Food Climate Research Network (2017) Food systems and greenhouse gas emissions. FoodSource. University of Oxford Environmental Change Institute. Retrieved: https://foodsource.org.uk/chapters/3-food-systems-greenhouse-gas-emissions

82. OECD (2019) Managing water sustainably is key to the future of food and agriculture. Retrieved: https://www.oecd.org/agriculture/topics/water-and-agriculture/

83. The Water Footprint Calculator. (2018) The Water Footprint of Beef: Industrial vs. Pasture Raised. Retrieved: https://www.watercalculator.org/water-use/water-footprint-beef-industrial-pasture/

84. Hoekstra, A. (2017) Water footprint of food – Product Gallery. Retrieved: https://waterfootprint.org/en/resources/interactive-tools/product-gallery/

85. World Resources Institute (2013) One quarter of the worlds food is grown in water scarce areas. Retrieved: https://www.wri.org/blog/2013/10/one-quarter-world-s-agriculture-grows-highly-water-stressed-areas

86. International Panel of Experts on Sustainable Food Systems (IPES Food) (2018) Breaking away from industrial food and farming systems – Seven case studies in agroecological transformations. Retrieved: http://www.ipes-food.org/_img/upload/files/CS2_web.pdf

87. FAO (2011) Global food losses and food waste – Extent, causes and prevention. Rome. Retrieved: http://www.fao.org/3/a-i2697e.pdf

88. UN (2013) UN report: one-third of world's food wasted annually, at great economic, environmental cost. UN News. Retrieved: https://news.un.org/en/story/2013/09/448652#.UjHwAdKwlAK

89. ibid.

90. Kyama, R. (2018) For tanzanian farmers, grain harvest is in the bag. VOA Africa. Retrieved: https://www.voanews.com/africa/tanzanian-farmers-grain-harvest-bag

91. World Economic Forum (2019) Which countries spend the least on food? Retrieved: https://www.weforum.org/agenda/2016/12/this-map-shows-how-much-each-country-spends-on-food/

92. FAO (2013) Toolkit: Reducing the Food Wastage Footprint. FAO, Rome. Retrieved: http://www.fao.org/3/i3342e/i3342e.pdf

93. Food Bank (2019) Hunger in Australia: The Facts. Retrieved: https://www.foodbank.org.au/hunger-in-australia/the-facts/

94. Food Wise (2019) Reduce Food Waste: Fast Facts on Food Waste. Retrieved: https://www.foodwise.com.au/foodwaste/food-waste-fast-facts/

95. Khoury, C. et al., (2014) Increasing homogeneity in global food supplies and implications for food security. Proceedings of the National Academy of Sciences Mar 2014, 111 (11) 4001-4006

96. National Geographic (2014), Evolution of Diet. National Geographic Magazine September 2014, Retrieved: https://www.nationalgeographic.com/foodfeatures/evolution-of-diet/

97. FAO (2019) Biodiversity reveals the treasures all around us. FAO. Retrieved http://www.fao.org/fao-stories/article/en/c/1133432/

98. Bioversity International (2014), Bioversity International's 10 Year Strategy, Bioversity International, Rome, ISBN: 978-92-9043-992-9

99. University of British Columbia. (2019). Natural biodiversity protects rural farmers' incomes from tropical weather shocks. ScienceDaily. Retrieved: www.sciencedaily.com/releases/2019/06/190627121246.htm

100. National Research Council of the National Academies (2006) Lost crops of Africa Volume II Vegetables. Retrieved: https://www.nap.edu/read/11763/chapter/1#ii

101. Mitchell, R., Becker, J. (2019) Bush food industry booms but only 1% is produced by Indigenous people. ABC Rural. Retrieved: https://www.abc.net.au/news/rural/2019-01-19/low-indigenous-representation-in-bush-food-industry/10701986

102. Alkon, AH., Guthman, J. (2017) The new food activism. Opposition, cooperation and collective action. University of California Press.

103. WFP (2019) Women and Hunger: 10 Facts. Retrieved: https://www.wfp.org/our-work/preventing-hunger/focus-women/women-hunger-facts

104. Roth, G. (2011) Women Food and God: An Unexpected Path to Almost Everything. Scribner

105. Eufic (2006) The Factors That Influence Our Food Choices. Retrieved: https://www.eufic.org/en/healthy-living/article/the-determinants-of-food-choice

106. Kessler, D. (2010) The End of Overeating: Taking Control of the Insatiable American Appetite. Rodale Books.

107. de Macedo, I. C., de Freitas, J. S., and da Silva Torres, I. L. (2016). The Influence of Palatable Diets in Reward System Activation: A Mini Review. Advances in pharmacological sciences, 2016, 7238679. doi:10.1155/2016/7238679

108. Lenoir, M., Serre, F., Cantin, L., Ahmed, H. (2007) Intense Sweetness Surpasses Cocaine reward. PLoS One, 2(8): e698

109. WHO (2016) Tackling food marketing to children in a digital world: trans-disciplinary perspectives. WHO Regional Office for Europe, Denmark.

110. Willett, W., Rockström, J., Loken, B., et al. (2019) Food in the Anthropocene: the EAT–Lancet Commission on healthy diets from sustainable food systems. Lancet; 393: 447-492

111. Willett, W., Rockström, J., Loken, B., et al. (2019) Food in the Anthropocene: the EAT–Lancet Commission on healthy diets from sustainable food systems. Lancet; 393: 447-492

112. Storz M. A. (2019). Is There a Lack of Support for Whole-Food, Plant-Based Diets in the Medical Community? The Permanente journal, 23, 18–068. doi:10.7812/TPP/18-068

113. Jacka, F. N., Cherbuin, N., Anstey, K. J., Sachdev, P., and Butterworth, P. (2015). Western diet is associated with a smaller hippocampus: a longitudinal investigation. BMC medicine, 13, 215. Retrieved: https://www.ncbi.nlm.nih.gov/pmc/articles/PMC4563885/

114. American Dietetics Association (2013) Position of the American Dietetic Association: Vegetarian Diets. Retrieved: https://www.vrg.org/nutrition/2009_ADA_position_paper.pdf

115. Watanabe, F., Yabuta, Y., Bito, T., and Teng, F. (2014). Vitamin B_{12}-containing plant food sources for vegetarians. Nutrients, 6(5), 1861–1873.

116. Tuso, P., Stoll, S. R., and Li, W. W. (2015). A plant-based diet, atherogenesis, and coronary artery disease prevention. The Permanente journal, 19(1), 62–67. Retrieved: https://www.ncbi.nlm.nih.gov/pmc/articles/PMC4315380

117. Burlingame, B., Dernini, S. (Eds.) (2010) Sustainable diets and biodiversity – directions and solutions for policy, research and action. UN FAO, Rome. Retrieved: http://www.fao.org/3/a-i3004e.pdf

118. Barilla Center for Food and Nutrition (2016) Double Pyramid 2016: A more sustainable future depends on us. Retrieved: https://www.barillacfn.com/m/publications/doublepyramid2016-more-sustainable-future-depends-on-us.pdf

119. Macdiarmid, J. (2014). Seasonality and dietary requirements: Will eating seasonal food contribute to health and environmental sustainability? Proceedings of the Nutrition Society, 73(3), 368-375. doi:10.1017/S0029665113003753

120. ibid.

121. Poore, J., Nemecek, T. (2018) Reducing food's environmental impacts through producers and consumers. Science Vol. 360 Issue 6392 pp. 987-992

122. World Health Organization (2015) QandA on the carcinogenicity of the consumption of red meat and processed meat. Retrieved: https://www.who.int/features/qa/cancer-red-meat/en/

123. O'Mara, F. P. (2012) The role of grasslands in food security and climate change. Annals of Botany, 110: 1263-1270

124. Personal correspondence with Dr Adrian Müller, Senior Researcher, ETH Zurich and Research Institute for Organic Agriculture.

125. UN FAO (2011) Major gains in efficiency of livestock systems needed. Rome. Retrieved: http://www.fao.org/news/story/en/item/116937/icode/

126. Guibourg, C., Briggs, H. (2019) Climate change: which vegan milk is best? BBC News. Retrieved: https://www.bbc.com/news/science-environment-46654042

127. Carman, T. (2019) Burger King is rolling out a meatless Whopper. Can McDonalds be far away? Washington Post. Retrieved: https://www.washingtonpost.com/news/voraciously/wp/2019/04/01/burger-king-is-rolling-out-a-meatless-whopper-can-mcdonalds-be-far-behind/?utm_term=.7cc4fe7f1edb

128. An, R. (2016) Fast-food and full-service restaurant consumption and daily energy and nutrient intake in US adults. European Journal of Clinical Nutrition 70, 97-103. Retrieved: https://www.nature.com/articles/ejcn2015104

129. Science Daily (2018) Adolescents' cooking skills strongly predict future nutritional well-being. Science News. Retrieved: https://www.sciencedaily.com/releases/2018/04/180417181125.htm

130. Wilson, B. (2019) The Lunchbox Renaissance. Wall Street Journal. Retrieved: https://www.wsj.com/articles/the-lunchbox-renaissance-11548348864

131. Hever J. (2016). Plant-Based Diets: A Physician's Guide. The Permanente Journal, 20(3), 15–082. doi:10.7812/TPP/15-082

132. Pohjolainen, P., Vinnari, M., Jokinen, P. (2015) Consumers perceived barriers to following a plant-based diet. British Food Journal Vol. 117 No. 3, pp. 1150-1167

Figure Endnotes

i. FAO (2018) Agroecology Knowledge Hub. Retrieved: http://www.fao.org/agroecology/en/

ii. Hanson, C. (2016) From why to how: reducing food losses and waste. World Resources Institute. Retrieved: http://ec.europa.eu/newsroom/horizon2020/document.cfm?action=displayanddoc_id=13622

iii. Food Climate Research Network (2019) What are the influences on our food choices? FoodSource. Retrieved: https://www.foodsource.org.uk/102-what-are-influences-our-food-choices

Index

A

almond(s). See also almond butter
    in chocolate cherry and coconut truffles, 193
    in lemon tarts, 221
    in make your own chocolate, 213
    in pineapple ginger carrot cake, 197
    in rooibos apricot and maple granola, 107
    in stracciatella overnight oats, 97
    in summer pea salad, 143
    in vitamin bites, 207
    in warm pumpkin spinach and quinoa salad, 165
almond butter
    honey lemon, 247
    in icing, for pineapple ginger carrot cake, 197
apple
    cinnamon compote, 110, 112, 113
    in green elixir, 238
    juice, in apfelshorle, 239
    in refreshing coconut lime and nut slaw, 145
    sauce, in spiced orange upside down cake, 217
    sauce, in vegan pancakes, 109
    in spiced harissa carrot and lentil soup, 159
    in sweet potato prune and hazelnut muffins, 203
apricot (dried)
    in aprichoc hazelnut blondies, 227
    rooibos and maple granola, 106, 106–7
    in vitamin bites, 207
aquafaba, in beetini brownies, 211
artichoke
    and easy green pesto pasta, 184, 185
    in Mediterranean rice salad, 139
aubergine
    in lasakopita, 175
    napoletana pasta, 166, 166–67
    in Sri Lankan jackfruit curry, 181
avocado
    in guacamole, 125, 169
    in mint mousse, 119

B

balsamic strawberry salad with roasted puffed grains, 140, 140–41
banana
    bread, date and chestnut, 194, 194–195
    in chai spiced breakfast smoothie, 101
    in go to green smoothie, 235
    in stracciatella overnight oats, 97
    in turmeric mango smoothie or popsicles, 237
bean(s)
    black, and rice, Dominican, 172, 172–73
    borlotti, in meditative minestrone, 153
    cannellini, in beetroot sweet potato and feta layered bake, 177
    cannellini, in creamy roast potato lemon and dill soup, 157
    edamame, in mint mousse, 119
    edamame, in tropical soba noodle salad, 137
    mix, for sweet potato burrito bowls, 169
    sprouts, in sweet potato noodle pad thai, 171
beetroot
    beetini brownies, 208, 209–11
    sweet potato and feta layered bake, 176, 176–77
bell pepper, in sofrito, 173
beluga lentils, in Mediterranean rice salad, 139
berry(ies). See also specific berries
    in blushing oatmeal, 105
    cherry crumble cake, 228, 229
    chia compote, 110, 111, 112
    millet and oat bake, 102, 103
black beans. See under bean(s)
black (beluga) lentils, in Mediterranean rice salad, 139
black rice noodles. See also brown rice noodle(s)
    in quick vegan ramen, 151
    in roasted tofu and greens noodle bowl, 183
blondies, aprichoc hazelnut, 226, 227
blood orange. See under orange
blueberries, in chia fresca, 241
blushing oatmeal, 105
bok choy, in quick vegan ramen, 151
borlotti beans, in meditative minestrone, 153
bowls
    roasted tofu and greens noodle, 182, 182–83
    sunshine Buddha, 188, 189
    sweet potato burrito, 168, 168–69
Brazil nuts
    in aprichoc hazelnut blondies, 227
    in beetini brownies, 211
bread, in recipes
    pita, for falafel and fries, 179
    shiitake truffle and mustard crostini, 123
bread, recipes for
    date and chestnut banana, 194, 194–195
    easy (and possibly Turkish), 120, 121
broccoli
    in green magic soup, 161
    in roasted tofu and greens noodle bowl, 183
broccoli rabe, in roasted tofu and greens noodle bowl, 183
brownies, beetini, 208, 209–11
brown rice. See also brown rice noodle(s)
    in Dominican black beans and rice, 173
    puffed, in chocolate nut rice crackles, 199
    puffed, in strawberry balsamic salad, 141
    salad, Mediterranean, 138, 139
    for Sri Lankan jackfruit curry, 181
brown rice noodle(s)

in quick vegan ramen, 151
in roasted tofu and greens noodle bowl, 183
salad, tropical, 137
in sunshine Buddha bowl, 189
in sweet potato noodle pad thai, 171
buckwheat. See also soba noodle(s)
    blood orange and raspberry smoothie, 242, 243
    flour, in vegan pancakes, 109
Buddha bowl, sunshine, 188, 189
burgers, mini millet, 126, 126–27
burrito bowls, sweet potato, 168, 168–69

C

cabbage, red
    in meditative minestrone, 153
    pickle, for sweet potato burrito bowls, 169
    in refreshing coconut lime and nut slaw, 145
    in summer pea salad, 143
    in tropical soba noodle salad, 137
    in warm winter salad, 147
cacao butter
    in make your own chocolate, 213
    in raspberry cherry rose chocolate kisses, 205
cacao nibs
    in make your own chocolate, 213
    in stracciatella overnight oats, 97
cacao powder
    in beetini brownies, 211
    in chocolate cherry and coconut truffles, 193
    in chocolate nut rice crackles, 199
    in chocolate orange and maple overnight oats, 99
    in make your own chocolate, 213
    and nut butter popsicles, 225
    in raspberry cherry rose chocolate kisses, 205
    in summer peach tart, 201
cake
    berry cherry crumble, 228, 229
    pineapple ginger carrot, 196, 196–97
    spiced orange upside down, 214, 215–17, 216
cannellini beans. See under bean(s)
capers
    in artichoke and easy green pesto pasta, 185
    in easy mac and sundried tomato sauce, 170
    in Mediterranean rice salad, 139
carrot
    cake oatmeal, 104, 105
    harissa and lentil soup, 158, 159
    in mini millet burgers, 127
    pineapple ginger cake, 196, 196–97
    in vitamin bites, 207
cashews, in tangy salad boats, 117
cauliflower
    with mint mousse and hazelnut sumac dukkah, 118, 118–19
    in Sri Lankan jackfruit curry, 181
    in sunshine Buddha bowl, 189
chai spiced breakfast smoothie, 100, 101

cherry
    berry crumble cake, 228, 229
    chocolate and coconut truffles, 192, 193
    raspberry rose chocolate kisses, 204, 204–205
chestnut and date banana bread, 194, 194–95
chia
    berry compote, 110, 111, 112
    in chocolate orange and maple overnight oats, 99
    in date and chestnut banana bread, 195
    fresca, 240, 241
    jam filling, for raspberry cherry rose chocolate kisses, 205
    in mixed berry millet and oat bake, 103
    orange compote, 110, 111, 112
    in stracciatella overnight oats, 97
chickpea(s). See also aquafaba, in beetini brownies
    in aprichoc hazelnut blondies, 227
    flour, in easy (and possibly Turkish) bread, 121
    flour, in mini millet burgers, 127
    in sunshine Buddha bowl, 189
    zucchini and pomegranate salad, 134, 134–35
chilli, red
    in pesto, 185
    in watermelon gazpacho, 149
chocolate. See also cacao butter; cacao nibs; cacao powder
    in aprichoc hazelnut blondies, 227
    in beetini brownies, 211
    cherry and coconut truffles, 192, 193
    indulgence tart, 218, 219
    make your own, 213
    nut rice crackles, 198, 199
    orange and maple overnight oats, 98, 99
    raspberry cherry rose kisses, 204, 204–5
    stuffed dates, 222, 223
chowder, warming vegetable and corn, 154, 154–55
cinnamon apple compote, 110, 112, 113
coconut
    in blushing oatmeal, 105
    in carrot cake oatmeal, 105
    chocolate and cherry truffles, 192, 193
    in chocolate indulgence tart, 219
    lime and nut slaw, 144, 145
    milk, in icing, for pineapple ginger carrot cake, 197
    milk, in lemon tarts, 221
    milk, in Sri Lankan jackfruit curry, 181
    in mixed berry millet and oat bake, 103
    in pineapple ginger carrot cake, 197
    in summer peach tart, 201
    in tangy salad boats, 117
    in vitamin bites, 207
    yoghurt, in Sri Lankan jackfruit curry, 181
compote
    apple cinnamon, 110, 112, 113
    berry chia, 110, 111, 112
    orange chia, 110, 111, 112
    rhubarb ginger, 110, 112, 113

corn
    in sauce, for mini millet burgers, 127
    and vegetable chowder, 154, 154–55
cranberries, dried, in make your own chocolate, 213
creamy beetroot sweet potato and feta layered bake, 176, 176–77
creamy honey mustard, 246
creamy roast potato lemon and dill soup, 156, 157
crostini, shiitake truffle and mustard, 122, 123
cucumber
    in green elixir, 238
    in tropical soba noodle salad, 137
    in watermelon gazpacho, 149
cumquats, in warm winter salad, 147
curry, Sri Lankan jackfruit, 180, 180–81

D
date(s)
    and chestnut banana bread, 194, 194–95
    in chocolate cherry and coconut truffles, 193
    chocolate stuffed, 222, 223
    in pineapple ginger carrot cake, 197
    in salted cacao and nut butter popsicles, 225
    in turmeric mango smoothie or popsicles, 237
    in vitamin bites, 207
dill potato and lemon soup, 156, 157
dip, sundried tomato harissa, 248
Dominican black beans and rice, 172, 172–73
dressing. See also salad; sauce
    for falafel and fries, 179
    garlic, 189, 247
    lemon mustard tahini, 143
    mustard, 139
    for roasted tofu and greens noodle bowl, 183
    sesame vinaigrette, 246
dukkah
    hazelnut sumac, and mint mousse, roasted cauliflower with, 118, 118–19
    zaatar hazelnut, 249

E
easy (and possibly Turkish) bread, 120, 121
easy green pesto and artichoke pasta, 184, 185
easy mac and sundried tomato sauce, 170
edamame beans. See under bean(s)

F
falafel and fries, 178, 178–79
fennel
    in refreshing coconut lime and nut slaw, 145
    in strawberry balsamic salad with roasted puffed grains, 141
    in warm winter salad, 147
feta
    beetroot and sweet potato layered bake, 176, 176–77
    in lasakopita, 175
    in roasted chickpea zucchini and pomegranate salad, 135
fries and falafel, 178, 178–79

G
garlic dressing, 189, 247
gazpacho, watermelon, 148, 149
ginger
    pineapple carrot cake, 196, 196–97
    rhubarb compote, 110, 112, 113
go to green smoothie, 234, 235
goats' cheese
    in roasted chickpea zucchini and pomegranate salad, 135
    in strawberry balsamic salad with roasted puffed grains, 141
goji berries, in make your own chocolate, 213
granola, rooibos apricot and maple, 106, 106–7
green elixir, 238
green magic soup, 160, 161
green peas
    in mint mousse, 119
    in summer pea salad, 143
greens and roasted tofu noodle bowl, 182, 182–83
green smoothie, go to, 234, 235
guacamole
    potato bites, 124, 125
    for sweet potato burrito bowls, 169

H
harissa
    carrot and lentil soup, 158, 159
    sundried tomato dip, 248
hazelnut
    aprichoc blondies, 226, 227
    in beetroot sweet potato and feta layered bake, 177
    in chocolate cherry and coconut truffles, 193
    in chocolate indulgence tart, 219
    in lemon tarts, 221
    in pineapple ginger carrot cake, 197
    in rooibos apricot and maple granola, 107
    in spiced orange upside down cake, 217
    in stracciatella overnight oats, 97
    sumac dukkah and mint mousse, roasted cauliflower with, 118, 118–19
    in summer peach tart, 201
    sweet potato and prune muffins, 202, 202–3
    in warm pumpkin spinach and quinoa salad, 165
    zaatar dukkah, 249
honey
    mustard, creamy, 246
    tahini lemon, 247

J
jackfruit curry, Sri Lankan, 180, 180–81

K
kale
    in green magic soup, 161
    in meditative minestrone, 153
    in Sri Lankan jackfruit curry, 181

in sunshine Buddha bowl, 189
in warm pumpkin spinach and quinoa salad, 165
in warm winter salad, 147
kisses, raspberry cherry rose chocolate, 204, 204–5
kohlrabi, in Sri Lankan jackfruit curry, 181

L
lasagne sheets, in lasakopita, 175
lasakopita, 174, 175
latte, turmeric, 251
lemon
    mint polo, Syrian, 232, 233
    mustard tahini dressing, for summer pea salad, 143
    potato and dill soup, 156, 157
    tahini honey, 247
    tarts, 220, 221
lemongrass
    in Sri Lankan jackfruit curry, 181
    in tangy salad boats, 117
lentil(s)
    black (beluga), in Mediterranean rice salad, 139
    red, harissa and carrot soup, 158, 159
lime
    coconut and nut slaw, 144, 145
    in guacamole, 125, 169
    in roasted tofu and greens noodle bowl, 183
    in Sri Lankan jackfruit curry, 181
    in tangy salad boats, 117

M
macadamia nuts
    in sweet potato noodle pad thai, 171
    in tropical soba noodle salad, 137
mac and sundried tomato sauce, 170
make your own chocolate – three ways, 212, 213
mango
    in tropical soba noodle salad, 137
    turmeric smoothie or popsicles, 236, 237
maple
    chocolate and orange overnight oats, 98, 99
    rooibos and apricot granola, 106, 106–7
meditative minestrone, 152, 152–53
Mediterranean rice salad, 138, 139
millet
    berry and oat bake, 102, 103
    burgers, mini, 126, 126–27
    in carrot cake oatmeal, 105
minestrone, meditative, 152, 152–53
mini millet burgers, 126, 126–27
mint
    lemon polo, Syrian, 232, 233
    mousse and hazelnut sumac dukkah, roasted cauliflower with, 118, 118–19
mixed berry millet and oat bake, 102, 103
mousse, mint, and hazelnut sumac dukkah, roasted cauliflower with, 118, 118–19
muffins, sweet potato prune and hazelnut, 202, 202–3
mung bean sprouts, in sweet potato noodle pad thai, 171
mushrooms
    in meditative minestrone, 153
    in quick vegan ramen, 151
    shiitake, truffle and mustard crostini, 123
mustard
    creamy honey, 246
    dressing, for Mediterranean rice salad, 139
    honey, 123
    lemon tahini dressing, for summer pea salad, 143
    shiitake and truffle crostini, 122, 123
    in Sri Lankan curry powder, 181

N
napoletana pasta, aubergine, 166, 166–67
noodle(s). See also pasta
    bowl, roasted tofu and greens, 182, 182–83
    quick vegan ramen, 150, 151
    salad, tropical soba, 136, 137
    in sunshine Buddha bowl, 189
    sweet potato pad thai, 171
    zucchini, in aubergine napoletana pasta, 167
nut. See also specific nuts; nut butter
    coconut and lime slaw, 144, 145
    rice crackles, chocolate, 198, 199
nut butter. See also almond butter; peanut butter
    and cacao popsicles, 224, 225
    in chocolate stuffed dates, 223

O
oat(s)
    in base for chocolate indulgence tart, 219
    in base for lemon tarts, 221
    in base for summer peach tart, 201
    in blushing oatmeal, 105
    in chai spiced breakfast smoothie, 101
    in carrot cake oatmeal, 105
    chocolate orange and maple overnight, 98, 99
    mixed berry and millet bake, 102, 103
    in rooibos apricot and maple granola, 107
    stracciatella overnight, 96, 97
olives
    Kalamata, in Mediterranean rice salad, 139
    Spanish, in sofrito, 173
orange
    blood, in chocolate indulgence tart, 219
    blood, raspberry and buckwheat smoothie, 242, 243
    blood, upside down cake, 214, 215–17, 216
    chia compote, 110, 111, 112
    chocolate and maple overnight oats, 98, 99
    in warm winter salad, 147

P

pad thai, sweet potato noodle, 171
pancakes, vegan, 108, 109
parmesan
    in artichoke and easy green pesto pasta, 185
    in meditative minestrone, 153
    in warming vegetable and corn chowder, 155
pasta. See also noodle(s)
    artichoke and easy green pesto, 184, 185
    aubergine napoletana, 166, 166–67
    easy mac and sundried tomato sauce, 170
    lasakopita, 174, 175
    in meditative minestrone, 153
peach tart, 200, 200–201
peanut(s). See also peanut butter
    in quick vegan ramen, 151
    in refreshing coconut lime and nut slaw, 145
    in roasted tofu and greens noodle bowl, 183
    in sweet potato noodle pad thai, 171
    in tangy salad boats, 117
peanut butter. See also peanut(s)
    in chocolate nut rice crackles, 199
    in chocolate stuffed dates, 223
    in dressing, for refreshing coconut lime and nut slaw, 145
    in dressing, for roasted tofu and greens noodle bowl, 183
    and salted cacao popsicles, 225
    in sauce, for tangy salad boats, 117
    sesame tamari, 247
    in sweet potato noodle pad thai, 171
pear, in chai spiced breakfast smoothie, 101
peas. See green peas; snow peas, in tropical soba noodle salad
pecans
    in beetini brownies, 211
    in chai spiced breakfast smoothie, 101
    in rooibos apricot and maple granola, 107
    in strawberry balsamic salad with roasted puffed grains, 141
    in sweet potato prune and hazelnut muffins, 203
    in warm winter salad, 147
pecorino, in artichoke and easy green pesto pasta, 185
pesto
    and artichoke pasta, 184, 185
    red, in lasakopita, 175
pickle, red cabbage, for sweet potato burrito bowls, 169
pineapple ginger carrot cake, 196, 196–97
pistachios, in Syrian lemon mint polo, 233
pita, falafel, 179
polo, Syrian lemon mint, 232, 233
pomegranate chickpea and zucchini salad, 134, 134–35
popsicles
    salted cacao and nut butter, 224, 225
    turmeric mango, 236, 237
potato(es)
    in green magic soup, 161
    guacamole bites, 124, 125
    lemon and dill soup, 156, 157
    in warming vegetable and corn chowder, 155
prune sweet potato and hazelnut muffins, 202, 202–3
puffed grains. See under brown rice; quinoa
pumpkin
    in spiced harissa carrot and lentil soup, 159
    spinach and quinoa salad, 164, 164–65
pumpkin seeds, in carrot cake oatmeal, 105

Q

quick vegan ramen, 150, 151
quinoa
    puffed, in strawberry balsamic salad, 141
    pumpkin and spinach salad, 164, 164–65
    in summer pea salad, 143
    in sweet potato burrito bowls, 169

R

raisins, in carrot cake oatmeal, 105
ramen, quick vegan, 150, 151
raspberry
    blood orange and buckwheat smoothie, 242, 243
    cherry rose chocolate kisses, 204, 204–5
red cabbage. See cabbage, red
red pesto, in lasakopita, 175
refreshing coconut lime and nut slaw, 144, 145
rhubarb ginger compote, 110, 112, 113
rice. See black rice noodles; brown rice; brown rice noodle(s); risotto, world's easiest; wild rice salad, Mediterranean
risotto, world's easiest, 186, 187
roasted cauliflower with mint mousse and hazelnut sumac dukkah, 118, 118–19
roasted chickpea zucchini and pomegranate salad, 134, 134–35
roasted puffed grains, strawberry balsamic salad with, 140, 140–41
roasted tofu and greens noodle bowl, 182, 182–83
roast potato lemon and dill soup, 156, 157
rocket
    in strawberry balsamic salad with roasted puffed grains, 141
    in summer pea salad, 143
romaine lettuce, for tangy salad boats, 117
rooibos apricot and maple granola, 106, 106–7
rosemary
    in meditative minestrone, 153
    in warm pumpkin spinach and quinoa salad, 165
rose raspberry cherry chocolate kisses, 204, 204–5

S

salad
- basics, 131
- boats, tangy, 116, 117
- Mediterranean rice, 138, 139
- refreshing coconut lime and nut slaw, 144, 145
- roasted chickpea zucchini and pomegranate, 134, 134–35
- strawberry balsamic, with roasted puffed grains, 140, 140–41
- summer pea, 142, 143
- tropical soba noodle, 136, 137
- warm pumpkin spinach and quinoa, 164, 164–65
- warm winter, 146, 147

salted cacao and nut butter popsicles, 224, 225

sauce. See also dressing
- for aubergine napoletana pasta, 167
- creamy honey mustard, 246
- for Dominican black beans and rice, 173
- peanut sesame tamari, 247
- sundried tomato, 170
- tahini drizzle, for beetini brownies, 211
- tahini honey lemon, 247
- tomato pasta, in lasakopita, 175

sesame seeds. See also sesame oil; tahini; zaatar
- in beetini brownies, 211
- in easy (and possibly Turkish) bread, 121
- in hazelnut dukkah, 119
- in roasted tofu and greens noodle bowl, 183
- in rooibos apricot and maple granola, 107
- in vitamin bites, 207
- in zaatar hazelnut dukkah, 249

sesame oil
- in dressing, for roasted tofu and greens noodle bowl, 183
- in dressing, for tropical soba noodle salad, 137
- in dressing, for warm pumpkin spinach and quinoa salad, 165
- in peanut sesame tamari, 247
- in quick vegan ramen, 151
- in refreshing coconut lime and nut slaw, 145
- in roasted tofu and greens noodle bowl, 183
- in sesame vinaigrette, 246
- in Sri Lankan jackfruit curry, 181
- in sweet potato noodle pad thai, 171

shiitake truffle and mustard crostini, 122, 123

slaw, refreshing coconut lime and nut, 144, 145

smoothie
- blood orange raspberry and buckwheat, 242, 243
- chai spiced breakfast, 100, 101
- go to green, 234, 235
- turmeric mango, 236, 237

snow peas, in tropical soba noodle salad, 137

soba noodle(s)
- in quick vegan ramen, 151
- in roasted tofu and greens noodle bowl, 183
- salad, tropical, 136, 137
- in sunshine Buddha bowl, 189
- in sweet potato noodle pad thai, 171

sofrito, for Dominican black beans and rice, 173

soup
- basics, 133
- creamy roast potato lemon and dill, 156, 157
- green magic, 160, 161
- meditative minestrone, 152, 152–53
- quick vegan ramen, 150, 151
- spiced harissa carrot and lentil, 158, 159
- warming vegetable and corn chowder, 154, 154–55
- watermelon gazpacho, 148, 149

soy. See also tofu
- cream, in creamy honey mustard, 246
- milk, in chocolate indulgence tart, 219
- yoghurt, in sauce, for mini millet burgers, 127

spaghetti, in artichoke and easy green pesto pasta, 185

spiced harissa carrot and lentil soup, 158, 159

spiced orange upside down cake, 214, 215–17, 216

spice mix
- for roasted chickpeas, 135
- turmeric latte, 250
- for warming vegetable and corn chowder, 155
- for warm pumpkin spinach and quinoa salad, 165

spinach
- in easy mac and sundried tomato sauce, 170
- in go to green smoothie, 235
- in green elixir, 238
- in green magic soup, 161
- in meditative minestrone, 153
- in Mediterranean rice salad, 139
- pumpkin and quinoa salad, 164, 164–65
- in quick vegan ramen, 151
- in roasted chickpea zucchini and pomegranate salad, 135
- in Sri Lankan jackfruit curry, 181
- in strawberry balsamic salad with roasted puffed grains, 141
- in sunshine Buddha bowl, 189
- for tangy salad boats, 117

spirulina powder, in green elixir, 238

sprouts, bean, in sweet potato noodle pad thai, 171

Sri Lankan jackfruit curry, 180, 180–81

stracciatella overnight oats, 96, 97

strawberry balsamic salad with roasted puffed grains, 140, 140–41

stuffed dates, chocolate, 222, 223

sumac hazelnut dukkah and mint mousse, roasted cauliflower with, 118, 118–19

summer peach tart, 200, 200–1

summer pea salad, 142, 143

sundried tomato
- harissa dip, 248
- in Mediterranean rice salad, 139
- red pesto, in lasakopita, 175
- sauce, easy mac and, 170

sunflower seeds
- in carrot cake oatmeal, 105
- in date and chestnut banana bread, 195
- in mini millet burgers, 127
- in rooibos apricot and maple granola, 107

sunshine Buddha bowl, 188, 189

sweet potato
- beetroot and feta layered bake, 176, 176–77
- burrito bowls, 168, 168–69
- in easy mac and sundried tomato sauce, 170
- in falafel and fries, 179
- in guacamole potato bites, 125
- in meditative minestrone, 153
- noodle pad thai, 171
- prune and hazelnut muffins, 202, 202–3
- in spiced harissa carrot and lentil soup, 159
- in vitamin bites, 207
- in warming vegetable and corn chowder, 155

Swiss chard
- in artichoke and easy green pesto pasta, 185
- in lasakopita, 175
- in meditative minestrone, 153
- in Sri Lankan jackfruit curry, 181

sultanas, in carrot cake oatmeal, 105

Syrian lemon mint polo, 232, 233

T

tahini
- in beetini brownies, 211
- in dressing, for roasted chickpea zucchini and pomegranate salad, 135
- in dressing, for roasted tofu and greens noodle bowl, 183
- in dressing, for warm pumpkin spinach and quinoa salad, 165
- honey lemon, 247
- lemon mustard dressing, for summer pea salad, 143
- in peanut sesame tamari, 247
- in sundried tomato harissa dip, 248

tamarind paste
- in sauce, for tangy salad boats, 117
- in Sri Lankan jackfruit curry, 181
- in sweet potato noodle pad thai, 171

tamari peanut sesame, 247

tangy salad boats, 116, 117

tart(s)
- chocolate indulgence, 218, 219
- lemon, 220, 221
- summer peach, 200, 200–201

tofu
- and greens noodle bowl, 182, 182–83
- in green magic soup, 161
- in quick vegan ramen, 151

tomato(es). See also sundried tomatoes
- cherry, in guacamole, 125, 169
- paste, in sauce, for Dominican black beans and rice, 173
- sauce, in aubergine pasta, 167
- sauce, in lasakopita, 175
- in roasted chickpea zucchini and pomegranate salad, 135
- in watermelon gazpacho, 149

tropical soba noodle salad, 136, 137

truffles, chocolate cherry and coconut, 192, 193

truffle shiitake and mustard crostini, 122, 123

Turkish (possibly) bread, 120, 121

turmeric
- latte, 251
- latte spice mix, 250
- mango smoothie or popsicles, 236, 237

two fancy oatmeals, 104, 104–5

V

vegan pancakes, 108, 109
vegan ramen, quick, 150, 151
vegetable and corn chowder, 154, 154–55
vinaigrette, sesame, 246
vitamin bites, 206, 207

W

walnuts
- in aprichoc hazelnut blondies, 227
- in beetini brownies, 211
- in garlic dressing, 247
- in garlic dressing, for sunshine Buddha bowl, 189
- in Mediterranean rice salad, 139
- in pineapple ginger carrot cake, 197
- in sundried tomato harissa dip, 248

warming vegetable and corn chowder, 154, 154–55
warm pumpkin spinach and quinoa salad, 164, 164–65
warm winter salad, 146, 147
watermelon gazpacho, 148, 149
wild rice salad, Mediterranean, 139
winter salad, warm, 146, 147
world's easiest risotto, 186, 187

Y

yoghurt
- coconut, in Sri Lankan jackfruit curry, 181
- soy, in sauce, for mini millet burgers, 127
- in summer peach tart, 201

Z

zaatar hazelnut dukkah, 119, 249

zucchini
- in artichoke and easy green pesto pasta, 185
- chickpea and pomegranate salad, 134, 134–35
- in Mediterranean rice salad, 139
- noodles, for aubergine napoletana pasta, 167
- in Sri Lankan jackfruit curry, 181
- in warming vegetable and corn chowder, 155

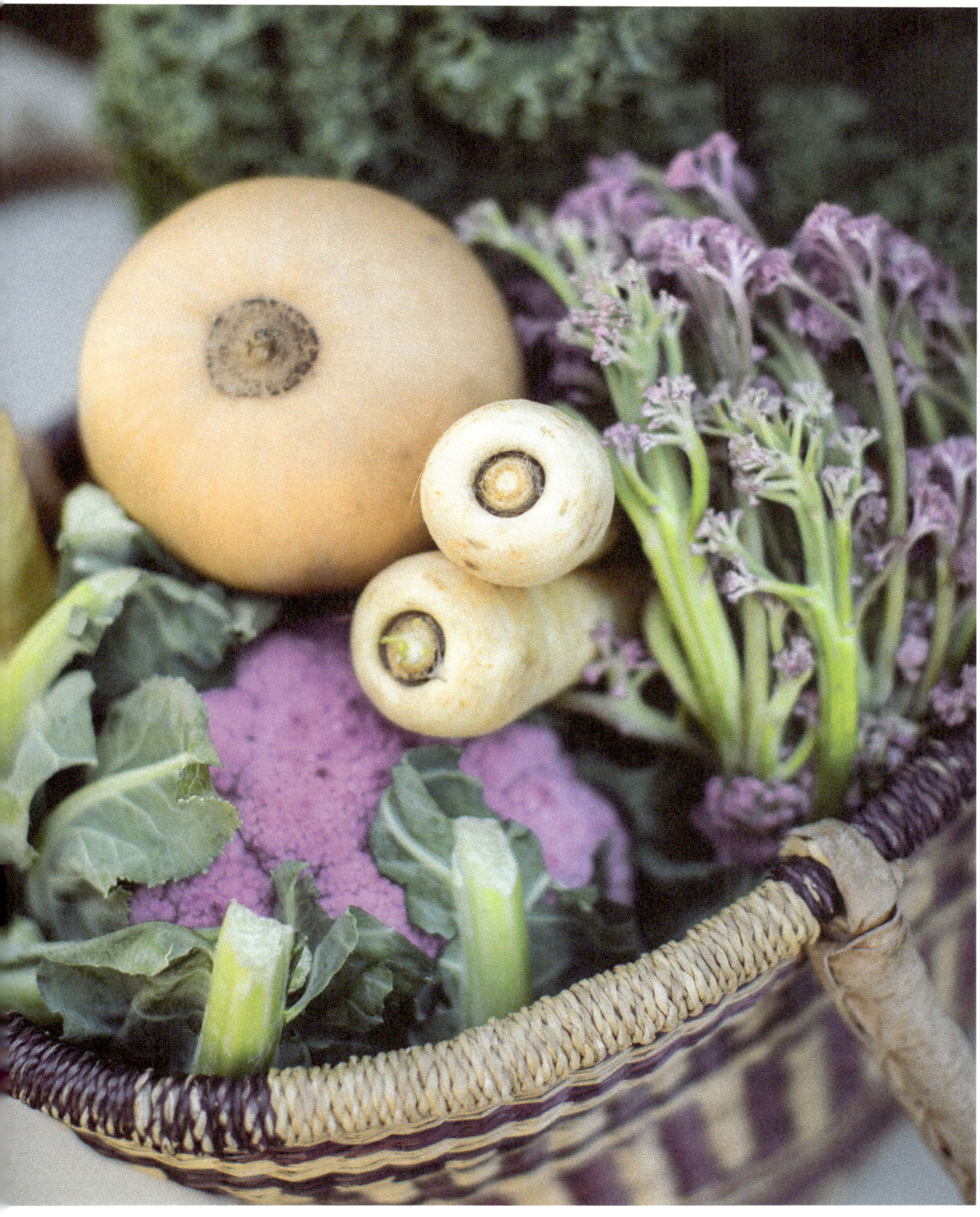

Copyright © 2019 by Michelle Grant

All rights reserved. No part of this book may be used or reproduced in any manner whatsoever without written permission from the copyright holder. For requests please contact www.thegreatfull.com.

Title: The Great Full
Author: Michelle Grant
Description: First Edition
ISBN 978-3-033-07457-6 (print)
ISBN 978-3-033-07458-3 (ebook)

Book and Cover Design: *Of* Note Designs
Editing: Katia Ariel
Recipe Development: Michelle Grant
Indexing: Iva Cheung
Food Photography and Styling: Michelle Grant
Photo Editing: Palina Zampieri

Additional Photography: **cover** The Picture Pantry Food Stock Photo Library with: Violeta Pasat; **page 4** Palina Zampieri; **page 6** Anna Brackmann; **page 12** William Felker; **page 18** Radoslav Bali; **page 22** Ellie Elien; **page 24** Martin Adams; **page 26** v2osk on Unsplash; **page 30** and **page 31** ©George Steinmetz; **page 32** Foto Murthy on Unsplash; **page 34** Pakka; **page 36** Sustainability Institute; **page 38** ©George Steinmetz; **page 40** Daniel Fazio; **page 44** OzHarvest; page 46 Mahdis Mousavi; page 48 OzHarvest; page 52 Peter Lüthi, Biovision; **page 58** Orlova Maria on Unsplash; **page 62** Brooke Lark; **page 66** Heather Ford; **page 70** Kirsty Russell, Of Note Designs; **page 74** Gaelle Marcel on Unsplash; **page 78** NordWood on Unsplash; **page 80** Kirsty Russell, Of Note Designs; **page 82** Joanie Simon; **page 84** Kirsty Russell, Of Note Designs; **page 90** Kirsty Russell, Of Note Designs; **page 114** Palina Zampieri; **page 124** Palina Zampieri; **page 126** Palina Zampieri; **page 162** Palina Zampieri; **page 180** Palina Zampieri; **page 186** Kirsty Russell, Of Note Designs; **page 224** Jennifer Pallian; **page 252** Lum3n on Unsplash

Lightning Source UK Ltd.
Milton Keynes UK
UKHW051105141219
355270UK00005B/58/P